BIG HOUSE, LITTLE HOUSE, BACK HOUSE, BARN

"Big house, little house, back house, barn" was a children's refrain recited on New England farms in the late nineteenth and early twentieth centuries. It is the only indigenous expression known to describe the region's unique connected farm buildings.

Facing page illustration: York, Maine, ca. 1885.

BIG HOUSE, LITTLE HOUSE, BACK HOUSE, BARN

The Connected Farm Buildings of New England

Thomas C. Hubka

University Press of New England

Hanover and London

UNIVERSITY PRESS OF NEW ENGLAND

Printed in the United States of America

Publication of this volume has been aided by a grant
from the National Endowment for the Humanities.

Library of Congress Cataloging in Publication Data

Hubka, Thomas C., 1946–
  Big house, little house, back house, barn.

  Bibliography: p.
  Includes index.
  1. Farm buildings—New England. I. Title.
NA8201.H8 1984   728'.67'0974   84-40303
ISBN 0-87451-310-3
ISBN 0—87451—356—1 (pbk.)

All farmsteads and houses described in
this book are privately owned and readers
are asked to respect that privacy.

To my mother and father

Contents

Preface, *ix*

Acknowledgments, *xiii*

I CONNECTED FARM BUILDINGS

  1 Appearance and Actuality, *3*

II PATTERN IN CONNECTED FARM BUILDINGS

  2 The Buildings, *32*
  3 The Buildings and the Land, *70*
  4 Permanence and Change, *86*
  5 Pattern in Building and Farming, *113*

III REASONS FOR MAKING CONNECTED FARM BUILDINGS

  6 Tobias Walker Moves His Shed, *161*
  7 Why Tobias Walker Moved His Shed, *179*

Notes, *205*   Bibliography, *213*   Glossary, *221*

Index, *224*   Figure Credits, *226*

Preface

This book, about the buildings that farmers made, traces the historical development of connected farm buildings, an architectural form common in rural New England. This is primarily a book of detailed architectural analysis, but it is also a cultural study. Buildings are seen as an expression of their culture and can be interpreted to reveal insights about the people who made them and the reasons they made them.

There are three parts: Part I provides an overview of connected farm buildings; Part II, the main body of the text, analyzes connected farms according to patterns of construction, usage, and change over time; and Part III explains why connected farms were built. This three-part organization follows an architectural logic in which building analysis precedes the explanation of historical development. I have found this strategy to be the most productive way of approaching an exceedingly complex problem of architectural interpretation, in which the late nineteenth-century product of connected farm builders is clear, but the way in which they developed this form in the first part of the century is not. My architectural training and respect for ethnographic inquiry have convinced me that a solid knowledge of how these buildings were made and how they were used will provide a basis for answering the difficult question of why they developed into their unique form. Consequently the major hypotheses of this study are derived from a detailed architectural documentation of many farms and an analysis of how they worked in the nineteenth century.

This study describes an example of American popular architecture. The term *popular* is used here to mean the buildings that most farmers made most of the time. This strategy differs from that in most architectural studies, which have usually recorded buildings of unique or original characteristics, and instead tells the story of buildings that were the common and traditional selection of a farming population. It focuses upon a striking change in New England's rural architecture between 1800 and 1900, when many farmers reorganized their detached house and barn arrangement into a connected house and barn plan.

Although the primary research data for this study was collected in southwestern Maine, fieldwork throughout New England has revealed a unified type of connected farm building most commonly found in northern New England, except western Vermont, and in some areas of southern New England. Since other building arrangements coexisted with it, my hypotheses are intended to apply to those farms that were arranged in or converted to the connected building plan. I have extended these ideas to include connected farmsteads in the entire region with great caution, because there is significant variation in architectural form even between adjacent counties and towns in New England. Nevertheless, the term *New England connected farm building* is appropriate because the remarkable similarity of most connected farmsteads suggests that a homogeneous agrarian culture once unified the entire region.

Although this book follows the architectural development of the connected plan during the nineteenth century, the end of the French and Indian War in 1763 and the beginning of the First World War in 1914 mark the outer boundaries of the study. The end of colonial Indian hostilities is significant because it marked the beginning of a major period of agricultural settlement in New England's interior. The beginning of the twentieth century concluded the era of connected farm building, although a few connected farms continued to be built until 1940.

One of the most controversial assertions in this book concerns the dating and origin of the connected farm building organization. Popular opinion and some historical studies have assumed a much earlier date, while my research has indicated that most farms achieved their connected configuration after the early nineteenth century. Both positions are partially correct. The subtle distinction I will attempt to make is that while buildings employing connected arrangements were built in colonial New England, they did not constitute a popular form for most farmers. The making of most connected farms will be shown to be a product of an intensive period of farm modernization and building experimentation that occurred during the nineteenth century.

While farm architecture is the principal concern, it is often difficult to distinguish farm buildings from other forms of rural architecture in New England. A large and diverse body of connected town houses in the small villages of the region share basic characteristics and origins with the more agrarian examples studied in this text. New England farms also have a long history of home-industry and nonagricultural activities, which blur distinctions between farm and town examples. In spite of these similarities, farm architecture maintains distinct differences in form and function from town and city examples, particularly because of its primarily agricultural nature. Perhaps a future study of New England's popular small-town architecture would parallel and complement this study.

A number of major ideas in this work are challenging to three prevailing orthodoxies within New England. The most pervasive I would describe as a New England antiquarian orthodoxy, which has romanticized the story of New England's past by glorifying old-time ways and rustic settings, often at the expense of historical accuracy. Second is a New England architectural orthodoxy, which has usually chosen to examine the houses of the region's wealthy classes and neglected examples of popular architecture. Unfortunately, data from these studies have often been applied inappropriately to the analysis of common farms. Finally, a popular opinion orthodoxy in New England has been a powerful shaper of ideas about New England's architectural heritage. It has often crystalized many imprecise stories about the region's farm architecture into brittle myths about its origin. While each of these orthodoxies contains important truths about connected farm buildings, all three have failed to analyze them in terms of the value system of the people who made them. It is this value system that I seek to portray.

A consistent goal of this study is to link the lives of farmers to the buildings that they made and to establish the relationship between the built form and the ideas that generated its making. This requires that common farmers be seen as active participants in the design and building of their farmsteads. Some readers will probably object to the designation of common farmers as designers, or even folk designers, because faculties such as design decision making and aesthetic preferences are usually associated with architects or urban people. Of course, pragmatically oriented farmers do not design their buildings in the same way as architects, but this study will show that they acted through the traditions of their building and their work to create their farmsteads. In Part III I develop this theme by examining the complete building history of one farmer, Tobias Walker, whose design decisions were rigorously shaped by the constraints of his environment, economy, and culture but who still exercised a considerable degree of individual choice in the organization of his farm.

Finally, this book attempts to answer the question, Why did New England farmers build connected farms? But the reader should be forewarned; there is no definitive statement that proves all. Rather, a case for understanding these structures is built out of their physical history and then set into a larger cultural history in order to understand the individual and collective motivation behind building decision making. This might seem like a weak and long-winded answer to a simple question, but the answer is not simple. It is similar in complexity to the problem of understanding the development of any popular architectural form. For example, the question could be asked, Why did millions of middle-class Americans build suburban ranch houses between 1950 and 1970? Having studied this phenomenon, I am confident that the answer cannot be summarized in one builder's statement or in specifications from a Federal Housing Administration manual, but must emerge from a careful artifact and cultural study of many buildings and the people and conditions that combined to shape them. It is this comprehensive approach that will provide an answer to the question, Why did New England farmers build connected farms?

Acknowledgments

I gratefully acknowledge the National Endowment for the Humanities in conjunction with Greater Portland Landmarks and the National Endowment for the Arts for the generous grants that have sustained this research. The University of Oregon has granted leave time and invaluable clerical support.

This book could not have been written without the cooperation of hundreds of residents who graciously allowed me to visit and document their homes. I would especially like to thank the Nuttings, the Bennetts, the Moshers, the Robert Walkers, and the Morses.

During the course of this study I have consulted with a group of dedicated local historians, including Mary Carlson, Sue Black, Stanley Howe, Ben Conant, Helen Prince, Robert Dingley, Sandra Armentrout, Ruth Landon, Jim Vickery, Harry Walker, Ernest Knight, Eleanor Walker, Margaret Sawyer, Betty Barto, Mary Bryant, Marion Carroll, Joy Malloy, Pat Townsend, Aubrey Palmer, George Allen, William Pierce, Randy Bennett, Roberta Chandler, and Phyllis Coolidge. Joyce Butler significantly contributed to the research and organization of Chapter 6. The dedicated assistance and untiring inspiration of Ursula Baier from the North Yarmouth Historical Society has immeasurably contributed to the entire work.

Four books have significantly influenced me and shaped many of the ideas in this work: *Folk Housing in Middle Virginia* by Henry Glassie; *The Machine in the Garden* by Leo Marx; *The Making of the English Working Class* by E. P. Thompson; and *The Interpretation of Cultures* by Clifford Geertz.

This work has benefited from the advice of a number of people, who are, however, not responsible for its content, including: Fraser Hart, Jere Daniell, Charles Clark, Richard Candee, Earl Shettleworth, Henry Glassie, Edward Ives, David Smith, Pierce Lewis, Robert Dalzell, Abbot Cummings, John Fitchen, Joyce Bibber, Wilbur Zelinsky, Ronald Brunskill, John Hakola, Joel Eastman, James Garvin, and Paul Frederic. I especially acknowledge the generous assistance of Leo Marx, who has helped me develop many of my initial ideas and has allowed me to appreciate the complexity of my task.

Mary Williams did a superb job of typing, Garry Fritz assisted with the graphics, and Kurt Brown took many of the photographs. Several of my architectural students assisted with the development and presentation of drawings, including: William Holland, Robert Kleinkopf, Scott Benson, Tom Stacey, Nancy Sussman, William Rudd, William Gould and Jeffrey Hoover. Finally I thank Mary, Terry, Sarah, and Rachel Hubka for providing a connected home away from home without equal.

But the people who most deserve acknowledgment are the most difficult to acknowledge. They are the hundreds of farmers who have contributed to this study. It is these farmers whom I especially thank with the hope that some measure of their lives will find a likeness in these pages.

Tobias Walker, a farmer from Kennebunk, Maine, described in his journal the events of April 11, 1850: "[The carpenters were] here putting shoes under the wood house to move it [to] the other side of the house. P.M. Moved the building over next to the barnyard. Had forty oxen." Walker recorded here the relocation of his large, multipurpose woodshed, carriage house, and workshop. Twenty teams of oxen were required to pull the 18-foot by 24-foot building onto its new site. It had previously been connected to the east side of his house, but he decided to move it to the west side into a position between house and barn. Walker's building realignment was an act integrally related to a large pattern of farm reorganization that transformed much of the rural landscape of New England in the nineteenth century. While not all farms were rearranged exactly like Tobias Walker's, thousands were formed in this manner and many thousands more were constructed in a similar connected house and barn arrangement.

I Connected Farm Buildings

Fig. 1. Nevers-Bennett Farm, Sweden, Maine.

1   Appearance and Actuality

The buildings on the old Nevers-Bennett farm stand at a small rural crossroads in the town of Sweden, Maine (fig. 1). Every summer tourists stop their cars to admire the impressive string of gleaming white buildings. The Nevers-Bennett farm is a striking example of a connected farm building commonly found throughout the New England region. Once it was the home of Charles and Charlotte Bennett, who converted a previous farm to the present arrangement of buildings in the 1880s. Their picture shows a proud, persevering couple who ran one of the finest farms in their town (fig. 2). Only Charles's roughened hands belie the genteel, late nineteenth-century appearance of the photograph, for in fact the Bennetts were the epitome of a hard-working farm couple.

Bill and Martha Gorman were also hard-working New England farmers. A 1919 photograph shows them standing before a loaded hay wagon on their farm in Newry, Maine (fig. 3). Here they continued the old ways of New England farming for as long as they were able, and when they died, their farm reverted to forest. Their story is legend in rural New England and has come to represent the plight of many farmers who continued to struggle against a tide of farm abandonment and rural readaptation in the late nineteenth and early twentieth centuries. Today, although there are still prosperous and active farmers in New England, the image of an old couple in a dilapidated house holding out against the encroachments of the modern world has, for many, come to represent the farms and the farmers of the region.

For this reason it is often difficult for people to perceive the region's characteristic farm buildings as anything more than quaint, picturesque relics from a distant rural past. And yet to understand connected farm buildings and the meaning they had for the people who made them, the modern viewer must relinquish any thought of backwardness or rigid conservatism on the part of their builders. To the farmers who made them, the connected farm building arrangement was eminently practical and was even a symbol of progressive agricultural improvement in New England throughout much of the nineteenth century. It was this conception that guided the Bennetts' reorganization of their farm, and it is to this concept of farm improvement that we must turn in order to understand why these structures were built.

The pictures of the Bennetts and the Gormans have been contrasted to emphasize a difference in the modern perception of these farmers, but in fact many aspects of their lives were quite similar. What was critically different, however, was that the Bennetts were able to build earlier and prospered within the social and economic traditions of a unified agricultural community. Both farms conducted similar agricultural operations, but the Gormans attempted to prolong older methods into the twentieth century only to find them increasingly obsolete. Had the Bennetts attempted to build and farm into the twentieth century, they too would have found their previous methods more and more

3

Fig. 2. Charles and Charlotte
Bennett, ca. 1900.

Fig. 3. Bill and Martha Gorman, 1919.

difficult to sustain. Although both the Bennetts and the Gormans have much to offer historians of New England's farms and their architecture, it is the Bennetts who most actively sustained the traditions of building improvement associated with the making of connected farm buildings. It is such farmers who will be investigated in order to understand the development of the region's farm architecture.

Connected Farm Buildings

Connected farm buildings are a conspicuous and remarkable aspect of the New England countryside. In the typical arrangement, house and barn are joined through a series of support structures to form a continuous building complex. The Sawyer-Black farm of Sweden, Maine, is a typical example of a connected farm building found in varying densities throughout the region, but most commonly in Maine and portions of New Hampshire (fig. 4). Although there is considerable visual variation, most connected

Fig. 4. Two views of Sawyer-Black Farm, Sweden, Maine. Barn, back house, and little house were constructed in mid-1800s, the big house in early 1800s (roof altered).

farms throughout New England were organized and functioned similarly and, like the Sawyer-Black farm, contain four distinct buildings. A children's verse from the nineteenth century describes the most typical organization: "Big house, little house, back house, barn." It is a refrain often repeated by old timers when asked to describe the unusual building arrangement. A few even recall childhood games played to its rhythmic cadence.[1]

From an architectural perspective, the verse succinctly summarizes the four essential components of the connected farmstead arrangement (fig. 5). First is the big house, the major farmhouse, and it is given the finest ornamentation. It usually faces the road and is the nearest structure to it. The big house is usually identified as the farmhouse by the farm family and contains the formal parlor room and the bedrooms or "chambers" on the second floor. In spite of its size and architectural refinements, it was seldom used for daytime activities in the nineteenth century and was primarily a place of rest. Second is the little house, which was, and still is, the kitchen building and active living center for the farm family. A workroom or "summer kitchen" usually adjoined the kitchen and was connected to the "wood house," used for firewood storage. The kitchen and its support rooms constituted the major work areas for the women of the farm. Third is the back house, a building extending from the kitchen or little house to the major barn. It usually contained a wagon bay and multipurpose work and storage spaces for house and barn. The farm outhouse or privy was usually located in the corner of this building closest to the barn and is also referred to as the back house. Together, the little house and the back house buildings are commonly called the ell, which was a term derived from the typical L-shaped plan relationship between the big house and its kitchen addition. During the middle of the nineteenth century, the little house and the back house were frequently combined into one continuous structure to produce a single uniform ell building between big house and barn. Today both differentiated and uniform ell plans are common (fig. 6). It is, finally, the barn that terminates the connected building complex and, as on most American farms, is the functional center of the farming operation. On the New England farm, it primarily sheltered farm animals and their food.

Although this four-part arrangement might sometimes appear haphazard, most nineteenth-century New England connected farm buildings shared similar patterns of spatial organization and usage. Most farms were aligned at right angles to the road with the major facades of the big house and the barn facing the road. Farmers then oriented their line of connected buildings to shelter a south- or east-facing work yard, called the dooryard, from north or west winter winds (fig. 7). A barnyard was usually located on the south or east side of the barn for similar reasons. Many farmers also added a formal front yard between the front door of the big house and the road. This three-yard system was the dominant pattern for connected farms during much of the nineteenth century and reinforced the functional organization of the farm. Thus the formal front yard was an extension of the architecturally formal big house, the working dooryard was an extension of the workrooms in the little house and the back house, and the animal barnyard was an extension of the barn.

As a physical unit in the landscape, the massing of a connected farm complex is roughly balanced between the larger, plainer bulk of the barn and the smaller but more intricate mass of the big house. Builders created a balanced relationship between house and barn by extending the architectural style of the big house to all the buildings in

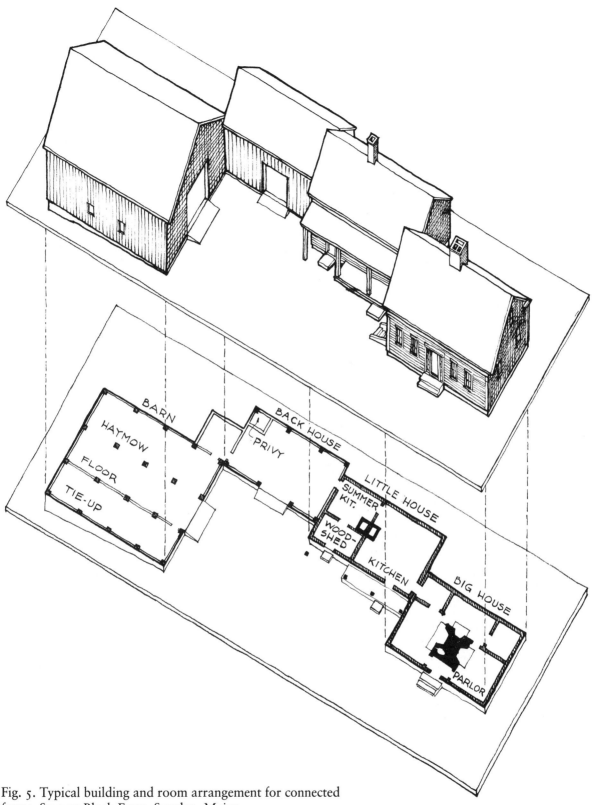

Fig. 5. Typical building and room arrangement for connected farms. Sawyer-Black Farm, Sweden, Maine.

Fig. 6. Connecting ells: *A*, the differentiated ell with multiple buildings connecting house and barn, Greenwood, Maine, area; *B*, the uniform ell with a continuous building connecting house and barn, Denmark, Maine.

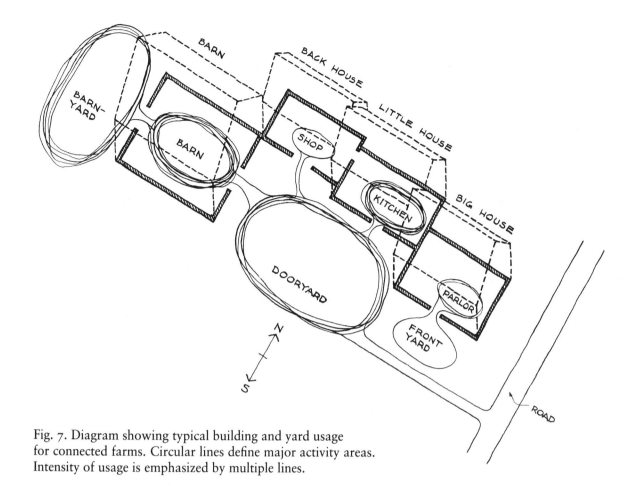

Fig. 7. Diagram showing typical building and yard usage
for connected farms. Circular lines define major activity areas.
Intensity of usage is emphasized by multiple lines.

the connected complex including the barn. Although most farmers chose to dilute the house's architectural ornament when they applied it to the barn, the fact that they applied it to the barn at all constitutes one of the most unusual and significant characteristics of New England's connected farm architecture.

The daily life on a nineteenth-century connected farm revolved around the work centers of the kitchen and the barn. The kitchen with its auxiliary rooms contained workplaces for the production of a variety of items such as butter, clothing, and handicraft products, as well as for the daily tasks of cooking, washing, and child care. The barn was commonly organized into side bays for animals and their food storage, with a central vehicle "floor" giving access to all areas. The centrally located dooryard provided an important focal point for all work activities originating in the kitchen, back buildings, and barn and was an important preparation and staging area for all outside activities.

New England farmers developed and popularized the connected farm building arrangement in the nineteenth century because it was well suited to the multipurpose agricultural production employed by most of the rural population. In the language of agricultural historians, it was a system of mixed-husbandry, home-industry, small-scale family farming. Mixed husbandry or mixed farming meant that the New England farmers never put all their agricultural eggs into a single product basket but produced a variety of crops and animal products. Home industry meant that they relied on non-agricultural sources of income to help support the family farm, including lumbering, clothing, and craft occupations. And the small-scale family farm with its limited production and its commitment to traditional cultural values has consistently characterized most of New England's agricultural community in all periods.

The distinctive form of the connected farm has spawned no indigenous architectural name.[2] Most farmers or present owners simply call the complex the farm, the farmhouse, or place (as in "the Walker place"). Perhaps it is because these buildings are so common that they have evoked no particular designation from New England's rural population. This is surprising to a visitor from outside New England because elsewhere the connected farm building organization is extremely unusual. What is even more surprising is the extent of its popularity within the region. For almost one hundred years the connected farm building plan flourished in New England, and in many areas it was the most popular form of rural and small-town domestic architecture before 1900. Throughout most of rural Maine and New Hampshire, about 50 percent of the dwellings follow this pattern, with lesser densities in areas further from Maine. In many Maine towns, over 70 percent of the pre-1900 dwellings followed the connected building arrangement.[3] It is the extraordinary popularity of this building arrangement over such a long period that makes the explanation of this construction more than the record of a few exotic buildings and central to an understanding of the nineteenth-century agrarian culture of New England. Furthermore, since so much of that culture has been lost, connected farm buildings offer a significant resource for interpreting the extensive agrarian society that once dominated this region.

After more than a century of decline in its agricultural fortunes, New England's connected farms have acquired an antiquated or picturesque appearance. Abandoned farms are a common site in rural areas, and many agricultural buildings have been allowed to disintegrate following the cessation of farming activities (fig. 8). But in the middle of the nineteenth century, connected farm architecture was often described as an efficient and stylistically progressive response to the requirements of the region's farmers.[4] An indication of the high esteem given this farm planning concept is clearly evident in a lithograph from Cumberland County, Maine, published in 1880 (fig. 9).[5] The drawing depicts a prosperous, model farm of the period and was produced to publicize the material accomplishments of its owner.[6] The drawing shows a continuous line of white buildings surrounded by neat, well-fenced fields. The roadway is lined by shade and fruit trees that also define the formal front yard of the big house. The overall impression is one of efficiency and order in which the buildings and the landscape were united into one uniform composition.

While details are generally accurate, the picture also tends to exaggerate characteristics of the buildings and the landscape that were highly esteemed by their owners. Consequently the scene becomes neater, whiter, straighter, and more uniformly organized than could actually have been the case at the time.[7] In their exaggeration the drawings reveal, far better than words, an idealized model for the buildings and environment that many New England farmers considered to be the most appropriate form for a farmstead. In 1880 this model clearly symbolized agricultural supremacy in New England, having emerged from many competing styles at the beginning of the century to become a popular and progressive style for many segments of the rural population.

Fig. 8. Disintegration of agricultural buildings on a connected farm, Windham, Maine, 1978. In 1858 Charles Hunnewell received wide publicity for the arrangement and efficiency of this model connected farm.

Fig. 9. A model for a progressive farm in New England in 1880. The Byron Kimball Farm, North Bridgton, Maine. From *History of Cumberland County, Maine*, by W. Woodward Clayton.

Popular Image and Historic Actuality

The high level of appreciation popularly accorded New England's rural architecture is based upon a complex mixture of facts, images, myths, and popular opinions. Although connected farm buildings are widely admired for their striking physical appearance, they have not received detailed historical study.[8] Consequently, several popular explanations have been given for the making of connected farm buildings that must be disentangled from their actual history.

WINTER PASSAGE VERSUS THE THREAT OF FIRE

The most popular reason given for the making of connected farms emphasizes the desirability of a winter passage from house to barn. Yankee readers will, of course, know the explanation I am going to quote. It has been repeated to me well over two hundred times in some variation of the following: Hundreds of years ago, New England farmers connected their buildings to provide a covered passage to their barns in order to feed their livestock during the heavy snows of long New England winters (fig. 10). This explanation is often given in terse, Down East fashion with the intent of underscoring the wisdom and practical good sense of the ancient Yankee way. It has a compelling logic, and it is not all wrong, but it omits much of the reasoning behind the making of connected farms. If the results of this study are correct, a climatic interpretation for building connection would not explain why the majority of New England farmers waited until the middle of the nineteenth century to connect their houses and barns. Furthermore, the popular explanation cannot account for the isolation of New England's connected farms. The snows are far deeper and the winters even more severe in other areas of the country (such as upstate New York and Michigan), where Yankee farmers settled in great numbers and where neither they nor other settlers chose to connect their houses with their barns.

Fig. 10. Winter passage between house and barn.

Like other popular New England legends concerning borning rooms and Indian shutters, the climatic argument for the making of connected farms isolates one of many factors and magnifies it as the entire story. While it is true that the connected buildings provided the farmer a convenient passage to the barn in severe weather, especially for morning and evening chores, other considerations had even more appeal. These factors, which will all be analyzed in greater depth, include: (a) weather protection for the critical dooryard created by the line of connected buildings, probably the most significant climatic determinant; (b) the convenient organization of agricultural and home-industry workrooms in the flexible, multipurpose ell, a system that responded to the increased commercial demands of nineteenth-century agriculture; (c) the influence of New England's progressive agriculturalists, who emphasized the practical efficiency of the new building system, which appealed to many farmers because it was similar to their existing system; and (d) the subtle but influential example of New England's connected town houses and gentleman farmer estates, which gave farmers a model for agrarian improvement. All these factors exerted an increasing influence upon New England farmers in the nineteenth century because they were under tremendous pressure to readapt their farming system in response to intensive western agricultural competition. Obviously, no single explanation for the making of connected farm buildings could possibly encapsulate these diverse causes in a simple tale about winter passage. Yet the unfortunate effect of the popular explanation is to conceal the intensive period of nineteenth-century agricultural development that created connected farms behind a benign tale of winter convenience. The complete story is far richer and more revealing of the Yankee farmer than the explanation of winter passage, but it is also more controversial and harder to tell.

There is another account of the connected farm building plan that is frequently told by old farmers, but it is not discussed as openly. As every New England farmer well knew, the connected complex was extremely vulnerable to total destruction by fire (fig. 11). The threat of fire was one of the most dreaded specters to haunt the records

Fig. 11. Fire spreading between house and barn. Gilead, Maine.

and diaries of nineteenth-century New Englanders. During interviews, some farmers would describe both the advantages of the winter passage and the disadvantages of the threat of fire inherent in the connected building system. Occasionally they have even described it as a reckless, headstrong way of building a farm because of its vulnerability to fire. Of course, Yankees who built these structures in the nineteenth century defended the connected system. In 1843 a Connecticut farmer acknowledged its fire hazard but recommended the connected scheme with a typical Yankee insight, "get insured and keep insured. Industry will pay for the policy."[9]

Both positive and negative interpretations exemplify strong opposing positions about the connected building arrangement. The objection to it on the grounds of fire danger symbolizes all the disadvantages of the new arrangement, including potential sanitary, siting, and expansion problems, which New England farmers needed to rationalize or at least accept before they could proceed with building in the connected style. Its acceptance based upon the convenience of winter passage symbolizes all the advantages of the new arrangement, including the convenience of workplaces in the ell and a certain amount of stylishness. These explanations provide outer boundaries of interpretation between which many other factors will be considered. Today it is not surprising that the more positive argument is usually offered by the descendants of the New England farmers who gambled upon the success of the new organization and converted their farms in this fashion.

ARCHITECTURAL PRECEDENTS

Many New England residents and regional historians have assumed that connected farm buildings existed in New England from the early colonial period.[10] The results of this investigation will show that, as a popular way of building, it was a relatively new tradition beginning in the early 1800s and reaching a peak of popularity after the Civil War. The discrepancy in dating, however, can be resolved. Buildings in connected arrangements existed in colonial New England, but they did not constitute a popular style for most of the rural population.

An early dwelling in a connected arrangement is shown in an 1801 watercolor of a house in Concord, Masssachusetts (fig. 12). It is a large town house with a staggered line of assorted buildings that constituted a regional style associated with town architecture by 1800. Similar types of buildings were usually found in the seacoast towns of New England and are shown in the 1824 painting *Morning View of Blue Hill Village* (Maine) by Jonathan Fisher. Here, in an assortment of town houses and farms with several forms of attached buildings, almost all the farms show a detached and clearly differentiated house and barn. Although the seeds of the connected farm building organization were clearly present in the early 1800s, the vast majority of New England farmers built in the detached house and barn arrangement, as continually pictured and cited in eighteenth- and early nineteenth-century accounts, paintings, maps, wills, samplers, and diaries, as shown, for example, in figure 13.[11] Where late eighteenth- and early nineteenth-century farms have survived in their original state, they are invariably built in the detached house and barn arrangement. For example, the well-documented Pettengill and Pote farms of Freeport, Maine, both preserve their original saltbox houses and were built with detached barns. Architectural historians of the colonial period have repeatedly observed this pattern, as in this description of early Connecticut farm buildings: "The barn was

Fig. 12. An early nineteenth-century connected town house with multiple building additions. *Dr. Hurd's House in Concord, Massachusetts*. Watercolor drawing by Henry Wilder, 1801.

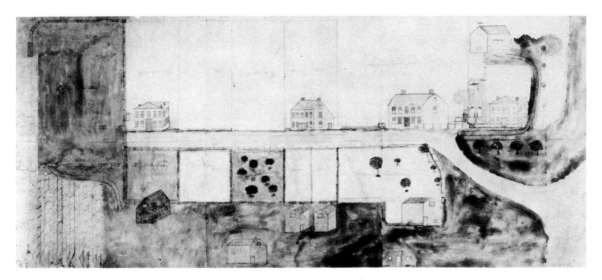

Fig. 13. Typical early nineteenth-century farms with detached houses and barns. Watercolor drawing by Charles Russell Sturgis, Point Shirley, Winthrop, Massachusetts, ca. 1815.

almost without exception free standing. . . . The basic agricultural unit carried from enclosed counties to America consisted of the house and separate barn." [12] It was this popular separated arrangement that was displaced by the connected house and barn arrangement during the nineteenth century, as it broadened from a loosely organized style of town dwellers and a few gentlemen farmers to become a dominant farm building organization in New England.

Two influences were critical to the popularization of the New England connected farm: first, a manor house tradition of Georgian and Federal style estates that employed extended outbuilding wings in a classical villa style, and second, a folk or vernacular building tradition of English origin in which domestic and agrarian structures were attached or closely clustered.

The genteel source was typified by the city and country estates of the early Federal period in New England. The Rundlet-May house of Portsmouth, New Hampshire, and the Deering estate of Portland, Maine, were two of the most influential examples of a large group of estate houses that frequently employed continuous ells, outbuilding wings, and attached carriage houses (fig. 14). Wealthy New Englanders had developed these practices in the colonial Georgian period by following an eighteenth-century English country house tradition. [13] Ultimately the sources for these buildings are English interpretations of Renaissance villa architecture, particularly Palladian examples, which incorporated farm buildings within symmetrical, classically ordered wings attached to the major house (fig. 15). [14] The leading European architects of the late eighteenth century combined these classical villa styles with the latest scientific farming theories of the Enlightenment to produce geometrical compositions in a grand connected building organization. [15] This classically inspired style of estate planning found its grandest American expression in the Virginia country estates such as Monticello, Mount Airy, and Mount Vernon, although the more severe, less publicized New England development of these ideas followed similar planning strategies. New England builders, like their southern contemporaries, were exposed to these ideas through numerous English planning treatises, such as the works of James Gibbs and Isaac Ware. Later, these styles were popularized by writers such as Joseph Gandy, William Pain, and J. C. Loudon in England and later by Asher Benjamin and A. J. Downing in America. [16]

A folk or vernacular source for the connected building arrangement paralleled the genteel development of the estate house. This folk tradition was practiced by most nineteenth-century New England farmers, who had maintained many aspects of their English building customs, including the practices of incremental, connected building growth and clustered pattern of outbuilding construction. [17] The English practice of constructing an individual building or "house" for each domestic or agricultural function was particularly responsible for the proliferation of multiple structures in New England. Farmers continued to develop these old-world customs in the New World to produce a popular building system with multiple ells and clustered outbuildings attached to house or barn.

By 1820 both genteel and folk sources had spawned specific building forms that were to influence directly the popularization of the connected house and barn arrangement. Wealthy merchants and gentlemen farmers inspired by grand estate houses in the Federal style continued to develop the connected town house with attached carriage house. An example of this type of building from Kennebunk, Maine, is shown in

Fig. 14. A Federal period town house with ells and attached carriage house.
Joseph Leland House, Saco, Maine, built 1801.

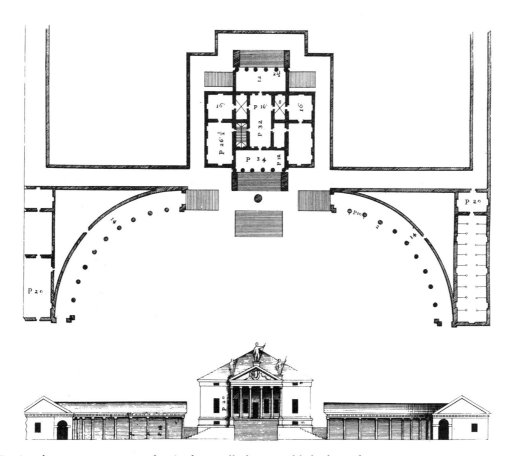

Fig. 15. Design for a country estate by Andrea Palladio as published in *The Four
Books of Andrea Palladio's Architecture* by the English designer Isaac Ware in 1738.

figure 16. Simultaneously folk builders in New England's rural communities continued to refine their old-world customs and developed several standardized ell arrangements that stretched outward from the major house. The ell in figure 17 was a typical example employed by most farmers in the early nineteenth century. Most farmers also continued to employ clusters of agricultural buildings in separate and connected arrangements. Throughout the first half of the nineteenth century, New England builders merged both genteel and folk traditions to produce the popular connected farm arrangement that we see today. The story of this merger unfolds in the following chapters.

The change from a detached to a connected house and barn arrangement was part of a broad movement of architectural development and must be repeatedly qualified by many exceptions and competing styles and organizations within the New England region. For example, in 1649 the town of Reading, Massachusetts, prohibited the joining of barns and dwellings in order to lessen the danger of fire.[18] During this early period, most Massachusetts settlements shared a compact, nuclear village plan in which the joining of house and barn would have been likely, especially inasmuch as this ancient practice was still used in some areas of England.[19] This compact settlement plan was rapidly changing, however, and by the early 1700s it was largely abandoned by yeoman farmers for a pattern of isolated farms and detached houses and barns. When Massachusetts and southern New England settlers entered the interior of northern New England after 1763, the tradition of building a separate house and barn had become firmly established with the largest segment of yeomen farmers, although various types of buildings employing connected structures continued to be built, especially in the towns of the region.

There is an obvious relationship between the New England connected house and barn and English examples of this organization. Many New England settlers came from regions of England that had traditions of connecting house and barn under the same roof.[20] Most English connected arrangements stemmed from ancient agrarian practices, especially those relating to the need for security and animal safety, and were generally declining by the seventeenth century.[21] The popular development of the connected farm in New England occurred alongside a similar type of movement in England. Both developments were intended to modernize and reform agriculture and had little relationship to ancient farming practices.[22]

Geographic Distribution

The areas where connected farm buildings are located and their approximate densities within the region are shown on the map of New England (fig. 18).[23] Perhaps even more surprising than its widespread popularity within New England is its abrupt confinement to this region. If New England had been settled by an isolated group of non-English Europeans (such as the Dutch, who developed a unique barn type in New York State),[24] it would be relatively easy to disengage New England's connected farm building traditions from the architecture of other agricultural regions of America. Yet the farmers who originally settled New England were overwhelmingly English, and a comparison of farm histories suggests that English farmers in New England shared many of the same patterns of building and life-style as English farmers in other areas of America, where con-

Fig. 16. A town house with connected carriage house. This remarkable pre-1870 photograph shows a grand connected town house and front yard with its full complement of family and employees. Nathaniel Jefferds House, Kennebunk, Maine, built ca. 1810.

Fig. 17. An early nineteenth-century vernacular farmhouse with common ell additions. Old Curtis House, Freeport, Maine.

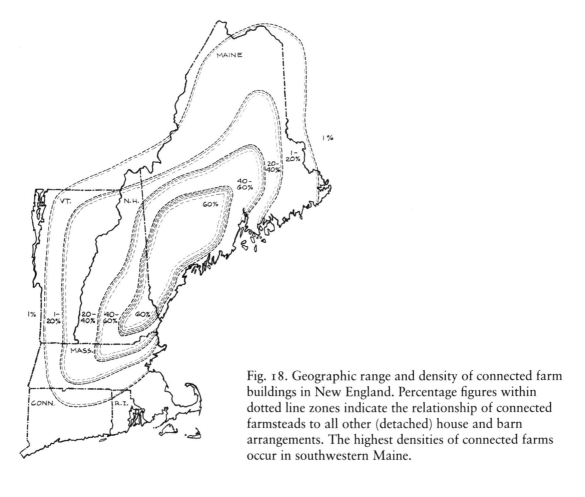

Fig. 18. Geographic range and density of connected farm buildings in New England. Percentage figures within dotted line zones indicate the relationship of connected farmsteads to all other (detached) house and barn arrangements. The highest densities of connected farms occur in southwestern Maine.

nected farms were never built.[25] The reasons for this surprising phenomenon can be found in the chronological record of emigration from New England.

OUTSIDE NEW ENGLAND

The confinement of connected farm buildings to New England is surprising to historians of America's frontier settlement, who would expect New England farmers to have brought this arrangement to the western states during their long period of emigration. That they did not do so is unusual in light of the significant and well-documented impact that New Englanders had upon the development of many areas across the northern third of the United States.[26] Yet the common New England pattern of connected house-to-barn construction was distinctly not exported to these regions. This phenomenon is also puzzling to folklorists, historians, and geographers, who have observed that some of the most commonly retained traditions during any cultural migration are the deeply ingrained practices of building construction and usage.[27]

These apparent contradictions are, however, quite easily resolved. New Englanders did migrate in great numbers from New England, and they did leave a strong cultural imprint and architectural style on many of the areas they settled, particularly in upper New York State and the upper Midwest. But they did not export the connected farmstead plan simply because they had not fully developed this style during the most extensive periods of their western migration (1790–1840). Only after the 1830s could they have imported the connected building arrangement, because that is when it began to become a popular style within the New England region. The domestic and farm buildings that Yankee farmers did construct across the northern third of the United States were, as one might expect, very similar to the ones they left behind in New England. For example, the effect of Yankee building practices is evident in a prime agricultural area, such as the Genesee region in western New York State, which was settled by many New England emigrants during the first quarter of the nineteenth century. This county still contains hundreds of older farmsteads that faithfully reproduce the most popular pre-1830 New England farmstead organization: a detached house and barn with kitchen-ell building extending toward the barn (fig. 19).[28] This does not mean the architecture that New England settlers constructed was identical to their previous farmsteads. When they came in contact with settlers from other regions and of other ethnic backgrounds, New Englanders did modify many aspects of their previous building practices. The stamp of New England's influence was, however, strongly felt in the architecture of America's western lands and particularly in the architecture that farmers built. But before 1830 this influence did not include the fully developed tradition of connecting house and barn.

After the first quarter of the nineteenth century, emigrant Yankee farmers to the western states could have begun importing the newly developing connected farmstead organization from New England, but by this time they were unlikely to do so. After the 1830s and 1840s, when much of the United States was initially settled, emigrants from New England entered into settled communities that had already established a nonconnected pattern of house and barn construction. This might have particularly influenced Yankee settlers to abandon their newly developed connected pattern, since most had left their farms to seek a better agricultural environment and were unlikely to import a unique building style from an area that even in the early 1800s was beginning to get a reputation as an unprofitable agricultural region.[29] During the second half of the nineteenth century, the spread of the connected style outside New England would have been extremely unlikely, since distinctive farm building patterns had already been strongly established in other agricultural regions and because New England's agriculture had such a negative reputation nationally.[30]

Fig. 19. A typical detached house and barn in western New York State. Genesee County, New York.

The confinement of the connected farm organization to New England is perhaps best summarized by the story of one emigrant from the region. In 1873 Elmer Calef returned from his mother's farm in Washington, Vermont, and began building his own house and barn in Lane County, Oregon.[31] Having been impressed by his mother's house with connecting barn, he commenced to reproduce it "exactly" as he had seen it. Elmer Calef finished his house much like the original, but he did not extend his ell and connect it to his barn "exactly" as had been done at his mother's house. Like all of his neighbors in Oregon, he chose to separate his barn and outbuilding from the house. Although Elmer Calef emigrated from New England after the connected building organization was fully established, he may stand for many emigrants from New England, who either left before the connected organization was established and could not have built a connected farm, or left after it was established, and chose not to build one. In either case, the connected farm building arrangement was not exported from New England.

INSIDE NEW ENGLAND

The geographic boundary for the connected farm building style within New England answers questions about the origin of these structures (see fig. 18). Connected farm buildings are found along the Atlantic coastline of Maine, New Hampshire, and Massachusetts. Generally, coastal towns have lower densities of connected farmsteads than inland towns, because competition from numerous maritime and trading enterprises curtailed intensive agricultural development, which contributed to the growth of many connected farms.

The southern boundary for connected farms gradually diffuses into southern Massachusetts, Connecticut, and Rhode Island. Such farms are infrequently found to the south of the present Massachusetts Turnpike, although isolated connected farms do occur in Connecticut and Rhode Island. The western boundary generally follows the spine of Vermont's Green Mountains. Although examples can be found in western Vermont, they are greatly outnumbered by detached house and barn arrangements similar to those in eastern New York State. The northern boundary for connected farms occasionally extends into Canada in areas of American influence or settlement, but usually terminates at the furthest line of nineteenth-century agricultural settlement in the United States. This line, therefore, dips into northern-central Maine, which was sparsely settled. The northeastern boundary in Maine and Canada is highly diffuse because French Canadian, British, and American building traditions blended together.[32] French Canadian farmers employed an ancient system of connected farm architecture in the New World, but this practice was declining in the nineteenth century and its influence upon New England farmers was minimal.[33]

The presence of connected farm architecture in northern New England (except western Vermont) and its relative absence in most of Connecticut and Rhode Island is surprising considering the basic cultural unity of the region, especially the similarity of English cultural and building traditions. Nevertheless, critical differences exist between the rural areas of these regions. The major reason that the connected farm building organization was not extensively adopted in southern New England was that its settlements were much older and agricultural development and building expansion were generally completed or even declining after the first quarter of the nineteenth century. The region had experienced soil depletion, overpopulation, and subsequent emigration

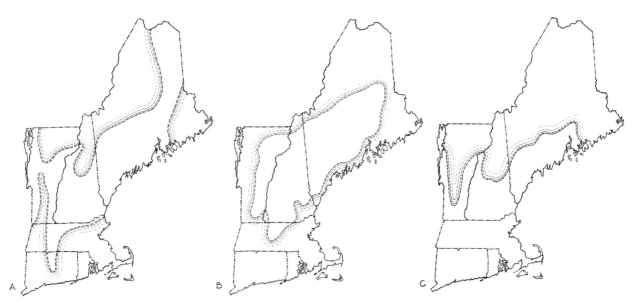

Fig. 20. Factors influencing the diffusion and concentration of the connected farmstead plan within New England: *A*, agricultural areas sustaining growth after 1850; *B*, rural areas sustaining English cultural homogeneity throughout the nineteenth century; *C*, furthest line of colonial settlement in 1780.

well before the major period of connected farm construction.[34] This does not mean that there was no agricultural activity or building construction in these regions, but the critical period of rural building expansion and remodeling that transformed many farms in northern New England between 1820 and 1880 was not generally experienced in southern New England. The southern region also experienced the earliest impact of large scale industrialization in the United States, which caused a significant disruption of the unity and homogeneity of its small-town agrarian culture.[35] Non-English immigration and cosmopolitan influences may also have spread new ideas into these areas, breaking down the rural building traditions that were essential to establishing the connected farm building organization.

The outer boundary for the spread of connected farms tells the story of its diffusion and competition with other farm building ideas, but the rings showing density tell the story of its popularity within the New England region (see fig. 18). The greatest densities occur in southern and western Maine and in the best farming areas of eastern New Hampshire. These regions of high concentration share three important characteristics that help to explain both the popularity of these structures and their confinement to New England (fig. 20).

First, connected farms were built in farming areas that were prospering and still expanding agriculturally in the mid to late nineteenth century. (Figure 20*A* is based upon the record of farm building activity on farms visited for this study and is highly generalized for the region.) Generally, areas that were stagnant or declining in overall agricultural production before 1850 have low concentrations of connected farm architecture. Large portions of eastern Massachusetts and central mountainous New Hampshire suffered significant declines in agricultural production and therefore have low densities of these farmsteads.

Second, areas with high concentrations of connected farms generally maintained a degree of English cultural homogeneity throughout the nineteenth century (fig. 20*B*). Many of the areas that produced connected farms continued to sustain strong, uninterrupted English building and social traditions essential to the development of the connected farmstead organization. It is important, however, to emphasize that the areas in which connected farms were built were not backwaters, isolated from new ideas. In fact, the region contained a rural population as cosmopolitan and literate as any group of farmers in America.[36] But, significantly, they did not live in proximity to farmers from other countries and other cultures, as did most farmers in the major agricultural regions of America.[37] This crucial limitation to the spread of rural ideas was extremely influential in sustaining their unusually long period of regional homogeneity.[38] Consequently areas of New England that came in greatest contact with non-English, industrial, and urban influences did not sustain their rural English homogeneity and thereby have the lowest densities of connected farm buildings. These areas include the cosmopolitan-industrial regions of eastern Massachusetts, the lower Connecticut River Valley region in contact with cultural influences from Hartford and the Long Island Sound, and much of Vermont, especially the lands to the west of the Green Mountains, which were in continuous contact with the commercial and cultural regions of New York's Hudson and Lake Champlain valleys.

Third, connected farms occurred in close proximity to older colonial towns and were influenced by the building traditions and architectural conventions of these areas (fig. 20C). Although nineteenth-century connected farm builders employed new methods and forms, much of their building repertoire was based upon earlier practices developed during the colonial period. Proximity to concentrations of early nineteenth-century Federal estates also seems to have been a factor in the popularization of connected farms. These pre-1760 settlements are located in a broad arc across south and seacoast New England.

The maps in figure 20 show the convergence of all three major characteristics influencing the location of connected farms in southwestern Maine. This region has some of the highest concentrations of connected farmsteads in New England. The map reveals that they were constructed in those areas of New England where farmers sustained a homogeneity of English cultural and building practices and enjoyed at least a modest degree of prosperity during the last three-quarters of the nineteenth century. When they sought to reform or expand their farms after 1820, farmers combined long-established vernacular building traditions with the example of prosperous gentleman farmer estates to produce the now common connected farm building arrangement.

The maps in figure 21 show the areas studied during the course of this investigation. The principal survey area, southwestern Maine and a small portion of eastern New Hampshire, was selected because of initial familiarity with the region. Within this study region, four Maine farming neighborhoods in the towns of North Yarmouth, Kennebunk, Bridgton, and Bethel provide the primary data for this investigation. The first two locations were selected to represent older colonial towns, the last two to represent newer inland towns. The primary criterion for selection was, however, availability of detailed historical information about farms, which is extremely rare. A detailed documentation was made of 120 farms in these neighborhoods, including measured drawings, photographs, census returns, title searches, and interviews. A total of 400 farms and houses were visited during a six-year period. Selective farmstead documentation and general

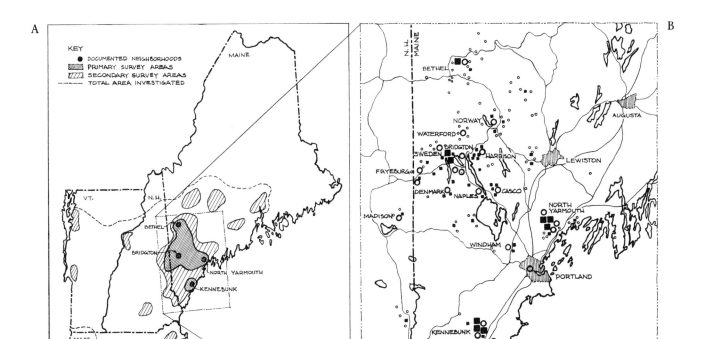

Fig. 21. Areas investigated for this study: *A*, New England region; *B*, southwestern Maine (insert).

neighborhood surveys were conducted in a wide area surrounding Bridgton, Maine, including the towns of Sweden, Denmark, Waterford, Fryeburg, Naples, and Windham, as well as Veazie, Phillips, Berwick, and Farmington, Maine; Madison and Hanover, New Hampshire; and Sturbridge and Topsfield, Massachusetts. A more general survey by car throughout most of New England corroborated regional comparisons.

An Obscure History

Considering the uniqueness of the connected farm building arrangement and the genuinely popular appreciation of this form of architecture in New England, one is surprised at just how little is known about these buildings. Although connected farms are invariably pictured in popular New England magazines, such as *Downeast* and *Yankee*, little is actually known about their history or development. The reason is not hard to find—the building history of most connected farms is extremely difficult to reconstruct. The complete building history of a farm such as the Dawes-Denison farm shown in figure 22 was difficult to obtain, requiring elaborate investigative procedures and a great deal of good luck. After one and sometimes two centuries, the history of most farms throughout New England remains obscure and difficult to decipher. Three principal reasons help to explain this difficulty and also provide a starting point for the analysis of connected farms.

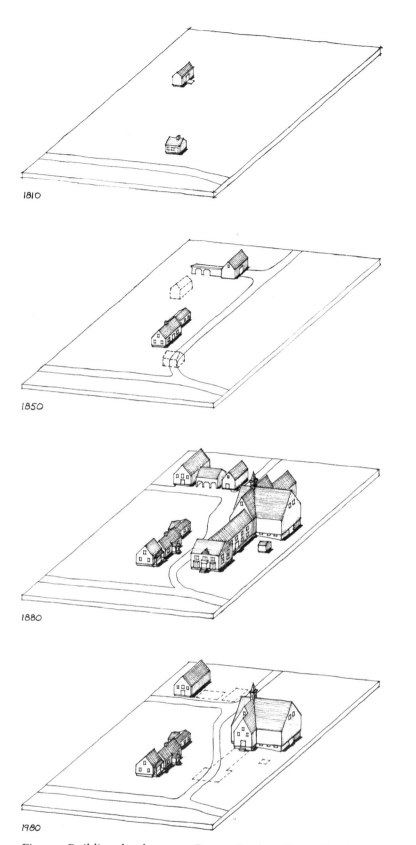

1810

1850

1880

1980

Fig. 22. Building development, Dawes-Denison Farm, Harrison, Maine.

First, connected farm buildings are often composed of distinctly different types of buildings—houses, barns, sheds, specialized agricultural buildings—as the record of the Dawes-Denison farm shows. Each building type contained different structural systems, architectural styles, and patterns of usage. Even within a specific class of building (barns, for example), there are a number of substantially different types often on the same farm. Unlike the study of a particular New England building type, such as the Cape Cod house or the Connecticut Valley tobacco barn, the architectural analysis of connected farms must simultaneously record the development of several different building types within the connected building ensemble, without losing sight of the connected complex as a unified whole. A problem with previous historical study has been that it focused upon one building in the connected complex, usually the major house, and assumed that its history portrayed or paralleled the history of the entire building complex. This, however, was seldom the case, as the development of the Dawes-Denison farm demonstrates.

A second problem of historical analysis is the interpretation of building permanence and change through time. Most connected farms must be analyzed over an extended period involving several major dates or periods of construction and often involving a variety of buildings constructed at different times and often different places. The four drawings that record the Dawes-Denison farm each represent a major phase or era of building construction. The popular idea of a single, fixed date for a building must be discarded for a more flexible assessment of multiple dates, periods, and styles that contribute to the complete history of most farms. The historical record of a connected farm is usually complicated because old and new portions continually intermingle. It is difficult to determine what has changed and what has remained the same. The interpretation and assessment of complex patterns of building permanence and change through time is, therefore, central to the study of connected farm architecture.

Third, perhaps the most serious problem of historical analysis is the general lack of historical data about the buildings and the people who constructed them. The Dawes-Denison farm could be documented primarily because descendants of the original settlers still live there and had preserved important data about the buildings. But even then there was need for considerable investigation and interpretation. The vast majority of connected farm structures, however, were built by farmers and craftsmen whose dates, ideas, processes, traditions, and influences were seldom recorded, and even when they were, much of that data has been lost. Information about farm buildings that does exist usually refers to larger or more prosperous farms, or town houses, and must be used cautiously when applied to the analysis of most connected farms. These are, of course, the consistent problems in the study of any building that might be labeled popular, nonacademic, anonymous, vernacular, or folk.[39]

It is precisely because the building history of most farms is so difficult to reconstruct that conflicting stories and legends are told about the connected farm building organization. This book challenges several popularly held beliefs about the making of connected farm buildings that I believe are misconceptions not supported by historical evidence. Through a detailed documentation of many farmsteads, this book analyzes the complex mixture of historical, contextual, and motivational factors that influenced farmers to build in this unique form.

The Nevers-Bennett Farm

To understand the development of the connected farm building system, this study focuses upon a particular moment of change—the abandonment of the detached house and barn and the adoption of the connected house and barn arrangement. Of course, this moment is actually many moments of quick and slow duration, of haphazard and deliberate action, of partial and complete fulfillment involving hundreds of thousands of farm families and extending over more than a century. These "moments" combine to produce a rich tapestry of developments as the connected farm organization was implemented according to the means, traditions, skills, and inclinations of individual farmers. It is a varied and frequently complex story, but occasionally a moment of change is dramatically isolated and made explicit by the suddenness of its impact and its contrast to the past. Such a moment occurred between 1885 and 1887 when Charles Bennett transformed the farmstead of Benjamin Nevers into a striking example of a fully connected house and barn (figs. 23, 24). The early photographs and drawings reveal the extent of the changes that transformed a typical detached house and barn farm of the early 1800s into a model connected farm of the late 1800s.

The first photograph of the Nevers farm was taken in the late 1860s, but it shows the farm as it probably looked in the 1840s and 1850s. It accurately conveys the basic characteristics of a prosperous farm of the early nineteenth century. The house with its kitchen ell (hidden) is separate from the barn and its outbuildings. The white, architecturally ornamented dwelling stands in sharp contrast to the blackened cluster of unadorned agricultural buildings, which included a large English barn, attached wagon shed, and stable. The fenced front yard might have remained from an earlier period or it might have been a more recent addition, but in either case it served to heighten the contrast between the refinement of the house and the functional organization of the barns.

A   1850

B   1890

Fig. 23. Nevers-Bennett Farm, Sweden, Maine: *A*, detached house and barn, ca. 1850; *B*, connected house and barn, ca. 1890.

A

B

Fig. 24. Two views of the Nevers-Bennett Farm, Sweden, Maine: *A*, ca. 1860; *B*, ca. 1890.

The second photograph shows the farm in the 1890s after Charles Bennett converted his new farm to the connected farmstead plan. In a three-year period he moved the old stable into line with the house and connected it with a new two-story ell. A new barn of a more advanced gable-door plan was then erected next to the stable. Mr. Bennett emphasized the uniformity of his creation by applying the same architectural style and a coat of brilliant white paint to the entire front facade including the barn. He also removed the formal front yard fence, which by 1890 was considered old-fashioned, and then he unified the entire area in front of his connected complex with a common yard or lawn.

The dramatic transformation of the Nevers-Bennett farm was not typical. Most farmers converted their structures to the connected plan in incremental fashion over a longer period. Mr. Bennett's remodeling project was so quickly implemented because of his wealth and because he employed a style fully perfected through a century of trial-and-error testing. The change is so striking because he applied the new style to a farmstead that had maintained an early nineteenth-century organization of buildings. The reorganization he accomplished can, therefore, be seen as a sudden, encapsulated version of a gradual change that rippled across rural New England throughout the nineteenth century. Thus Mr. Bennett's remodeling project accurately represents the full extent of the change that transformed much of New England's farm architecture between 1800 and 1900. The gradualness of this transformation by most farmers, however, does not imply that theirs was less profound than Mr. Bennett's. Most builders of connected farms achieved the same dramatic results; it just took them a little longer.

The change that Mr. Bennett enacted was certainly prodigious, but behind the striking new facade there remained a farm that he continued to operate in much the same way as his predecessor. This is surprising, considering the extent of the alterations. One might expect that such a change would signal a greater transformation and reorganization of the farmstead operation, but it did not. Mr. Bennett's changes only made the previous farm operation more efficient. The reasons why farmers like Charles Bennett dramatically altered the way the farm looked while simultaneously preserving many aspects of the way it worked hold important clues to why they chose this unique building system.

II   Pattern in Connected Farm Buildings

2   The Buildings

After 1850 a standardized version of the connected farm building organization became popular in many areas of New England. It was composed of four basic parts: the "big house, little house, back house, barn" of the children's rhyme. The Samuel Smith farm of Kennebunk, Maine, was a typical example. It included a one-and-a-half story, side-hall big house and a three-bays-deep New England barn (fig. 25). Unlike earlier farms built in incremental fashion over a long period, the Smith farm was built entirely in 1877 at a time when the connected style was fully developed.[1]

This chapter analyzes each of the four building components to determine its specific contribution to the connected complex. Also described is the practice of outbuilding construction that has always been an important component of the New England farm.

Big House (Main House, Front House, House, or Farmhouse)

The big house is the symbol of home and the focus for domestic pride on the New England connected farm. During the nineteenth century, the rooms in the big house were not utilized as extensively as those in the adjoining little house (or kitchen), which was the working center for the farm family. The importance of the big house was, however, clearly demonstrated by its size, frontal position to the road, and prominent architectural ornamentation. Prosperous farmers extended the architectural order or style of the big house to all buildings in the connected complex including the barn, while most farmers extended a simplified version of the big house style to other buildings.

There were two major periods for big houses on the connected farm: houses built before 1830 with a fireplace chimney and containing a kitchen within the big house, and houses built after 1850 with stove chimneys and a kitchen located in an attached ell (fig. 26). The most common early period big house in most of New England had one story with a center chimney and is popularly known as a Cape Cod house.[2] The most common big house of the later period was a one-story house, often in the Greek Revival style, with stove chimneys and a front door placed at one side of the gable end.[3] The significant differences between houses of these periods reveal a major transformation in building construction and social usage for rural dwellings in New England. This change in house form will be linked to the same process of reorganization that resulted in the making of connected farmsteads.

Figure 27 shows the most common house forms built by New England farmers in the late eighteenth and nineteenth centuries during the period when connected farmsteads were developed. (Although the terms accompanying figure 27 may appear cumbersome to those familiar with stylistic classifications commonly used, an expanded ter-

Fig. 25. A typical post-1850 four-part connected farm. Samuel Smith Farm, Kennebunk, Maine, built 1877.

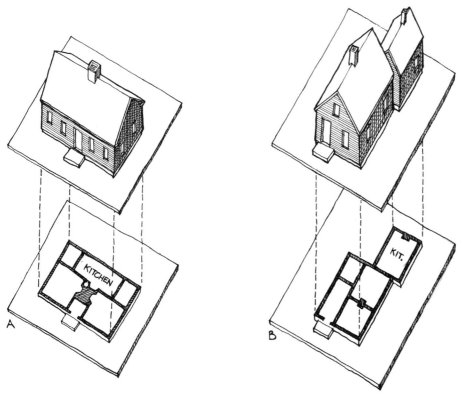

Fig. 26. Big house periods: *A*, pre-1830, fireplace kitchen within the big house; *B*, post-1850, stove kitchen in an ell attached to the big house.

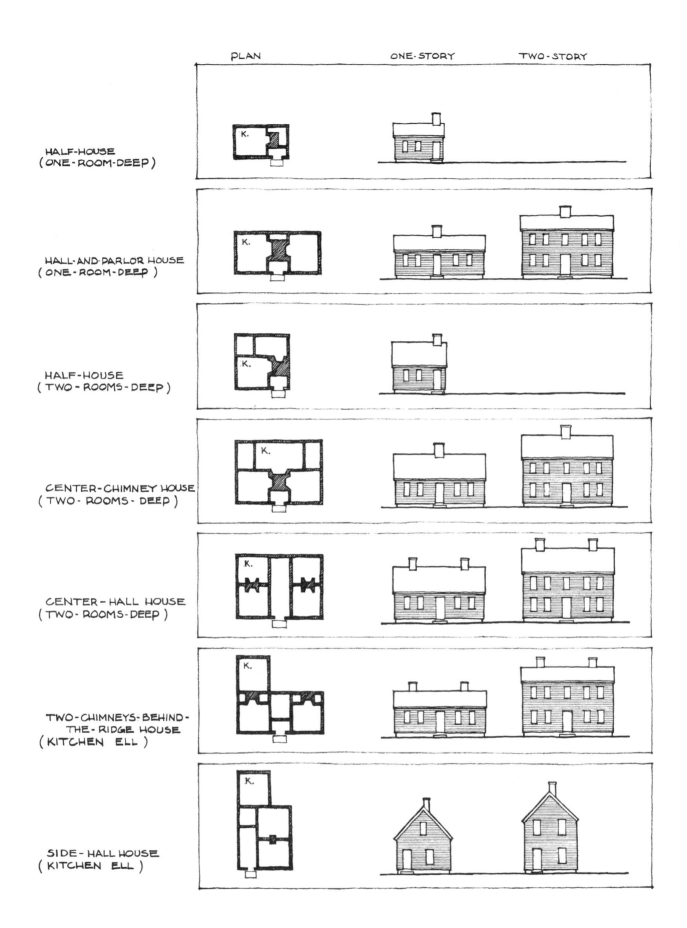

PLAN ONE-STORY TWO-STORY

HALF-HOUSE
(ONE-ROOM-DEEP)

HALL-AND-PARLOR HOUSE
(ONE-ROOM-DEEP)

HALF-HOUSE
(TWO-ROOMS-DEEP)

CENTER-CHIMNEY HOUSE
(TWO-ROOMS-DEEP)

CENTER-HALL HOUSE
(TWO-ROOMS-DEEP)

TWO-CHIMNEYS-BEHIND-
THE-RIDGE HOUSE
(KITCHEN ELL)

SIDE-HALL HOUSE
(KITCHEN ELL)

minology is essential for understanding the multiplicity of the region's early nineteenth-century house forms.) Before 1830 most rural houses were built in a few variations of the center-chimney house. Two distinct types of center-chimney houses had been developed in New England by the early 1800s: a one-room-deep house often referred to as the hall-and-parlor house, and a two-rooms-deep house like the commonly labeled Cape Cod house. One-room-deep houses are easily recognized by the narrow width, usually 15 feet to 20 feet; while two-rooms-deep houses are significantly wider, usually 25 feet to 35 feet. Both one-room-deep and two-rooms-deep houses could be modified to produce dwellings with one or two stories, rooms on one, two, or three sides of a fireplace chimney core, a variety of architectural styles and finishes, and later, multiple chimney arrangements.[4]

The group of one-room-deep, center-chimney houses was derived from the ancient English hall-and-parlor house and includes dwellings in half- and full-house units, in one- and two-story heights, with center chimneys and, later, two chimneys behind the ridge.[5] The group of two-rooms-deep, center-chimney houses includes the popular one-story, center-chimney Cape Cod house and a larger two-story version of the same house. Both types were commonly built throughout the eighteenth century in the styles of the period. In the early nineteenth century, most were built in the Federal style. Both one- and two-story houses were also built in half lengths, but these houses are now rare in most areas of rural New England. The now popularly appreciated saltbox house was an earlier colonial form that combined aspects of the one-room-deep and two-rooms-deep house, but it was seldom built by the end of the eighteenth century.[6] Another pre-1830 type was the center-hall Georgian house, but it is uncommon within the connected farm building organization and is usually found on farms of significant wealth and in the older towns of New England.

After the transitional period of 1820–50, farm builders produced versions of the side-hall, Greek Revival house, distinguished from all previous houses by its front door offset in the gable end. Side-hall houses in New England were often built in one-and-a-half- and two-story forms with two major parlor rooms. Although a major distinction will be made between pre-1830 and post-1850 houses, there was considerable overlapping. For example, many houses continued to look like the older center-chimney ones from the outside, but inside they were arranged without the center chimney and with kitchens in ells. After 1860 an increasing variety of Victorian house types makes strict categorization of all dwellings extremely difficult, but the basic side-hall house form continued to be the most popular farm dwelling throughout the entire second half of the nineteenth century.

One-room-deep and two-rooms-deep center-chimney houses of the pre-1830 period and the side-hall house of the post-1850 period constitute the three most common big house forms of rural New England. Each type possesses unique characteristics.

Fig. 27. Common house types in nineteenth-century rural New England. Classification is based upon spatial organization of rooms, room usage, and chimney location and type, progressing from houses with kitchens within the big house to houses with kitchens in the ell.

The most popular type of pre-1830 big house for connected farm buildings was the one-story, center-chimney, two-rooms-deep house. Also common was a two-story version, which was usually selected by farmers with greater income (fig. 28). Both forms were derived from English vernacular precedents perfected during the seventeenth century in New England.[7] From 1760 to 1830, during the major period of pioneer settlement in the areas where connected farms became popular, these houses were the most common choice of settlers for their major dwelling.[8] In the spatial arrangement for most two-rooms-deep houses, the major entrance hallway divides two front rooms, with a major back room flanked by two smaller rooms. Rooms were organized around a central chimney with fireplaces opening into each of the three major rooms.

The traditional English practice of building two principal rooms, the hall (kitchen) and parlor, was continued in the two-rooms-deep house with the kitchen located in one of the front rooms or in the major back room. Although the practice of locating the kitchen in one of the front rooms is older, both front and back room locations were popular in New England after 1800. In either arrangement, the parlor or "best room" was located in one of the two front rooms, usually on the side of the house closest to the road, furthest from the barn, or toward the northern side of the house. While popular literature has stressed the function of the parlor for formal occasions, such as ceremonies for deaths and marriages, farmers' parlors appear to have been used most of the time as a combination bedroom and storage room.[9] The third major room in this arrangement

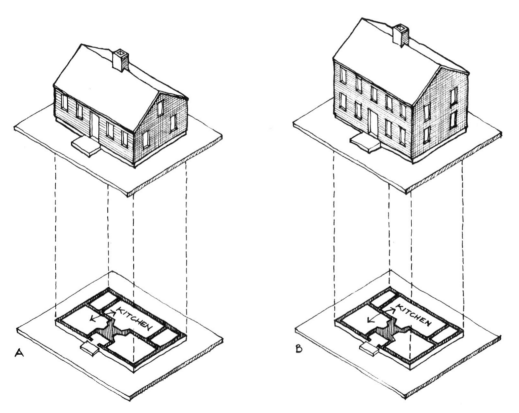

Fig. 28. Two-rooms-deep, center-chimney houses: *A*, one-story, popularly known as a Cape Cod house; *B*, two-story. Both types have similar floor plans.

could be either a less formal parlor room, a bedroom, an all-purpose storage room, or a combination of all three. The two smaller back rooms, connected by doorways to the principal back room, were typically used for kitchen storage (buttery, pantry, or larder) or a small bedroom. These rooms are commonly called borning rooms today, and though births did occur there, the term seems to be a product of the twentieth century.

The center-chimney house plan was built in either one- or two-story forms. Although architectural historians frequently differentiate the one-story from the two-story house on stylistic grounds, their room organization, usage, and structural systems are similar.[10] The plan of the two-story version, however, is frequently larger, with a major side entry and a second stairway located off the major back room. Two-story, center-chimney houses usually displayed the greater wealth of their owners with finely crafted architectural casing, molding, doors, windows, fireplace surrounds, and paneling. Attention to the front stairway, including delicate balustrades and stair ends, was a conspicuous change from the minimal attic stairways of the typical one-story, center-chimney house.

The distinction between the one-story house and the two-story house had important social meaning for the pre-1850 culture of New England. The societal gulf between people who lived in them was considerable. The two-story form conveyed the status of wealth and social distinction (or pretensions to both) in the rural communities of early nineteenth-century New England. In a typical inland agricultural community of Maine in 1802, the ratio of one- and two-story dwellings probably accurately reflected a typical social hierarchy. Out of one hundred and seven houses in Waterford "six were two storied, eighty-six were low framed or one-story, and fifteen were log."[11] Following the Civil War, the two-story house was more commonly used by farmers of modest means, who often "raised the roof" of their one-story houses to achieve a two-story form.

ONE-ROOM-DEEP HOUSES

There are two major types of pre-1830 one-room-deep houses in New England: the center-chimney, hall-and-parlor house and the two-chimneys-behind-the-ridge, kitchen-ell house (fig. 29). Both houses were built in one- and two-story forms with two major rooms divided by a central entry. The two house types differ substantially in the placement of fireplaces and chimneys and in room usage. In the hall-and-parlor house, one central chimney is located between the two major rooms. This room organization is a direct descendant of the Massachusetts Bay houses of the seventeenth and eighteenth centuries, including widely publicized examples such as the Parson Capen house of Topsfield, Massachusetts.[12] Here, the pattern of room usage continued the old English custom of hall (kitchen) and parlor, with the kitchen serving as the central focus of family life. In the two-story version the upstairs rooms had the potential for becoming finished "chambers" instead of minimal attic rooms. The front stairway between the hall and the parlor also tended to be a more finely crafted area in the two-story version. The one-room-deep, hall-and-parlor house was also built in a half version consisting of a single room with a fireplace at one end. This form will be analyzed in the following section on the little house.

In the second and later type of one-room-deep house, two chimneys were located near the back of the two major rooms, with a minor center room in between. (A variation on this type locates the two chimneys in the gable-end walls.) This small room did

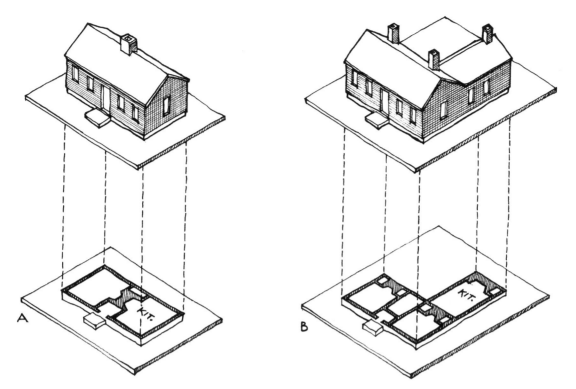

Fig. 29. One-room-deep houses: *A*, center-chimney, hall-and-parlor house; *B*, two-chimneys-behind-the-ridge, kitchen-ell house.

not open to the entrance hallway, as might be expected following the Georgian center-hall house plan, but usually served as a small bedroom behind the stairs. A critical difference in this house type was that neither major room was designed to be a kitchen following the traditional hall-and-parlor organization. The entire house was designed to be accompanied by a kitchen ell, which was an integral part of the overall plan. The earliest houses using this arrangement date from about 1800 and appeared in the seaport towns of New England.[13] It was one of the first known examples of a popular house form specifically designed to accommodate a kitchen addition in an attached ell. This type of kitchen organization was to become standardized in the connected farmstead organization after 1830.

THE SIDE-HALL HOUSE

Directly associated with the increased popularity of the connected farm building organization in New England was the emergence of a new popular house form after the 1830s, the side-hall house (see fig. 26B). Elaborate versions of this house employ accentuated gable ends that reinterpret features of the Grecian temple pediment in many versions of the Greek Revival style. Builders in New England's towns had perfected this gable form in the early 1800s before the popularity of the Greek Revival style, but most farmers adopted the gable-end house type with Greek Revival details after the 1830s.[14]

The typical plan of the side-hall house has two major parlor rooms (or later "sitting rooms" and "living rooms"), with a stair hallway along the side of the parlors and a small room at the back of the stairs producing a typical four-room plan. Although owners and builders varied this plan by the addition of bays, dormers, and porches, its basic form became a standard component of New England housing during the latter half of the nineteenth century. It is one of the most numerous house forms in the entire region.

Because the location of the kitchen was shifted to an attached ell, the plan and usage of the typical side-hall house is usually quite simple. The downstairs rooms were for parlor activities, with the front room usually reserved for formal occasions, and the back room used as a less formal sitting room, or later, a dining room. The small service room under the stairs often provided a downstairs bedroom; later, in the twentieth century it was frequently converted into a bathroom. The upstairs was usually divided into two bedrooms located in the front and the rear gable ends. A comparison of a typical pre-1830 center-chimney house with a typical post-1850 side-hall house emphasizes the changes between these two periods.

THE HAMILTON HOUSE

The house in figure 30 was built in the 1790s by John Hamilton III, of North Yarmouth, Maine.[15] It is a one-story, center-chimney, two-rooms-deep Cape Cod house, and is a well-preserved example of a common domestic dwelling of the late eighteenth and early nineteenth century. The structural system is typical of most pre-1830 houses that em-

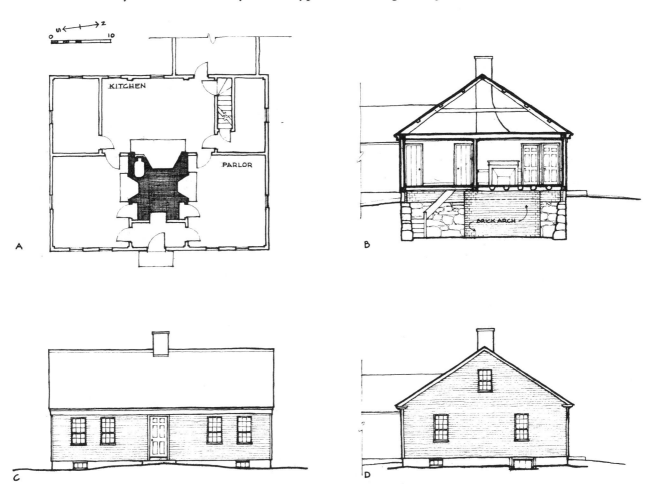

Fig. 30. A typical pre-1830 center-chimney house: A, plan; B, section looking north; C, east elevation; D, south elevation. Hamilton House, North Yarmouth, Maine, built ca. 1790.

ployed the older mortise-and-tenon, heavy-timber construction system (fig. 31). Its sills and plates form a double ring of structural members around the periphery of the house. The sills and plates, separated by vertical corner posts and smaller studs, are subdivided into three parts by the interior girts, which define the chimney and the two major rooms on either side. Studs are placed in between the sills and the plates to frame the openings for windows and doors. They also provide a nailing surface for horizontal sheathing on the outside, and for lathing for plaster on the inside. Most major timbers in pre-1830

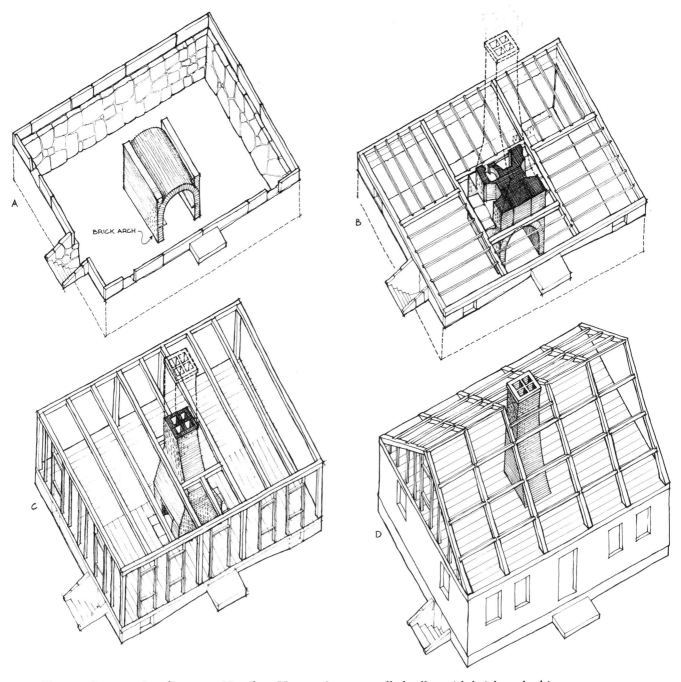

Fig. 31. Construction diagrams, Hamilton House: *A*, stone walled cellar with brick-arch chimney support; *B*, first-floor framing members with cut-away central fireplace chimney; *C*, side-wall studs with second-floor girts; *D*, roof framing members with fireplace chimney stack.

houses such as the Hamiltons' were hand hewn. Smaller studs and braces were either hand hewn or sawed; frequently floor joists, especially in the first floor, were minimally hewn logs.

The frame-raising operation for a dwelling like the Hamilton house in one- or two-story form is a side-wall assembly system. Early New England barns and houses shared a similar raising sequence (see fig. 46A). It was a framing tradition that dated from the earliest colonial settlement and was brought unaltered from England.[16] The roof frame in the Hamilton house, a major-rafter, minor-purlin system, is based on English framing traditions but is an American development of the early colonial period (fig. 32).[17] It is typical of pre-1830 dwellings in the eastern half of northern New England. In the western half, however, another type of roof framing was typically used, the major-purlin, common-rafter system. Thus the two roof systems mark a major cultural boundary between eastern and western New England.

The cellar below the big house was an early, colonial development introduced by English settlers primarily to protect perishable food from winter freezing. This was not widely practiced in England but was necessitated by the more severe New England winters.[18] A distinctive feature of most pre-1850 northern New England house cellars is the massive stone or brick arch supporting the central chimney structure (fig. 33). New England settlers refined the chimney support as a unique winter food storage area. As a farmer remarked at the beginning of December 1849, "I put the potatoes in the arch."[19] Larger pre-1830 houses had finely crafted brick arches, but smaller houses combined brick, split granite slabs, and boulders. Perhaps the most common form of cellar chimney support in northern New England did not employ brick but was composed of two parallel piles of granite topped by horizontal connecting slabs of granite or wood (see fig. 33B).

The cellar arch in the Hamilton house supported a massive brick structure containing three fireplaces and an oven on the first floor and a small fireplace on the second

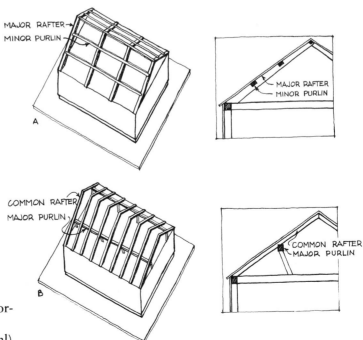

Fig. 32. Roof framing systems: *A*, major-rafter, minor-purlin; *B*, major-purlin, common-rafter (major purlin is optional).

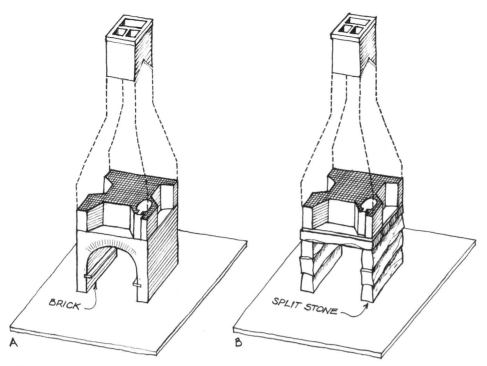

Fig. 33. Chimney arches: *A*, brick arch; *B*, split stone arch.

floor. Similar one-story houses may or may not have contained second-floor fire-places, although two-story houses almost always included two or three fireplaces for the second-floor rooms. The presence of an oven within the wide fireplace hearth identifies the location of the kitchen in the back room of the Hamilton house. In other examples, any one of the three major first-floor rooms could have been designed as a kitchen.

The interior detailing and woodwork in the Hamilton house is typical of most pre-1830 houses because it contains styles and interior finishes from different periods. The earliest woodwork in the northeast parlor was applied in the 1790s and follows the Georgian style. The southeast parlor was largely finished in a delicate Federal style of the early 1800s, while the kitchen was finished in a severe interpretation of the Georgian style. It is not known whether the rooms in the newer styles remained unfinished until the newer styles were applied or whether major remodeling was involved. Both se-quences were common, and even well-to-do New Englanders frequently left rooms unfinished for long periods.[20] All rooms bear evidence of multiple changes during several periods. Dwellings like the Hamilton house continued to be built into the 1850s in New England, but by then radical changes had been made to the popular pattern of building.

THE STAPLES HOUSE

The side-hall, Greek Revival big house of John Staples, Jr., in North Yarmouth, Maine, was a typical dwelling of the post-1850 period (fig. 34). Unlike the Hamilton house of the previous period, the Staples house was designed and built with the kitchen in an attached ell building. This allowed the big house to become a more formal building,

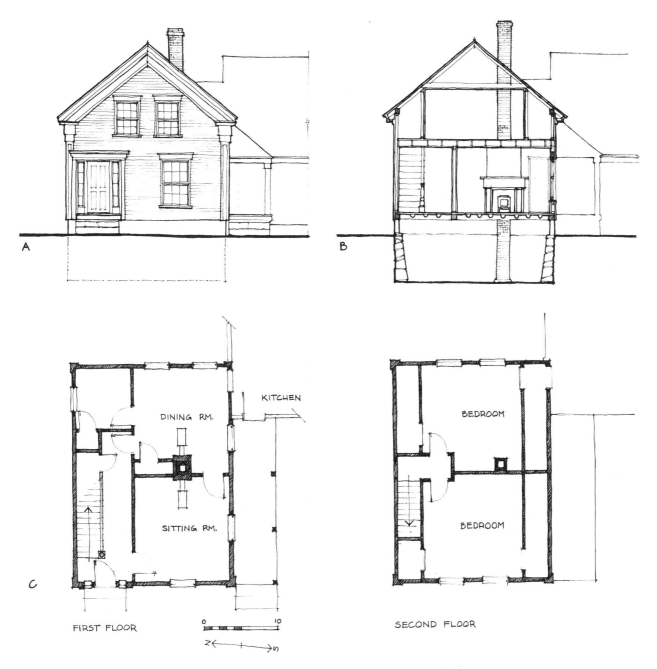

Fig. 34. A typical post-1850 side-hall house: *A*, west elevation; *B*, section looking east; *C*, plans. John Staples, Jr. House, North Yarmouth, Maine, built 1857.

used primarily for parlor and bedrooms. Thus the major focus of farm work activities shifted to the kitchen ell. The massive masonry core of the older center-chimney type house was replaced by a small stove chimney that could be placed in several locations. In the Staples house, it was constructed between the two parlor rooms so that stoves could be located in each room and served from one chimney, although end- and side-wall positions were also common.

When the side-hall Greek Revival house type was first introduced into rural New England, houses continued to be built using the heavy-timber mortise-and-tenon construction system, similar to that used in the Hamilton house. By 1857, however, the proportion of sawed to hewn structural members was reversed. In the Staples house, most structural members were sawed except for the longest hand-hewn sills and plates. The principal structural members and the vertical studs in the Staples house continued to be joined in the old mortise-and-tenon fashion of the Hamilton house, but the common rafters were nailed in a modern stud construction manner. The combination of old mortise-and-tenon with newer stud construction techniques is typical of most houses throughout the nineteenth century.

Although it has been widely recognized that balloon-frame construction was introduced in Chicago in the 1830s, New England builders had previously streamlined their house-building techniques into a system extremely close to this "new" method of stud construction.[21] Using a combination of hewn major structural members and sawed studs, rural New England builders were well prepared to accept the strategy of balloon-frame construction; they were already employing several of the most important components by the 1830s.

Unlike the Hamilton house, the architectural style of the Staples' first floor was uniform since it was completed in a short time. These first-floor rooms were finished in a severe version of the Greek Revival style, but the upstairs was not finished until the later part of the century. The entire house was probably completed in one year because many construction techniques and procedures had been greatly simplified.

The comparison of the Hamilton and the Staples houses emphasizes the tremendous changes in design and construction techniques that popularly occurred in a relatively short period between 1820 and 1860 (fig. 35). Except for the absence of twentieth-century conveniences, including electrical and plumbing equipment, the Staples house of 1857 is essentially a modern house. Only relatively minor refinements separate its basic form and arrangement from the housing of the twentieth century. The Hamilton house, on the other hand, is far closer to ancient postmedieval housing in seventeenth-century England than it is to the Staples house. The significant changes between these two house forms were enacted during a short period of the nineteenth century and represent the compression of a much longer period of English and American technological, social, and economic changes that suddenly burst upon the world of nineteenth-century New England farmers. This quickened period of change was also to effect the popularization of the connected house and barn arrangement.

Little House (Kitchen, Ell, Kitchen Ell)

The little house contains the kitchen area in a connected building complex (fig. 36). While it is possible to list specific house types for the big house, the little house is not so easily classified because the mixture of buildings and parts of buildings is so diverse. The little house usually resembles a less ornate miniature of the big house, hence the name.[22] The kitchen in an ell attached to the big house is a fundamental component of the connected farm building plan and is distinctly different from the earlier colonial practice of placing the kitchen within the big house.

The little house kitchen building originated in three typical ways: (1) as a later ad-

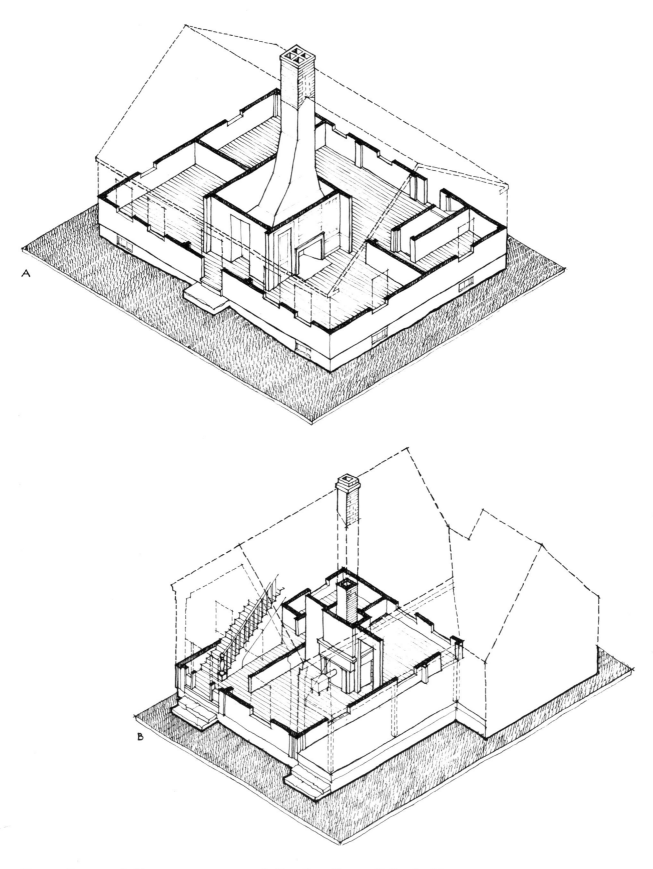

Fig. 35. Room and chimney arrangement: *A*, Hamilton House; *B*, Staples House.

Fig. 36. A little house (kitchen) located between the big house and an extended back house. Moulton Farm, Thorndike, Maine, ca. 1900.

Fig. 37. Historical patterns of development for the little house kitchen: A, the kitchen as an addition to the big house; B, a small original house converted to a kitchen ell; C, the kitchen ell and big house built at the same time.

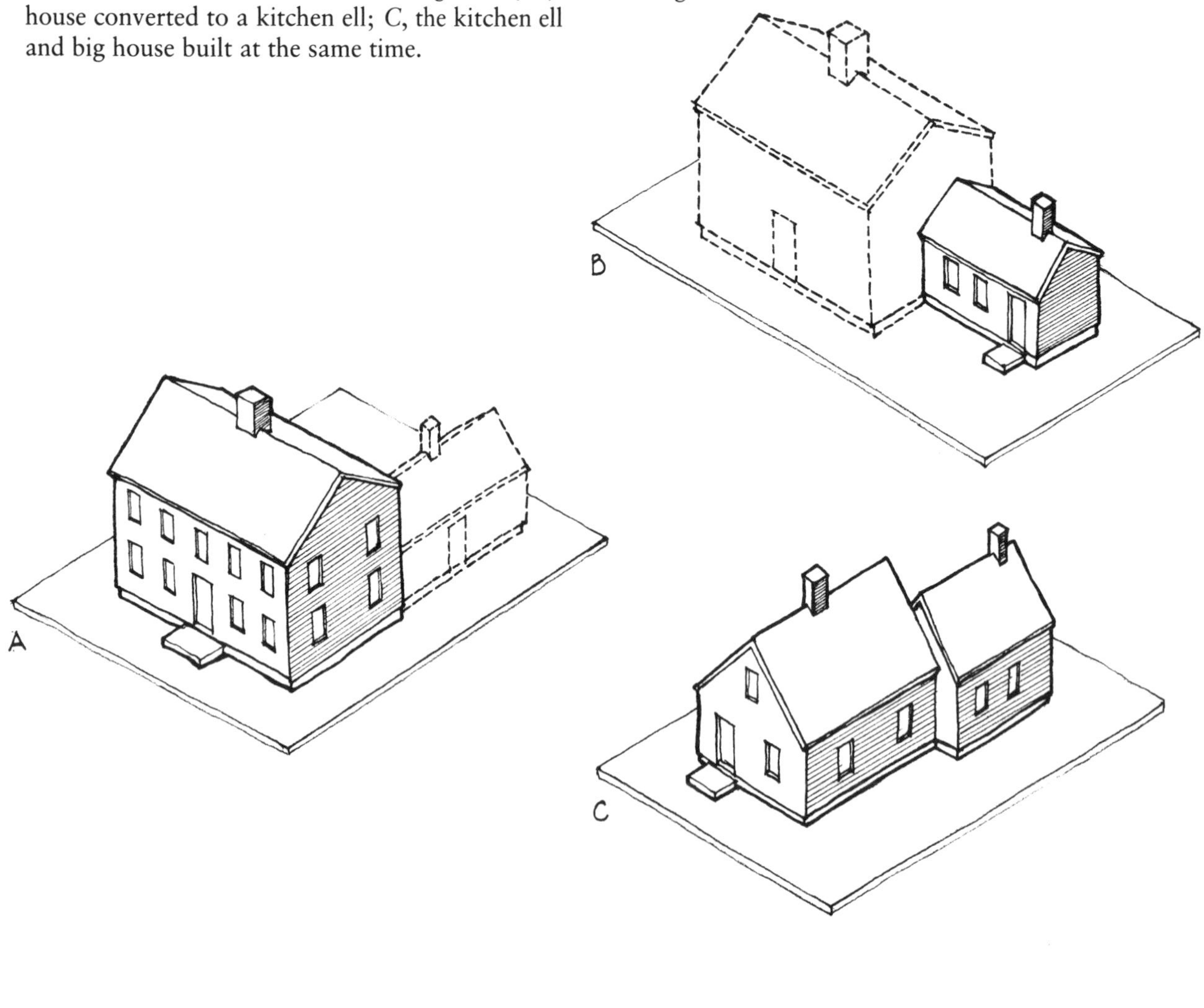

dition to the big house; (2) when an original house became the kitchen ell after a larger house was added on; and (3) as an ell built simultaneously and integrally with the big house, usually within a continuous ell type structure stretching out from the big house (fig. 37). Although all three practices are occasionally found throughout New England in all periods, the practice of placing the kitchen in the ell did not become widely popular for farmers until the first half of the nineteenth century, and it is this practice that was adopted by the builders of connected farms. After 1850, when local builders constructed both big house and little house simultaneously, the entire complex continued to look and function as if it were made from two different structures, following the older incremental tradition.

Present kitchen buildings that were once original houses are usually half versions of the one-room-deep and two-rooms-deep house plans described in the previous section on the big house. The two most numerous types are a simple one-room-deep, one-story, gable structure that contains one room of the hall-and-parlor house plan; and a slightly larger, one-story, two-room plan derived from the center-chimney Cape Cod house. Both versions were once built as original houses, or potential big houses, but they were seldom chosen to become big houses in the connected building complex. However, both half-houses have frequently been preserved as converted kitchens attached to larger and later big houses (fig. 38). Early forms of both houses in Maine and New Hampshire have hewn, tapered, corner posts with a major-rafter, minor-purlin roofing system similar to most early nineteenth-century houses and barns. Along with the larger center-chimney house types, these smaller half-houses were one of the most common houses of the late eighteenth century.[23]

The term *half-house* invites confusion. Today it denotes an uncommon one-half version of a full, two-rooms-wide house like the common Cape Cod house. In the eighteenth and nineteenth centuries, the term *half-house* does not appear. Because of its popularity, it was probably not perceived as a "half-house," but as a whole small house. The term *double house*, however, was widely used to describe a typical center-chimney house, which would be two smaller houses combined.[24] The change in emphasis is

Fig. 38. An original half-house attached to the rear of a later center-chimney Cape Cod house. The original dwelling was probably moved into its present location and its chimney relocated. Whitney-Scribner Farm, Bridgton, Maine, built early 1800s.

significant because earlier builders saw the now typical center-chimney dwelling, like the Cape Cod house, as composed of two smaller whole units that combined to make a double house. The shift in terminology probably also indicates that they perceived the smaller house to be a common and not unusual unit of construction.

The first type of half-house was a small, single-room, single-story structure with a chimney in one end. It had been common in New England since the initial colonial settlement, but, because it was a house form of poorer yeoman farmers, it has generally not survived into the twentieth century. It contained a single, all-purpose kitchen and living room with a large fireplace and doorway at one end and an attic sleeping loft above. In plan and elevation, it was a half version of the hall-and-parlor house with parlor room removed, leaving a hall (kitchen) and a fireplace. Similar structures are frequently cited as the original dwellings or first hewn structures in accounts of pioneer settlement, and in many areas of interior northern New England it was probably the most numerous house type before 1830.[25]

The second type of early dwelling frequently converted to a kitchen ell was a one-half version of a two-rooms-deep, center-chimney house. Its two major rooms were located to one side of the entrance hall and fireplace bay. Although this house form is rare in the connected farm plan today, evidence of it exists in many remodeled kitchen areas.[26]

It is extremely difficult to determine the age or origin of many little house kitchens because they have so often been extensively remodeled. Similar plan dimensions and structural details, however, reveal that a large proportion of kitchen little houses and smaller converted outbuildings originated from a group of uniform, early nineteenth-century structures.[27] The most common, a one-half hall-and-parlor building, is usually the same size as the minimum requirements for houses as stipulated in the 1762 charter of Fryeburg, Maine: "twenty feet by eighteen and seven foot stud."[28] This measurement was repeated in several other town charters in Maine and appears to indicate the presence of a uniform minimum house size for the eighteenth century, much as modern Federal Housing Administration standards dictate minimum housing sizes today. Many tapered-post kitchen ells measure 20 feet by 18 feet, and this supports the hypothesis that many kitchen buildings were the first framed houses on many farms. The kitchen of the Woodsum farm is a typical example of this smaller original house form (see Chapter 4, The Woodsum Farm, 1835–1845).

Between 1800 and 1850, kitchens began to be built within the bays of longer buildings that stretched outward from the main house (fig. 39). These ells were not copies of existing house types, like previous ells, but were designed to be connected additions to a principal dwelling house. This practice of making a long kitchen-ell addition probably developed slowly in the colonial period before becoming popular in the early nineteenth century. By 1830 a long continuous ell extending outward from the big house was a standardized addition to rural New England dwellings and became a critical component in the newly developing connected farm system. It was this house and ell organization that New England emigrants took with them to other areas of the country. Usually the ell addition contained a kitchen, kitchen workroom (or summer kitchen), and woodshed in a standardized room arrangement and structural system. After the middle of the century, when this practice was widely adopted, some observers began to have second thoughts about the wisdom of ell construction. In 1867 one farm writer strongly recom-

Fig. 39. A little house kitchen contained within a continuous ell structure between house and barn. This early 1900s photograph shows a farmer displaying a new horse-drawn mower. South Paris, Maine, area.

mended gathering kitchen workrooms nearer each other, "rather than stretching [rooms] off in a continuous line, as we too often see where ell upon ell is added to the main structure."[29] Obviously this advice was ignored by most farmers, who consistently implemented the practice throughout the nineteenth century.

The development of the outwardly modest-looking ell actually represented a decisive change in the traditional vernacular building system and allowed farmers to develop a new architectural form. The new system was not bound by vernacular construction and measurement systems, which maintained a fixed number of bay sizes, but could be built in any length by simply adding additional bays. This new modular component to planning also influenced interior building layout by permitting farmers to subdivide traditional room organizations into a variety of rooms at any point within the system (although subdivision was most easily accomplished at the structural bay interval). A module approach to building planning was probably developed slowly by trial-and-error testing during the colonial period, but during the early nineteenth century its rapid popularity signaled a radical break with traditional vernacular practices and the beginning of a modern, technological orientation toward building.[30] The system allowed farmers a high degree of design flexibility and permitted ell additions to be remodeled or changed with great efficiency. The ideas of incremental growth and flexible internal subdivision were also applied to a new type of nineteenth-century barn, which will be analyzed below. As we shall see, New England farmers were to have great need for a farm building system that could respond to changing conditions.

The kitchen interior has always been an area of continuous remodeling on the nineteenth-century farm. Early nineteenth-century features, such as the kitchen fireplace, wooden sink, multiple-paned windows and wooden wainscoting, were repeatedly replaced by the wood stove, the metal sink, two-over-two windows, and layers of paint and wallpaper. On the exterior of the little house, porches ("piazzas"), bay windows, dormers, and trellises became common "improvements" after 1850 (see fig. 40). Lengthening the side walls and raising the roof of the attic was a frequent modification for both the kitchen ell and big house. So common were these modifications that today it is extremely difficult to find a New England farmhouse kitchen that preserves even the faintest hint of its earliest interior or exterior origins. The deeper logic behind these frequent changes becomes evident when the kitchen is compared to the usually well-preserved parlor room. Kitchens were assumed to be adaptable and changeable, while the parlor was assumed to be permanent and unchanging. This practice is a very old and still sensible tradition of maintaining distinct realms of formal and working areas and acknowledges the diverse requirements of daily living and family tradition in the same house.

Back House (Ell, Shed, Carriage House, Stable, Back Buildings)

The back house is a general term for a wide assortment of domestic and agricultural buildings (fig. 40). One, two, or even three separate buildings may connect the little house kitchen with the principal barn (see fig. 99). Back buildings may be converted houses (with vertical studs and horizontal sheathing), or barns (with bands of horizontal beams and vertical sheathing), or a combination of both. The standard back building is 30 feet wide by 16 feet deep. It is usually three bays wide and one bay deep with openings for wagons or people entering from the dooryard. Most back buildings in the connected complex were composed of wooden members from previous buildings, which were often joined using later nineteenth-century nail-and-stud construction techniques. This indicates their relative newness on most New England farms.

A relocated barn, no longer used as an animal barn, is a common type of back building. Frequently, an older English style barn was moved next to a little house or kitchen (see Chapter 4, The Woodsum Farm, 1845–1880). Back buildings of this type are usually 30 feet wide by 20 feet deep (the standard size for an older English barn), and have almost always been moved to or reconstructed on their present connected location. In another common arrangement, no distinction is made between little house and back house so that a continuous ell building stretches from house to barn. Usually this type of back house was constructed with sawn studs and built after 1850.

The back house, while not as glamorous as the big house or as dominant as the barn, was actually an important unit in the daily operation of the connected farm, and its function is critical to understanding the popularity of connected farm architecture (fig. 41). The back house in combination with the kitchen was a small-scale farm production center of agricultural and home-industry products for home consumption and commercial sale. The workrooms in the back house closest to the kitchen were often used as a dairy or milk room, buttery, cheese room, laundry or wash room, woodshed, workshop, canning room, loom room, summer kitchen, farm laborer's quarters, or a general kitchen storage area. The seasonal movement of the stove from the major kitchen to a summer kitchen or workroom alongside the kitchen was a frequently recorded back house event.[31] The areas of the back house closest to the major barn were frequently the wagon or carriage shed and the privy, but also might serve as a tool shed, stable, garage, small animal barn, barn workshop, home-industry shop (such as a leather shop), grain and crop storage area, slaughter house, or barn storage area. Some farmers even included a post office or a wagon shop within the connected farm complex (see fig. 118).

Although widely varied according to individual wealth, farm production, local traditions, and personal choice, the basic organization for kitchen and back buildings became standardized in the New England farm ell between 1800 and 1850. In the most

Fig. 40. Back house with three Gothic dormers, Fryeburg, Maine (garage doors are recent additions).

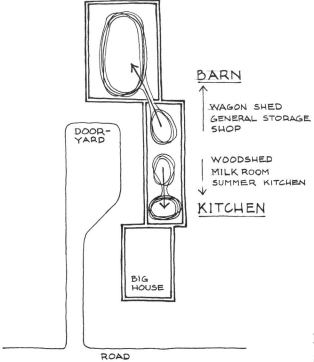

Fig. 41. Rooms of the back house showing their relationship to kitchen and barn.

common pattern, farmers chose to locate an all-purpose kitchen workroom or summer kitchen next to the kitchen, followed by a woodshed, an all-purpose workshop and storage area, and a vehicle storage area. Upstairs, the back buildings served as summer bedrooms for children or hired help and as general storage or cold storage areas. In the simplest version of the ell, a kitchen, woodshed, and all-purpose storage and vehicle shed extended between big house and barn.

The outhouse, known to old timers in satirical terms such as the "deacon's seat," is almost always located on the north side of the back buildings or ell nearest the barn (one of the most consistent patterns in the connected farm arrangement). In the children's rhyme, "big house, little house, back house, barn," the back house is the third building in the connected complex, but the term *back house* is also regionally used to describe the privy or outhouse which is commonly located there. To some old-timers, the term *back house* is used only for the privy. In old English usage, *back house* is a common term used for a building or shed attached to a kitchen, and it is possible that both meanings have influenced the usage in the children's rhyme.[32]

Barn

A major barn usually terminates the connected building complex (fig. 42). In the most common type of connected farm, the house and barn appear roughly balanced in size and importance. Just as the big house marks the domestic portion of the farm, so the barn signifies the importance of its agricultural operation and is the traditional symbol for the agrarian values and life-style of its builders. Old farmers often recall the story of a neighbor who lived in a fallen-down house while maintaining a magnificent barn, or the story of an old barn that valiantly resisted repeated onslaughts of chain saws and bulldozers. Based on fact, these stories convey the significance of the barn for farming people.

The form of the ubiquitous New England barn with its door in the gable end has remained practically unchanged since its introduction in the early 1800s. Internally, however, most barns have undergone extensive and continuous periods of remodeling. Farmers throughout New England began building this type of barn in the early 1800s, and by 1860 it had become the most popular form.[33] The new barn replaced an earlier English barn, which had been brought by settlers to the New World. Barns on New England farms before 1900 should, therefore, be seen in two generically related but distinct chronological and typological groups: the side-door English barn usually built before 1830 and infrequently seen today, and the gable door New England barn usually built after 1830 and now the most common barn form in the region (fig. 43). In this book this later barn will be called the nineteenth-century New England barn or simply the New England barn. The change from old English to New England barn is properly associated with a series of major economic and social changes that transformed many aspects of New England's rural culture in the late eighteenth and early nineteenth centuries. Generally, the new barn form was an outgrowth of a more commercial agricultural operation. The selection of this new barn was initially implemented by large-scale, progressive farmers in the early 1800s and gradually adopted by most farmers between 1830 and 1880. Its selection represented a modest but fundamental step toward a mid nineteenth-century model of commercialized agriculture while simultaneously retaining many of the older patterns of mixed-farming production and traditional barn construction.

Fig. 42. The typical gable-door New England barn in a connected farm building complex. This barn was moved from its original location across the road and connected to the house in the 1880s. Emerson-Ames Farm, Bridgton, Maine.

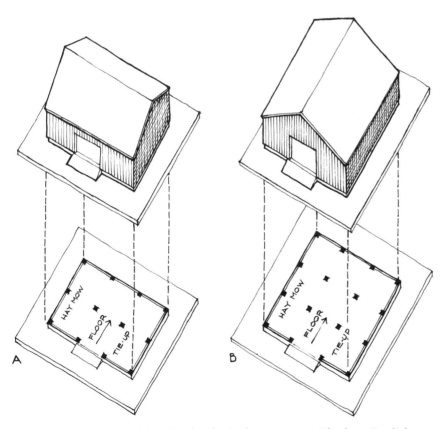

Fig. 43. Barn types in New England: *A*, the pre-1800 side-door English barn; *B*, the post-1850 gable-door New England barn.

The barn in figure 44 is a typical example of an early nineteenth-century English barn (also called an Old English, Yankee, or Connecticut barn).[34] In plan and elevation the English barn is organized in a three-bays-wide system with a central threshing floor separating two usually equal bays. This barn is easily recognized because its major door is located in the middle of the side wall and not in the gable end. Although similar barn forms are also found in other northern European countries from which settlers came to North America, the source for the colonial New England barn is exclusively English.[35]

The barn that New England settlers developed was used differently from the barns they had known in Great Britain. The English tradition of differentiating and separating barns with different functions gradually gave way to an American desire to centralize barn functions under one roof. The severity of the winters in the New World seems to have been the major motivating factor behind this development. New England farmers combined their English hay barn and cow barn and occasionally their stable into an expanded version of the traditional barn form they had brought with them from England.[36] Samuel Deane, New England's famous agriculturalist, recognized this new American development in the definition for a barn in his 1790 dictionary as "a sort of house used for storing unthreshed grain, hay and straw, and all kinds of fodder. But the other uses of barns in this country, are to lodge and feed beasts in, to thresh grain, dress flax, etc."[37] By the early 1800s New England farmers had generally standardized the arrangement of their barns; one side was used for a tie-up or livestock bay and the other side for a haymow or hay storage bay. The central floor continued to be used for threshing but was also used as a vehicle platform to unload hay wagons containing loose cut grass or hay for storage in the barn. In many English type barns, the threshing floor had double doors at both ends to provide a continuous wagon drive and to facilitate air circulation for the winnowing of grain during the hand-threshing process. The primary area for hay storage was the haymow bay, but additional storage was provided by a hayloft (or second floor above the cattle tie-up bay), and also by temporary "scaffolds" constructed in the "high timbers" over the threshing floor.

In the older agricultural areas of southern New England, the English barn was frequently enlarged laterally with bays added to either side of the central drive. This produced a long, multiple-door barn type similar to earlier English examples (see fig. 47A). However, this method of barn enlargement is rarely found in areas of northern New England where connected farms are most numerous because there the English barn was more extensively replaced by the New England barn.[38]

One of the distinguishing characteristics of the English barn is its elaborate framing system, particularly the complex corner joint, often called a flared or gunstock-post system (see fig. 44B). This method of joining structural members predates the fourteenth century in England, and it is a remarkable example of the persistence of a medieval construction system into the middle of the nineteenth century.[39] Although complicated from a modern perspective, this elaborate connection solved a difficult jointing problem involving the junction of four major structural members within a system of all-wood construction (without the use of metal connectors or nails for structural reinforcement).

The roof framing system of English barns in Maine, eastern Massachusetts, and New Hampshire is generally a major-rafter, minor-purlin system (see fig. 32A). Its distinctive tapered or gunstock rafter and multiple purlins are identical to those employed in almost all pre-1830 houses of the region. The eastern New England roofing system differs from that in western Massachusetts and New Hampshire and Vermont, in which minor common rafters rest upon two major purlins.[40] The assembly and raising system used for the English barn is similar to the one used for houses of its period. Like earlier houses, the key framing element of an English barn is its side wall, which is the major structural unit and is raised first in the framing operation (see fig. 46A).

Foundations for old English barns, where original, are usually made of boulders or rough granite slabs, although the finest barns of all periods often had split granite slabs. Barn cellars do not appear to have been widely employed in the early nineteenth-century English barn, although they were highly recommended.[41] It is extremely difficult to confirm the existence of early nineteenth-century cellars from site inspection because of the frequency of barn movement and remodeling. From the criticism that New England farmers received in the agricultural press for not using cellars, it must be assumed that cellars were not commonly constructed before the middle of the nineteenth century. In 1840 a Maine farmer recommended the barn cellar for root crop storage but added that "very few (farmers) have barn cellars."[42]

Today English barns can still be found on older pre-1820 farms and in farming areas of New England that did not maintain high levels of agricultural productivity after the middle of the nineteenth century. For example, there are high concentrations of English barns in eastern Massachusetts, which lost agricultural productivity and leadership in the early nineteenth century. This also suggests that the old English barn was replaced by the New England barn after the first quarter of the nineteenth century.

THE NEW ENGLAND BARN

Today the most common barn in New England has no specialized designation; it is simply "the barn" to most farmers and present owners (see fig. 42). Only when compared to barns of the previous period and to barns in other areas of the country does an architectural label seem justified. The term *nineteenth-century New England barn* is used here because the structure was built throughout the nineteenth century, and although it is most common in the northern region, it was built throughout New England (fig. 45). The basic form of the present New England barn is found in almost every part of the country and, although there are distinct regional variations, it is probably one of the most ubiquitous architectural forms of North America.[43]

The nineteenth-century New England barn is easily differentiated from the earlier English barn by the major door centered in the gable end. It was frequently built in a three-bays-wide, three-bays-deep grid and organized around a central vehicle floor that runs the length of the barn parallel to the roof line and the side wall. Since mechanical threshers generally replaced hand threshing between 1830 and 1860, it is inappropriate to label this central bay a threshing floor, as in the earlier English barn. Most farmers simply call it the floor. Although many observers assume that the central drive floor and its barn door are located in the exact center of the barn, this is infrequently the case.[44] Most New England barns were designed to accommodate a wide haymow bay and a narrow cow tie-up bay, and consequently the barn door is usually offset from the exterior view (see fig. 42). The large hay storage bay (12 to 15 feet) was consistently located on the colder northern or western side and the narrow cow bay or tie-up or linter (9 to

12 feet) on the warmer southern or eastern side, a further example of the sensitive climatic response of most farm builders.

During the second half of the nineteenth century, the unequal size of the bay system was gradually modified so that by the end of the century barns were often built with uniform or nearly equal bay spacing. The reasons for this change are that the increasing importance and the larger physical size of cows, oxen, and horses necessitated the expansion of the traditionally narrow, early nineteenth-century tie-up bay, and that New England farm builders had standardized nonuniform procedures and measurements of their building construction system.[45]

The structural framing for all nineteenth- and twentieth-century New England barns was a heavy timber, mortise-and-tenon system. Most barns were constructed from both hewn and sawn timbers, but generally hewn timbers were gradually replaced by sawn ones during the nineteenth century. Therefore, an early nineteenth-century English barn might be constructed of all hewn structural members except perhaps the small sawn braces, and a later nineteenth-century one might be framed with all sawn members except the longest plates or sills. Although the old medieval system of flared or gunstock posts continued to be employed until the latter part of the nineteenth century, many barns built after 1840 employed standardized 8 inch by 8 inch straight-sawn major structural members with a greatly simplified timber jointing and connection system. The complex gunstock post design was simplified by early nineteenth-century builders, who separated the major structural members and accomplished the same structural tasks as the old English barn connection in a greatly simplified system (compare fig. 44 with fig. 45).

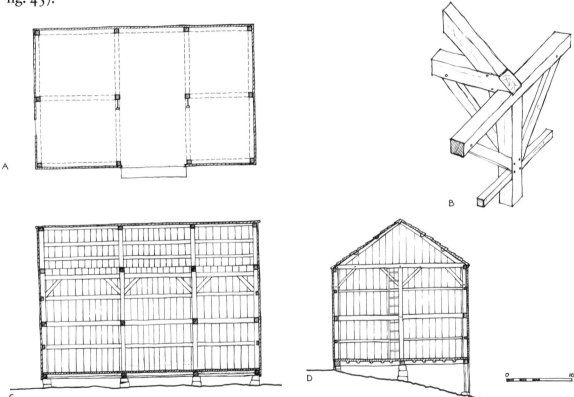

Fig. 44. A typical English barn: *A*, plan; *B*, framing detail at plate; *C*, longitudinal section; *D*, transverse section. Chase-Sawyer House, North Yarmouth, Maine.

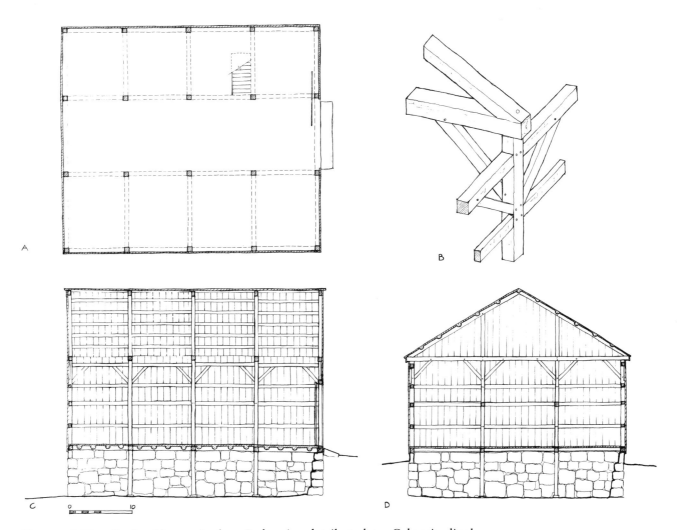

Fig. 45. A New England barn: *A*, plan; *B*, framing detail at plate; *C*, longitudinal section; *D*, transverse section. Sawyer-Black Farm, Sweden, Maine.

The major structural unit in the simplified framing system of the New England barn was the bent (or transverse section), which is the key component in the raising sequence (fig. 46). The adoption of the bent system heralded a distinct break with the earlier and more complex medieval side-wall assembly system of the English barn and can be seen as an example of the trend toward simplification and standardization of construction techniques during the nineteenth century.

The major-rafter, minor-purlin roof framing system of the old English barn of eastern New England was commonly maintained in the nineteenth-century New England barn, although the distinctive flared rafter was often relinquished for a standardized 8 inch by 8 inch sawn one. This late seventeenth-century roofing system of Maine and eastern New England was relinquished only late in the nineteenth century for the major-purlin and common-rafter system previously employed in most areas of western New England. At the beginning of the present century, farmers began to employ stud construction techniques for the roof in the distinctive gambrel roofed barn. This new style roof, however, was only added to a structural framework made in the traditional heavy-timber mortise-and-tenon fashion.[46]

Barn cellars were commonly adopted after 1850. Generally barns built before 1830 did not have a cellar, and those built after 1850 usually had a full or partial cellar. Many New England barns have a half-dug and half-exposed basement. (In other parts of the country, similar practices were labeled a bank barn, but this term was not used in New England even though the practice has been common since 1850.) Stone walls might line the cut-away banks under barns (split stones for prosperous farmers, roughly fitted boulders for most) while the open sides might be left partially open or enclosed with stud walls. Livestock was not normally quartered in the cellars of nineteenth-century New England barns.

Architectural refinements for New England barns became popular after 1860 (see fig. 1). A line of small windows over the door was a helpful addition to a dark, windowless pre-1800 barn (the origin of this early practice is not known but it probably developed in the early 1800s).[47] When clapboard and architectural refinement became more popular for barns after 1850, most farmers limited this embellishment to the front or road-facing facade and sheathed or shingled the sides and back of their barns.[48] Farmers added barn cupolas, lightning rods, and weather vanes during the last quarter of the nineteenth century.

The change from the English barn to the New England barn was a decisive break from the building and agrarian traditions of colonial origin to more modern procedures of the nineteenth and twentieth centuries. The new barn plan offered a distinct advantage over the old English barn because it could be expanded to the rear by the addition of new bays that were easily serviced by wagons moving along the continuous central "long floor" (fig. 47). This could not be accomplished in the English barn "short floor" plan, which required a lateral expansion system with multiple doors and wagon floors. In 1847 a farmer summarized the advantages of the new barn type by emphasizing "that if it is wished to make an addition, it is simply necessary to extend the length, which is readily done without in the least interfering with the original building" (fig. 48).[49] The potential for expanding the New England barn was critical to the acceptance of the connected farm concept, because it gave the New England farmer a means of accommodating the increased yields of nineteenth-century crops and livestock production in a

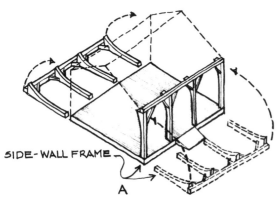
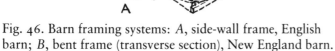

Fig. 46. Barn framing systems: *A*, side-wall frame, English barn; *B*, bent frame (transverse section), New England barn.

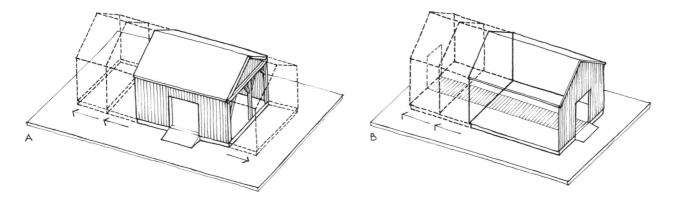

Fig. 47. Barn expansion systems: *A*, English barn; *B*, New England barn.

Fig. 48. A New England barn showing a three-bay addition to the rear of the original six-bay barn. Bethel, Maine, area, ca. 1890.

large, expandable barn without moving the barn away from its attached position with the house.

The change from English barn to New England barn occurred gradually from about 1800 to 1850 as farmers, sensing the advantages of the newer barn, nevertheless had to accommodate the new plan within their existing farm buildings. Consequently they used several common transitional methods to transform their old English barns into the new gable-door arrangement. One popular method was to change the door location from the side to the gable end (fig. 49). This usually required the realignment of the existing posts from a two-bay system of the English barn to produce the standard three-bay alignment of the New England barn. This realignment was often initiated after the movement or reassembly of an old barn on a new site and was the method used to remodel three English barns along Ingalls Hill Road in Bridgton, Maine.

A second popular method involved a similar relocation of the doorway into the gable end, but in this procedure the door was moved to one side of the gable end and an additional shed was constructed along the side wall to produce the desired three-bay arrangement. This was the method of modernization used to transform a large English barn on the Anderson farm in Windham, Maine, into a modern mid nineteenth-century

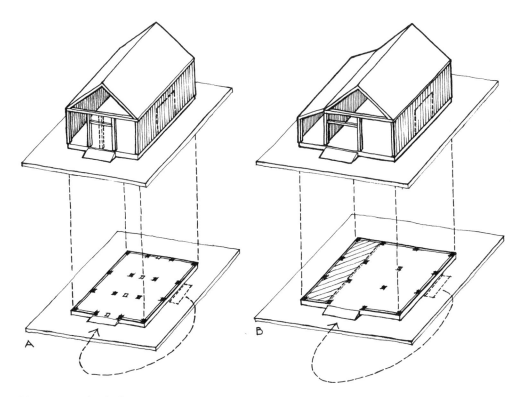

Fig. 49. Methods for converting an English barn to a New England barn: *A*, center bay realignment; *B*, side bay addition.

New England barn, for which the owner received wide publicity in 1858.[50] (This bay addition to the side of an old English barn should not be confused with a similar looking, later nineteenth-century bay expansion that enlarged the tie-up bay of the New England barn; see the section on animal shelters below.)

Four significant changes are associated with the change from the English barn to the New England barn: (1) the realignment of the main barn door and its central drive to allow for expandability and easily serviced additions; (2) the acceptance of a centralized large barn while retaining aspects of an older outbuilding tradition; (3) the construction of barn cellars for the storage of manure and crops; and (4) the streamlining, standardization, and simplification of many construction techniques. Each of these changes is associated with the transformation of the entire farmstead and the adoption of the connected farm building concept.

In the record of building history, few buildings have accommodated change and survived as successfully as the nineteenth-century New England barn. From a modern standpoint, we could attribute this to adherence to unchanging antiquarian ways. But considering the amount of change and remodeling that have occurred on the New England farmstead during the last hundred and fifty years, it is likely that the New England barn persisted because it served the purposes for which it was intended. The New England barn persisted and even prospered because good original design decisions have proven remarkably adaptable and successful. The endurance of this barn will be examined later in relation to the stabilization of farming methods employed by New England farmers during the nineteenth century.

Today, in the areas that are still actively farmed, single-story prefabricated steel barns with concrete floors are replacing the older barns. Of course, those who appreciate the older structures lament the loss, but those associated with farming know that it is extremely difficult to make a living using the old buildings for modern farming practices. However, the older barns have served the modern farmer as valuable storage buildings, particularly for hay. Now, however, even this use might become obsolete if a new method of open rolled hay eliminates the need for covered storage. If this practice becomes widespread, it will probably signal the abandonment of many older wooden barns.

Outbuildings

The children's rhyme "big house, little house, back house, barn" does not mention outbuildings or other attached buildings, but these structures form an integral part of the building history of New England farms. *Outbuilding* is an old English term used by New England farmers and may refer to any building not part of the major building core, including small attached buildings or sheds. The English tradition of constructing separate buildings for separate agricultural functions was continued by New England farmers in the New World. In the seventeenth- and eighteenth-century English system, a cluster of agricultural buildings of more or less equal importance formed the farm center. A typical eighteenth-century farmstead for a prosperous English yeoman farmer would commonly include many of these separate buildings: a stable for horses, a barn for threshing grain and storing hay, a byre or shippon for sheltering cows, a granary for crop storage, and a sty for pigs.[51]

Outbuildings have sheltered a variety of farm and domestic functions on New England farms and were produced in many building types, including converted houses and barns, smaller versions of those structures, and parts and pieces from previous buildings. The history of many outbuildings is difficult to reconstruct because many have been continuously remodeled, reassembled, and reused for different functions. Many outbuildings look alike because they were originally houses or barns or styled after existing buildings. Only outbuildings with highly specialized functions, such as hop barns or corncribs, received a unique architectural form.

The history of outbuilding construction presents a vivid picture of the variety of farm and nonfarm occupations that were attempted by New Englanders within their nineteenth-century system of mixed-farming and home-industry agriculture. Perhaps, more than any other tradition, the continuous practice of outbuilding construction demonstrates the extent to which a changing agricultural context forced New England farmers to diversify their farm production system and constantly readjust their building organization. New England outbuildings have been organized here into six categories: animal shelter, produce storage, vehicle storage, home industry, domestic, and miscellaneous activities. Although combining several activities in one building was common, the traditional English preference for maintaining separate buildings for separate agricultural activities has created an extensive body of outbuildings on the New England farm.

ANIMAL SHELTERS

Stable (Carriage House, Horse House, Chaise House, Shed). Connected farms have three types of stables or carriage houses: structures for horses only, for vehicles only, and for both horses and vehicles. All three types were built throughout the nineteenth century in separate or attached positions with house and barn. Before 1830 few common farmers had enough horses or carriages to justify a separate structure, and most farmers housed their first horses in their barn. After 1830 the stable or carriage house was sometimes located in a separate structure, although by 1850 it had become increasingly popular to locate it within the connected farm arrangement. During the second half of the nineteenth century, horses began to supplant oxen for pulling farm machinery and wagons. (Most New England farmers, however, never relinquished oxen and continued to use both animals.)[52] Generally the stable or carriage house was absorbed into the connected building complex, but separate stables and carriage houses also continued to be constructed into the twentieth century (see Chapter 4, Nevers-Bennet Farm, 1835–1880).

Sheep Barn (Sheep House or Shed). Periods of intensive sheep raising appeared in New England throughout the nineteenth century after the first major period in the 1820s.[53] Although the sheep barn was occasionally built as a separate structure, many farmers found it convenient to attach this building to the major barn in order to facilitate winter feeding. Nineteenth-century agricultural census figures show that many farmers kept a small flock of four to eight sheep. The sale of wool added a small cash income for the New England farmer, but western competition generally rendered sheep production only marginally profitable until by 1900 it had become unprofitable.

Pigsty (Pig House, Sty, or Shed). Early colonial records frequently mention problems associated with unfenced pigs.[54] By the beginning of the nineteenth century, most farmers probably housed their pigs in crude sheds near the principal barn, although well-to-do farmers continued to follow the English tradition of building a separate building for sheltering pigs. In the early 1800s attention was called to the pig's natural rooting ability as a way of mixing livestock manure with soil.[55] Consequently more farmers began to make specific accommodations for their pigs in buildings referred to as pig houses or sties (see Chapter 6, 1840–1850). After 1830 farmers began housing their pigs in the cellars of their barns and stables to facilitate the mixing of manure, although they continued to build separate pig houses into the twentieth century.

Chicken Shed (Chicken House, Hen House). Chickens were present on the earliest New England farms, but they seldom were given a separate building until they became more commercially important in the last quarter of the nineteenth century. Most existing chicken sheds were built in the twentieth century and range in size from small coops to long, continuous sheds. They were made in light frame stud construction, and because they were built cheaply to buttress a declining agricultural economy, they have generally not survived, even though they were among the most recent and numerous outbuildings on the New England farm.

Chicken Barn. Although there is no rigid distinction between a chicken shed and progressively larger chicken barns in New England, the advent of the egg industry in the early 1900s signaled a major change in the previous scale of chicken raising and egg production.[56] Most large pre-1950 chicken barns are actually converted dairy barns with continuous rows of windows placed into the side walls and additional floors inserted between the existing barn floors to accommodate greater numbers of chickens (fig. 50). After 1950 chicken barns began to be built in long, single-story, metal-sheathed structures.

Fig. 50. A New England dairy barn converted to a chicken barn. Baston Farm, North Yarmouth, Maine.

Cow Tie-Up Expansion (Shed). The customary small width of the barn's cow tie-up bay was a problem for late nineteenth-century farmers because the larger size and greater number of dairy cows made milking and cleaning extremely difficult. Some New England farmers solved this problem by enlarging their cow tie-ups and constructing a bay addition along the side of their barns. This distinctive addition is easily recognized from the main gable end because it appears as if an awkward-looking bump has been added to one side of the symmetrical barn facade. Unlike the open manure shed that was constructed in the same location, the tie-up expansion is completely enclosed in order to shelter the dairy herd. These additions were usually made after 1900.

PRODUCE STORAGE STRUCTURES

Corncrib (Corn House, Grain House). After the expansion of corn production following the Civil War, a special building for corn storage, or corncrib, was constructed (fig. 51).[57] This building is easily identified by its conspicuous slanted walls with ventilation slats for air circulation and its unique stilt foundation for protection against rodents or vermin. Similar structures are found throughout the Midwest and South, although the corncrib in New England is usually smaller.

Hop Barn (Hop House). Periods of hop growing occurred in the mid-1800s and led farmers to develop a distinctive hop-drying barn. One barn in Harrison, Maine, contains an insulated drying room, where hops were dried by the smoke and heat from a large open hearth (see Chapter 4, The Woodsum Farm, 1845–1880). By 1880 this crop had almost ceased to be cultivated in northern New England.

Granary (Barn). Grain storage in a separate structure was not widely practiced in New England, perhaps because the yields were so small. Most existing structures are combined with other outbuildings like the pig house. Figure 52 shows the granary on the Nutting farm in Otisfield, Maine, which served as a grain storage area above and a hen house and pig house below. Many farmers stored small quantities of mixed grains in a corn house or in their barns or back buildings, particularly in the attic of the ell.

Manure Shed (Cow Shed, Shed). To protect manure from exposure to the weather and to preserve its valuable nutrients, farmers often added a manure shed to the south side of the barn. Both the manure shed and the barn cellar became popularly accepted after

Fig. 51. A corn crib (*right*) and milk house (*left*) in front of a New England barn. Foster Farm, East Bethel, Maine.

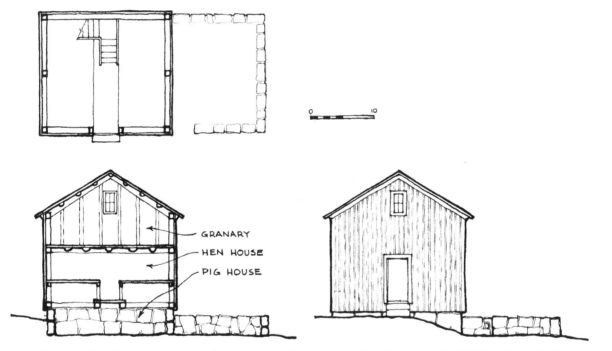

GRANARY

HEN HOUSE

PIG HOUSE

Fig. 52. Combination granary, hen house, and pig house. Nutting Farm, Otisfield, Maine, built ca. 1825.

1830, when most farmers began to give more attention to the conservation of manure for fertilizer. Although the most common location for manure storage was the barn basement, older barns without cellars or barns where cellars could not be constructed were often equipped with a manure shed, which also served as a shelter for livestock during inclement weather.

Milk House (Milk Room). The post-1920s milk house was spawned by state regulations to promote sanitary standards for milk processing and storage (see fig. 51).[58] A milk storage building or milk house was required to be separate from the milking room or tie-up. Most farmers chose to attach this building close to their tie-up at the front of the barn. Today this small building beside the front of the barn is the conspicuous mark of a New England dairy farm.

Apple Barn. After 1850, when large-scale orcharding became profitable, farmers occasionally built separate barns for apple processing and storage.[59] Most apple barns were merely converted barns or sheds, but by the end of the nineteenth century a specialized insulated and heated apple barn was perfected to store apples and prevent frost damage. Most farmers grew apples for home consumption, particularly for cider making, but only a few specialized enough to devote an entire barn to apple storage. Apple barns are found in areas that have continued to raise large commercial orchards during the twentieth century.

Silo. A common silo on Maine farms was constructed inside the barn, usually within a bay of the haymow. Exterior silos were probably built as early as the 1880s after corn production increased throughout Maine.[60] The silo works on the principle of ensilage, in which an airtight container permits the fermentation of fodder without spoilage. The introduction of the silo in New England is usually associated with the widespread expansion of the dairy and the sweet corn industry after 1880 and was used to store corn or corn silage for animal consumption. The earliest circular wooden silos on the outside of barns were introduced in the early 1900s and continued to be built until the Second World War. Silos made of brick and tile came into use after 1920, but they were rare in New England. Concrete and sheet metal silos were developed after 1930 and are a common barn appendage today.

Sap House (Sugar House). The sap house was a building for boiling the sap of the sugar maple tree into maple sugar syrup. It was usually located near a stand of sugar maples, often at a great distance from the major farm buildings. The production of maple syrup was a messy, seasonal job, which also contributed to the separation of the sap house from other farm buildings and functions. Most sap houses were small, temporary structures that generated a cash crop for a small farm operation and consisted merely of a roof covering an open fire pit. Large permanent maple sugar houses were more likely to have been constructed for larger commercial enterprises.

Root Cellar. A few isolated root cellars demonstrate an alternative method of food storage in the winter, although the traditional method established very early in the colonial period was to store food in the cellar of the house. An early root cellar probably dug between 1800 and 1820 still exists on the Carlson farm in Harrison, Maine. The Aroostook County potato barn of northern Maine is a specialized one-crop structure accomplishing a similar purpose, but this building was not widely developed until the late 1800s. A modern method of low-grade fodder storage is an open concrete bin or excavated silage ditch.

Field Barn (Barn). The practice of building a separate barn away from the major farm center was probably an old English tradition, and it lingered in New England until the nineteenth century.[61] A field barn might be any barn located at a distance from the major house, although most were used as hay storage barns. Old-timers will occasionally recall such an isolated barn, although they were never common.

VEHICLE STORAGE STRUCTURES

Wagon Shed (Carriage or Tractor Shed). A structure for sheltering farm and domestic vehicles was one of the most common additions to both houses and barns throughout the nineteenth century. After 1840 this structure became increasingly integrated within the connected farm complex. The wagon shed was often an open structure, usually two or three bays wide with a single pitched shed roof.

Tractor Barn (Model T Garage, Garage). After 1910 early gasoline-powered cars and tractors were generally separated from the connected building complex, probably because of the fear of fire. Automobile garages were usually located near the house and the major road, while tractor barns were placed near the barn or at the rear of the building complex.

HOME-INDUSTRY WORKSHOP (SHOP)

The tradition of home-industry shops is an essential component of the New England farm (fig. 53). Over two-thirds of the farms surveyed in this study supported at least one of the following home-industry shops during some period in their farm history: blacksmith's shop for farm metalworking, particularly the shoeing of animals (later to become the machine shop on the mechanized farm); tannery for the curing of animal hides and production of a wide range of leather products, such as harnesses and shoes; carpentry shop and a variety of specialized wood product shops like the shingle shop and the cooper shop for barrel making; slaughterhouse (although many farmers slaughtered their own animals, a neighbor who specialized in this task was common); and a wide variety of specialty shops including wagon and toolmaking facilities. Many of these home industries were housed in converted barns and domestic buildings or in structures

Fig. 53. A typical home-industry shop (*far right*). The shop served a succession of tradesmen owners: cooper, shoemaker and carriage painter. A well sweep visible behind the shop raised water from a hand-dug well. The early barn for this house was not connected but stood to the left of the house. Ephraim Andrews House, North Yarmouth, Maine.

indistinguishable from smaller barns and house types. A small standardized shop, known as a ten-footer, often housed these roadside shops.[62] Although they were common buildings on nineteenth-century farms, these workshops have not generally survived. Because of their limited scale of production, most farm shops were family operated, although one or two employees or apprentices were not uncommon (see Chapter 6, 1770–1820). Less common shops also existed, including specialized smithing shops such as a gun shop, and together these shops testify to Yankee resourcefulness in a highly competitive rural farm economy.

DOMESTIC STRUCTURES

Wood House (Woodshed). Early nineteenth-century accounts have sometimes listed a detached wood storage building, but the overwhelming majority of farmers stored their cut firewood near the kitchen within the connected building complex.

Icehouse. Icehouses were built in great numbers after the Civil War because increased commercial production of dairy products required improved methods of refrigeration. The icehouse was usually located on the shady north or west side of the connected building complex. It was often insulated by sawdust-filled walls, a technique widely recommended in the agricultural journals during the middle of the nineteenth century.[63] Most icehouses were situated close to but separate from the connected complex because of the constant problem of building rot and deterioration caused by the melting ice. Consequently, the icehouse, although one of the most common New England outbuildings, has generally not survived in great numbers. In some rural communities, farmers used icehouses until the Second World War, when electric refrigeration finally replaced hand-cut ice.

Summerhouse. The term *summerhouse* can be applied to a wide variety of open pavilions used for relaxation, from tiny garden gazebos (not an indigenous term) to large screened-in buildings or porches for outdoor relaxation and eating. Although the summerhouse was more popular among nonfarmers and townspeople, farmers employed these buildings as early as 1870, both in emulation of genteel urban styles and, more commonly, for the attraction and use of summer tourists, whose boarding fees supported declining farm income.

Pump House (Well House, Windmill, Spring House). Old photographs show early buildings and covers atop wells, but few original structures remain. True pump houses protected the valuable pumping mechanisms (wood and metal) from the weather, while ornamental well covers satisfied aesthetic needs. Elaborate wooden windmills and the more common metal windmills were introduced in the late 1800s. Frequently pump houses were built to protect twentieth-century pumping machinery.

MISCELLANEOUS STRUCTURES

Stores. Many early stores were located on the farmstead, although they were usually separate from the connected farm buildings. Frequently stores were located along the road near the farm complex, as evidenced by the placement of Bennett's store in Sweden, Maine (see Chapter 4, The Nevers-Bennett Farm, 1820–1835).

Mills. Many neighborhood sawmills, gristmills, and cider mills were full-time occupations for nineteenth-century New England millers and do not generally fit the category of an outbuilding on the farm, but there were also a large number of mills located near the main house that were small enough to be considered outbuildings in the traditional part-time occupational sense.

Camps (Cabins). A camp is a New England term for a minimal cabin, usually a summer vacation cabin. To attract the tourist trade, some farmers constructed hotels, guest-houses, cabins, children's summer camps, and vegetable stands in the late nineteenth and early twentieth centuries. This category of building constitutes a large percentage of the post-1890 buildings in many areas of northern New England.

PATTERN IN OUTBUILDINGS

Overall patterns for the construction of outbuildings are difficult to discern because of the vast number of structures involved, their rapid change, and their generally poor documentation. Nevertheless, overall patterns do emerge if individual farms are carefully studied over time. The two farms depicted in figure 54 show the locations of all the outbuildings constructed on these farms. Despite first impressions, the placement of these outbuildings is not random or haphazard. Just as the location of the major buildings in the connected farmstead was highly structured, so the placement of outbuildings followed a set of commonly accepted conventions that made good sense to most farmers (fig. 55). Of course, many farmers deviated from these normally accepted patterns for various reasons, but most located their outbuildings in similar positions because trial-and-error decisions and local traditions reinforced the selection of particular locations.

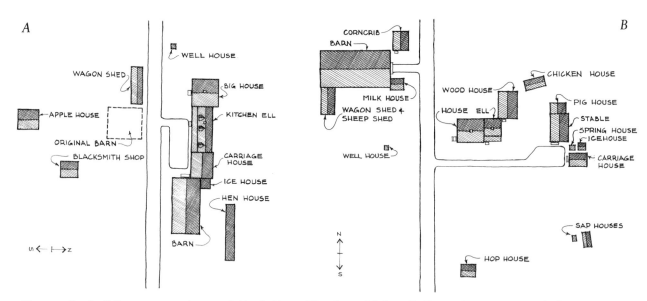

Fig. 54. Outbuildings on two farms: *A*, Buck Farm, Harrison, Maine; *B*, Foster Farm, East Bethel, Maine.

The construction of outbuildings and specialized attached structures continued an older English agrarian idea of differentiation and separation of individual work activities. This ancient practice came into direct competition with newer nineteenth-century American ideas of centralization and standardization of various farm functions. The latter idea is best typified by the development of the large, multipurpose New England barn, which combined the hay and cow barns into one larger unit. Throughout the nineteenth century, New England farmers combined the old concept of differentiation with the new concept of unification and centralization in the construction and arrangement of their farm structures. These planning practices gradually stabilized in the popular late nineteenth-century pattern of a unified, connected farm complex with a diversified outbuilding arrangement in which both ideas actively influenced farm building organization. The record of multi-outbuilding construction and repeated modification to these buildings accurately records the continuous, almost heroic effort of New England farmers to develop stable, long-range markets for their farm production. It is also the record of their failure finally to achieve this goal.

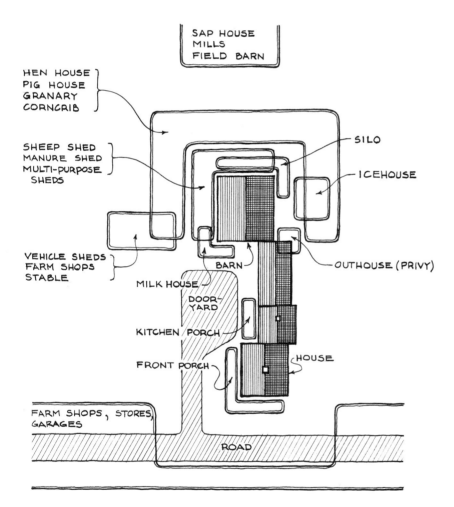

Fig. 55. The pattern of outbuilding location. Zones indicate the typical location for outbuildings and connected sheds surrounding the connected farmstead.

3 The Buildings and the Land

The land that surrounded the typical connected farmstead was organized according to the same influences and ideas as those that shaped the buildings. Like the buildings, the landscape also underwent a significant transformation during the nineteenth century (fig. 56). The magnitude of this change is indicated in a comparison of the two scenes of the Nevers-Bennett farm (see fig. 24). Although the first photograph was taken in the 1860s, it may stand for the pre-1820 farm landscape, which was organized in a similar fashion. The differentiation between house and barns is reinforced by the formal, symmetrical front yard defined by its formal fence. The white house stands in distinct contrast to the darkened cluster of barns and outbuildings. In the post-1890s picture, the connected house and barn are unified by a similar spatial order that extends from the uniformly white buildings into the entire landscape surrounding the complex. This dramatic change can be followed in the development of the yards and fields that surrounded New England farms.

Yards

The yards that immediately adjoined the connected farmstead reflected the spatial and functional arrangement of buildings. By the fourth quarter of the nineteenth century, many connected farms contained three principal yards: the front yard, the dooryard, and the barnyard, which followed the functional distinction between the formal big house, the working kitchen ell, and the animal barn (fig. 57).

THE FRONT YARD

Before 1820 common farmers maintained a working dooryard and a barnyard but did not usually construct a fenced or distinctly delineated front yard. The popular acceptance of the farm front yard with its sharply delineated white picket (or "paling") fence accompanied the building of many connected farms between 1820 and 1860. After 1880 many farmers began to relinquish the idea of a rigidly defined, formal front yard for a less formally ordered lawn. Today most front yards have lost their fences and distinctive formal character because the front lawn now blends into the kitchen dooryard. But during the middle of the nineteenth century, the front yard was a crowning component of the newly popular connected farmstead organization.

The front yard on the typical connected farm was intended to enhance the big house by establishing a zone of formality between the house and the road. It was often laid out in a symmetrical alignment with the formal front door of the big house. Many farmers constructed a picket fence to define this area as recommended in an 1829 farm

Fig. 56. A typical farm landscape without common nineteenth-century improvements: barnyard with oxcart (*left*); granary on stilts (*far left*); half-gable, wagon shed attached to one-story, center-chimney house (*right*). Alonzo Fifield Farm, Riley Township, Maine, 1905.

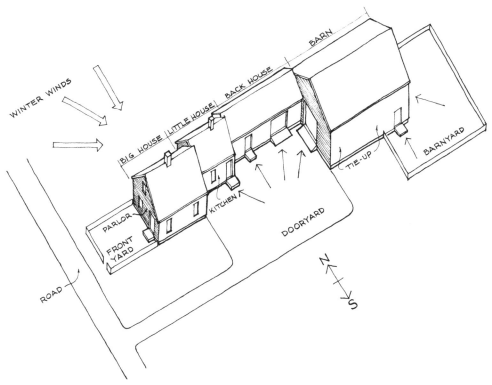

Fig. 57. The three-yard system.

A

B

Fig. 58. Two views of the front yard of a farm in Minot, Maine: *A*, ca. 1870, newly constructed front yard with young sugar maple trees and a variety of garden shrubs behind the white picket fence; *B*, 1982, more than a hundred years later, the same farm without an articulated front yard.

journal: "In front of the house there should be sufficient room for a convenient yard, which should be made perfectly level and smooth, and enclosed with a suitable fence."[1] Figure 58 shows a farm family from Minot, Maine, proudly gathered in their newly completed front yard. This often recorded scene contains all the essential ingredients of a mid nineteenth-century formal yard including a white picket fence, symmetrically planted trees about the front door, and ornamental shrubs. Although many chose a more modest interpretation, most farmers did create the outlines of a formal front yard, so that between 1820 and 1880 the essential elements of this scene became part of the dominant rural landscape in New England.

Before 1820 the area in front of the major house on most common farms was a much more barren, undifferentiated landscape. A Massachusetts farmer probably spoke for most New England farmers when he recalled his boyhood in the early 1800s: "I remember that my father caused the ample front yard to be plowed, and instead of planting out shrubbery and flowers, it was filled with bush beans."[2] This farmer was probably describing an accepted treatment for the environment around the house. William Cobbett, an Englishman, commented upon the condition of this farm landscape. Unlike many Europeans, and Englishmen in particular, he did not make a habit of belittling American accomplishments. Cobbett was sympathetic to the American cause, yet he commented unfavorably on the environment of rural residents of Long Island, noting "the general slovenliness about the homesteads, and particularly about the dwellings of laborers." His observations may also be applied to New England farmers: "Instead of neat and warm little cottages [in England], we here see the laborer content with a shell of boards while all around him is as barren as the sea-beach . . . there is no English shrub or flower."[3] When one compensates for homeward-longing exaggeration, such comments convey a sense of the stripped down, antinaturalist American folk aesthetic that characterized most yeoman farmers at the beginning of the nineteenth century.[4] Photographs of New England from as late as the 1880s and 1890s still show farms that followed this minimalist aesthetic, and although it seems bare and almost shocking today, it probably characterized most farms in the early 1800s (fig. 59).

To modify this bleak picture, it must quickly be added that the typical New England farm was not devoid of vegetation or care. There was always vegetation near the farmhouse, particularly in the dooryard, where the planting of day lilies and lilacs, assorted herbs, and a variety of fruit trees was a popular tradition that probably was maintained from the earliest colonial settlements.[5] The kitchen garden was usually located nearby, and the planting of roadside trees in front of the house was another early colonial tradition.[6] Thus the pre-1820 yard near the house was not devoid of order, vegetation, or care, but it was not the same front yard that many farmers developed during the next eighty years with a keen eye for symmetry and a desire for greater quantities of natural vegetation. Most farmers achieved the look of a formal front yard by setting off their big house with symmetrical groupings of roadside trees and shrubs, although many also included a stylized organization of fences, gates, paths, trellises, and formal plantings about the front door. When the physical setting of many farms is assessed over time, it is clear that the popular acceptance of the formal front yard played a significant role in the transformation of New England's rural landscape in the nineteenth century. Although the distinction between the formal front yard and its surrounding landscape lessened with the gradual disappearance of the fence in the later nineteenth century, its organizing principles are still an important component in what we recognize today as the picturesque New England countryside.

The idea for creating a formal yard in front of the main house, especially by means of a formal fence, was borrowed from the example of New England's wealthy gentry and merchant classes. Late eighteenth- and early nineteenth-century estate and manor houses are continually shown with a rectangularly fenced yard stiffly defining a formal zone in front of the major house.[7] While not all farmers adopted this strategy, the practice of creating a more formal, fenced front yard gradually became popular throughout all levels of society by the middle of the nineteenth century (fig. 60). For example, in 1856 William Walker remodeled a small, modest farm and constructed a white picket fence in his front yard. He recorded the project in his diary: "I built some board fence from the corner of the house to the road, turning the door yard [front yard] into the road."[8] What is so unusual about this farmer's account is the hint he gives of the motivation behind his improvement project. His intent was to turn or focus the yard of the front door toward the road. It is this often assumed characteristic of the formal front yard that was a distinctly new idea to farmers like William Walker, who instituted the change during the middle of the nineteenth century.

Fig. 59. A vernacular landscape. The rough appearance of this farm was probably similar to most common farms in the early nineteenth century. A kitchen garden and a small orchard are grouped together near the connecting ell. A rough roadway cuts across the foreground with a post-and-rail fence on the near side and a version of the common crossrail fence on the far side. The strewn boulders give some idea of the original condition of the land before farmers cleared their fields and stacked their stone walls. Cobblestone Farm, Grover Hill, Bethel, Maine, ca. 1900.

A photograph from the Bethel, Maine, area, probably taken in the 1860s or 1870s, summarizes the development of the front yard and shows a typical farm at a critical moment of transition from an older, traditional farm landscape to a more carefully organized front yard and building group (fig. 61). The farm family sits in front of their newly remodeled big house displaying a new shingled roof, stove chimney, two over two windows, and two young sugar maples defining the front yard. The rocks have been removed in a small area where the family sits, but clearing the remainder of the front yard, like clapboarding the buildings, would probably wait until more important tasks were completed. It is this gradual, relatively modest scale of improvement to the appearance of the New England farm that characterized the projects of most farmers during the nineteenth century. But because improvements such as these were outwardly modest and gradually accomplished does not mean they were minor or insignificant. Together, the concerted action of thousands of farmers effected a profound reinterpretation of the traditional vernacular landscape of nineteenth-century New England.

During the early 1800s a few wealthy New Englanders began to abandon the idea of a formally defined front yard with its white fence for a picturesque or pastoral concept of landscaping imported from Europe. An early indication of this changing style was summarized by John Codman in 1800. While touring English country estates he described future improvements to his estate in Massachusetts: "All it wants is the fore-yard all knocked away and the house to stand in the midst of a lawn."[9] Codman's removal of the formal front yard and the establishment of an undifferentiated lawn in a more natural setting heralded the emergence of an American picturesque landscape movement that became popular with progressive farmers after the middle of the nine-

Fig. 60. The front yard of a small farm. The simple picket fence defines a lush garden while the working dooryard (*left*) is barren. The dwelling is a small version of a center-chimney, one-room-deep house. A twentieth-century photograph shows a much altered view from the dooryard (see fig. 63 C). George F. Hamilton House, North Yarmouth, Maine, 1899.

Fig. 61. The beginning of a formal front yard. Bethel, Maine, area, ca. 1870.

teenth century and was to influence the majority of New England farmers modestly by
the end of the century.

Today it is difficult to perceive the nineteenth-century distinction between the front
yard and kitchen dooryard on most connected farms for two important reasons. First,
since most connected farmsteads are no longer active farms, the normally busy kitchen
dooryard no longer contains the residue of multiple domestic and agricultural activities
that once clearly separated it from the seldom used and carefully maintained front yard.
Second, and more important, the entire concept of the front yard has been seriously
undermined since the late 1800s by the reversals in New England's agricultural prosperity. Many former front yards that once proudly displayed picket fences, exotic shrubs,
and stately trees have completely disappeared, so that only old photographs and memo-
ries record their existence. This transformation is dramatically evident in the comparison
of past and present photographs of the farm from Minot, Maine (see fig. 58).

The planting of roadside trees in front of the house was one of the most distinctive
characteristics of the front yard. The tradition of planting "marker" or "marriage trees"
commemorated a significant event like a marriage, a birth, or the construction of a
house.[10] Many late nineteenth-century houses still stand in back of trees planted to mark

their construction. Generally, however, most farmers planted trees to enhance their farms. As one farmer wrote in 1858 during a slack period, "It rained by spells, we dug up two maple trees and set-out [them] before the house."[11]

The earlier traditions of roadside tree planting practiced by both common farmers and gentlemen farmers were significantly augmented in the early nineteenth century by a widespread movement for town and rural improvement. This "spirit of beautification" began in the towns during the first quarter of the century and quickly became an extraordinarily popular and unifying aesthetic force throughout the region.[12] Tree planting societies became the mark of progressive rural communities by the middle of the century and probably influenced farmers to intensify their previous tree planting traditions.

The elm and the sugar maple were by far the most popular trees planted in front of the main house. In southwestern Maine, the sugar maple or rock maple was favored by rural or farming people, while the elm was more popular with town dwellers, although both species were widely planted in all areas during the nineteenth century. The elm, sugar maple, and the occasional oak were most frequently arranged in symmetrical groupings of two, four, or six trees and often planted at the same time.

Symmetrical groupings of trees might be planted on either side of the front door of the big house or on either side of the entrance drive to the kitchen dooryard. The visual impact of both arrangements is slight, but the meaning is significant: a symmetrical alignment of trees in the front yard probably indicated an emphasis on a more formal spatial organization of the big house. Symmetrically planted trees flanking the entrance drive probably indicated a slight shift in attention and care from the front yard to the dooryard and the establishment of a less formal, more agrarian idea of farm order.

Today various species such as black locust, horse chestnut, and white pine are found in front of farmhouses, but these varieties usually date from the twentieth century and were often, but not always, planted by people who no longer farmed for their major source of income. The loss of most elm trees to the Dutch elm disease has had a tremendous impact upon many farms, which is evident when the photograph of an old house showing large elms is compared to the present house with its elms removed (see fig. 76).

THE DOORYARD

The dooryard is an old English term still commonly used in rural New England. In the connected house organization, the dooryard is the area in front of the ell between the house and barn, and it receives its name from the kitchen door of the little house, which opens onto it. In the later nineteenth century, the kitchen dooryard, like the front yard, became a more refined area on some farms with a greater frequency of flower gardens, shrubs, trellises, summerhouses, and porches. The dooryard is probably best understood as a working porch for the active farm. More than just a place of work, it was the place to meet neighbors and talk, a place to leave from and come back to; it was the outside center of the farm in much the same way as the kitchen was the inside center. Even today the combination of the kitchen and its dooryard provides a spatial and experiential focus to life on the family farm, just as it did over a century ago.

On a typical farm in the middle of the nineteenth century, the dooryard was the workplace of multiple domestic, agricultural, and home-industry activities. It gathered

Fig. 62. Work activities adjacent to the dooryard. Sheep
shearing in the barn doorway. York, Maine, 1890s.

the various labors of the kitchen, back buildings, and barn, which literally spilled
outward from the various doors that lined the ell and barn (fig. 62). Most frequently the
dooryard served as a place for chopping firewood and harnessing horses and oxen, and
as a general vehicle staging and loading area, but it also served as a critical outdoor or
overflow area for work conducted in the buildings, including crop processing, butchering, tool and vehicle repair, and many domestic chores. Consequently it was often an
active and sometimes cluttered place in contrast to the seldom used front yard.

The physical condition of the dooryard attracted considerable attention from agricultural writers, who consistently advised farmers to keep it neat and orderly and
recommended that they evaluate their neighbors by these standards. Usually these writers emphasized the connection between the physical and moral organization of the farm
and went on to recommend a neat and orderly farmyard appearance on economical
grounds.[13] The twentieth-century observer, however, should be careful not to construct
too static or idealized an image of the dooryard or any yard on the typical connected
farm (fig. 63). Just as today people maintain different front yards for a variety of
reasons, so New England farmers developed their individual dooryards according to a
variety of factors including wealth, social class, local traditions, and personal tastes.
Photographs from the nineteenth century reveal that the appearance of dooryards ranged
from barren and immaculate to lush and picturesque, from functional and full of work,
to cluttered and hardscrabble.

But in spite of these individual differences, the general trend of nineteenth-century

A

B

C

Fig. 63. Dooryards: *A*, William Walker Farm, Arundel, Maine, ca. 1880; *B*, Windham, New Hampshire, area, 1890s; *C*, George F. Hamilton House, North Yarmouth, Maine, early 1900s.

agricultural improvement tended to increase consciousness and attention to the spatial and visual aspects of the farm dooryard. It remained, of course, a working place, but as this book will show, New England farmers gradually but significantly altered their previous attitudes about its care and upkeep during the nineteenth century. A summary of that previous attitude is provided by William Cobbett, again describing Long Island farmers in the early 1800s, but probably also describing their New England neighbors: "round about the house, things do not look so neat and tight as in England. Even in Pennsylvania, and amongst the Quakers too, there is a sort of out-of-doors slovenliness, which is never hardly seen in England. You see bits of wood timber, boards, chips, lying about here and there, and pigs and cattle trampling about in a sort of confusion, which would make an English farmer fret himself to death, but which here is seen with great placidness."[14] In spite of the exaggerated style of the period, these remarks probably typify an industrious, American, make-do approach to the care of the environment that was the normal operating procedure for most farmers in the early nineteenth century. New England farmers were to reexamine this common attitude to the buildings and the land when they spruced up the general appearance of their farms and adopted the connected building plan.

THE BARNYARD

The barnyard is also an old English term, and, as the name implies, it is connected to and associated with the barn (fig. 64). It is usually the fenced livestock yard, and on New England farms after 1880 it was increasingly the dairy cow yard. In 1790 Samuel Deane recommended, "It is best that a barn yard should be on the south side of a barn."[15] This advice was usually followed because of considerations for animal warmth and the desirability of a dry yard. The barnyard was separated from the work activity area of the dooryard because livestock fencing, manure storage, and general sanitation considerations made it desirable to separate animal areas from other areas of farm activity. Fencing was therefore an important consideration, and elaborate pens and yards were frequently constructed near the barn to separate different animals, commonly cattle, horses, and sheep, and different breeds, sexes, and ages of the same animal. It is important that a reader unfamiliar with farms not confuse the use of the major barn door and its dooryard with the activities of the barnyard. The major barn door did not connect to the barnyard but was used by vehicles and people entering from the dooryard. Farm animals, except horses or oxen pulling vehicles, did not use this entrance. Therefore the barnyard did not connect to the kitchen dooryard but was connected to the barn through a series of smaller side doors or larger openings in the cellar. The funneling of animals into a separate barnyard away from the dooryard was critical to the success of the connected farmstead organization, which required the close functioning of a variety of nonrelated agricultural and home-industry activities.

The early nineteenth-century barnyard was slightly modified after mid-century by the popular introduction of the barn cellar. Slight adjustments in fencing and yard layout had to be made to allow vehicular access to the cellar and major barn floor while still maintaining animal passage to both floors and to the barnyard. There were, however, extreme variations in individual barnyards in all periods depending upon farm wealth, agricultural production, site topography, and barn type.

Surrounding the connected farm building complex was a group of outside areas and

Fig. 64. A barnyard. A farmer stands alongside a team of oxen in the barnyard. Behind the oxen, a pile of dung shoveled from the cow tie-up stands ready to be carted to fields and pastures. York, Maine, 1890s.

physical amenities that were common to most farms but did not develop a consistent location within the three-yard system. Almost all farms had a kitchen garden, containing vegetables, herbs, and flowers; wagon paths about the buildings; fruit trees; wells (usually two, one for the house and one for the barn); and perhaps a small recreational area on the north side of the complex (usually added after 1860). The most consistent landscape feature near the house was the kitchen garden. It was often located directly outside the kitchen on the north side of the building complex, although the location of fertile soil was the most important consideration for its placement.

The basic three-yard system for connected farms became popular between 1820 and 1860, when New England farmers gradually added a more formalized front yard to their previous dooryard and barnyard organization. The question of the source and the motivation for this effort will be examined in the last chapter, but it does appear that, during the middle of the 1800s, many New England farmers intensified their normal efforts to create an agrarian order. One of the products of that effort was a vastly restructured and visually refined outside area.

Fields

The fields that surrounded most connected farms were organized and farmed in generally consistent patterns. Although the crops were frequently rotated and changed to maintain soil fertility, the overall field organization for many New England farms remained uniform throughout the nineteenth century because most farmers operated their farms according to a system of mixed-farming, home-industry agriculture.

ORGANIZATION

A four-part field system employed by New England farmers was probably well established by the time Reverend Samuel Deane described its organization in his agricultural dictionary of 1791: "When it can conveniently be so ordered, the lots for tillage should be nearest to the house and barn, to save labor in hauling manure and prevent loss in getting in the crops. . . . The mowing lots should be next, if the soil permits; as these must be dunged, and their crops carted—The lots for pasturage should be next—and the wood lots furthest of all the lots from the house" (fig. 65).[16] He further recommended that house and barn be located along the major road nearest the center of the property with vegetable, herb, and flower gardens and yards located close to the house and barn. Deane's plan for a judicious farm layout remained the basic pattern for a small, mixed-farming New England farmstead well into the twentieth century and was only enlarged, not fundamentally altered, by mechanized farming techniques during the second half of the nineteenth century.

New England farmers followed this plan by locating their crop fields close to the farm building and usually adjacent to the road. Fields were most frequently planted in potatoes, corn, beans, and a variety of grains, including oats, barley, and wheat. Throughout the nineteenth century there were wide fluctuations in the production of these staples due to market conditions, crop failures, soil quality, localized traditions, and personal preferences. Farm diaries, farm censuses, and agricultural literature of the nineteenth century list a variety of other crops including turnips, flax, and hops.[17]

Mowing fields and pastures were planted in a variety of English grasses and grains or were allowed to mix with indigenous species. The difference between mowing fields and pastures is that grazing animals were kept out of mowing fields, so that the grain or hay might be harvested for winter consumption or sold for profit. Pastures on many nineteenth-century farmsteads were usually the poorest agricultural lands, unfit for plowing, mowing, or fertilization, although the wealthiest farmers in all periods maintained fertilized pastures for greater productivity, as progressive agriculturalists recommended.[18] The woodlot was an important economic unit on the majority of nineteenth-

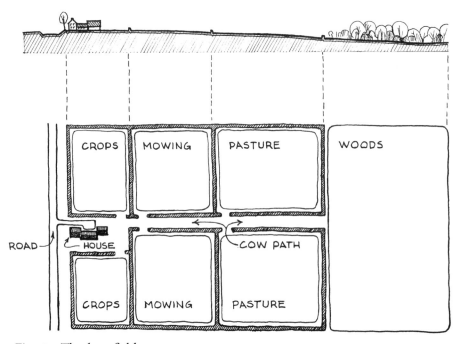

Fig. 65. The four-field system.

Fig. 66. A typical New England hilltop farm showing cultivated fields near
the farmstead and uncleared pasture in the lowland. A small orchard ajoins the
road in the center of the photograph. Shrewsbury, Massachusetts, 1890s.

century farms, supplying an important winter cash crop of timber and cordwood, as
well as household firewood. As in other areas of the country, woodlots were situated on
leftover areas, which contained the hilliest, rockiest, least productive farming soils furthest from the house. A late nineteenth-century photograph shows a hilltop farm with
this four-field system extending from the house to the bottom of the hill (fig. 66).

Of course, not every farmer in New England laid out fields in this manner. As
Samuel Deane emphasized, this four-field system was to be applied when it was convenient to do so. It was a model that was developed over many years of trial-and-error
testing in the New World and was based upon a group of shared assumptions about the
New England mixed-farming system. One of its chief tenets was that the most economic
and labor-intensive crops should be concentrated and crops of less worth and requiring
less labor should be dispersed.[19]

A cow path or lane was a ubiquitous feature of the New England farm. Farmers
built cow paths to solve a consistent problem in their four-field system that necessitated
the movement of cows and horses from the barn through crop and mowing fields to
distant pastures. Although its layout varied, the common purpose of the cow path was
summarized by Samuel Deane, who recommended that it "should not be very narrow,

lest it be blocked up too much with snow in winter. The land it contains will be useful in pasturing. . . . On this plan, the labor of driving cattle out and in morning and evening will be halfed, as the lane may be always in common with the pasture which is in the present use, the gates of all the rest being shut."[20]

One common crop that did not fit into the basic four-field model was the orchard, usually for apples. Farmers integrated the orchard into their field system by planting large field orchards or by planting orchards along the boundaries of existing fields. Both practices were recommended by agriculturalists at mid-century. Many farmers followed both methods by filling in small orchards on less productive crop land and by bordering fields with fruit trees (see fig. 66). As a general rule, farmers located their small family orchards in close proximity to the house, with several apple trees frequently near the dooryard or on the north side of the house. In 1858 a farmer recorded a common occurrence: "Dug apple trees in field and set them by door yard."[21]

The distinction between fields for crops, mowing, and pasture and woods was not rigid. Farmers continually changed their field systems according to both time-tested methods and new progressive ideas.[22] Therefore, a pasture might be fertilized one year and mowed the next year, or a long-abandoned field might be plowed and planted. The idea that there were strict patterns for the use of fields must be applied cautiously and should be seen only as an idealized model, which would be followed unless there was a good reason to change it. For example, a farmer who owned a fertile nonadjoining field, as was often the case, would plant it to crops regardless of the distance from the farmstead. Still, the adjacency of crop fields to the farmstead made good, practical sense and was the practice most frequently employed by nineteenth-century New England farmers.

BOUNDARIES

An elaborate system of stone walls and wooden fences gave definition to the rural landscape of New England. As a general rule, the construction of eighteenth-century field boundaries kept grazing animals (particularly cows and pigs) out of crop and mowing fields. In the nineteenth century, field boundaries were increasingly intended to keep animals inside pasture fields, as the frontier landscape became more populated and increasingly structured by farmsteads. The frequency of fencing and animal pound debates in New England town meetings in the eighteenth and early nineteenth centuries clearly indicates the degree to which the practice of fixed-field fencing vied with older traditions of minimal fencing and the remnants of the English open field system.[23] By the 1830s grazing animals were allowed to roam unfenced in only the most marginal farming areas, as the practice of the fixed field and fenced livestock boundary system was firmly established in most settled areas of New England.

The fencing and field boundary systems on connected farms in New England were constructed of either stone, wood, or combinations of these two materials (see fig. 64). Today usually only the stone walls of this system remain, but they serve as a most fitting symbol for the effort to create the New England farm. No account of the region's agriculture can neglect the momentous toil that their making represented for the farmer. It was a staggering investment of labor conducted over a long period of time, usually by several generations on a farm. Perhaps the only positive advantage of New England's rocky soil was that the stones that were so laboriously removed from fields could be used to make permanent walls. Or, at least, this is what New England's agricultural propagandists told farmers at mid-century.[24] Although there is considerable regional subtlety in construction depending on the size, amount, and shape, two types of walls were common in northern New England: a single-thickness rock wall and a double-thickness rock wall with infilling. Perhaps the most common type of nineteenth-century field boundary was the pole or rail fence, which usually combined an in-progress stone wall with a crossrail structure of poles and a top rail guard. This system is by far the most commonly observed field boundary in early photographs (see fig. 59).

Wooden fences were used for field boundaries where rocks were not available or not collected. They were made with poles or half-cut or split poles or boards, and were constructed by a number of methods in a variety of woods and styles. One of the most durable fences was a split-rail cedar fence recommended by agriculturalists.[25] A sawed board and nail fence appeared more often after the Civil War. It had previously been the mark of a wealthy farmer. Barnyard fencing was made in many combinations of wood, stone, and occasionally iron depending upon farm wealth, although most farmers continued their combination system of pole and stone fencing into the barnyard. Wire fencing was not widely used until after 1900.[26]

There was a wide variety of ornamental or front yard fencing in the nineteenth century, with considerable regional variation in New England. For example, a stone post with cast iron rail fence became popular with farmers of greater than average means in the Kennebunk, Maine, area between 1860 and 1890. Early photographs indicate that variations on the white picket fence with corner posts were the most popular ornamental fencing for front yards (see fig. 102).

The field boundary was a vital component in New England's mixed-farming system because of the adjacency of crop and animal fields. Furthermore, New England's poor soil and lack of large quantities of fertilizers necessitated constant field rotation to sustain soil fertility, and this exacerbated fencing problems. New England farmers, therefore, had to devote considerable time and resources to their field boundary maintenance. By itself this was not a major problem, but it was one of many factors that gradually worked against the possibility of their long-range success in agriculture.

The overall layout and boundaries for fields were strongly influenced by the site a farmer chose to build upon. In the two most popular patterns of site selection, farmers frequently chose the higher elevations of gently sloping hills for their building site (or the highest elevation of their particular parcel of land) or the lower intervale plains near streams or rivers. Because flat intervale land was so rare, the agricultural settlement of many inland towns throughout New England was along the upper ridges of gently sloping hills.[27] The principal reason for selecting the higher elevation was probably to avoid problems such as muddy roads and barnyards, late drying fields, and spring freshets (washouts) caused by water accumulation. Higher elevations were also less susceptible to sudden frosts in an area with an already short growing season. In many areas, the upper ridges contained less surface rock than valley locations, which were also associated with stagnant air and diseases of people and animals. Although these hilltop sites were poor selections by modern agricultural standards, they afforded enough advantages to most farmers to make them the overwhelming selection during the late eighteenth and early nineteenth centuries (see fig. 66). On the back roads of rural New England today one of the invariable signs of agricultural presence is the location of farms (or traces of previous farms) atop the crests of gently sloping hills.

4 Permanence and Change

The building histories of four farmsteads reveal typical patterns of development for connected farms. First described is the Nutting farm of Otisfield, Maine, an excellent example of a pre-1830 detached house and barn farmstead. It typifies the popular building arrangement for most farmsteads before the second quarter of the nineteenth century and before the connected arrangement became popular. The other farms demonstrate the variety of sizes, buildings, dates, and arrangements of the connected farmstead organization. The histories of all four farms span the nineteenth-century period before and after the connected farm concept was popularly accepted. The last three farmsteads have a distinct pre- and postconnected phase, as do most connected farmsteads that were settled before 1820 and reorganized in the later nineteenth century. The last farm,

Fig. 67. Nutting Farm, Otisfield, Maine.

the Woodsum farm of Harrison, Maine, represents a typical connected farmstead. Although the first three farms follow the popular pattern of farmstead development, for one reason or another, atypical wealth allowed them to be built more extensively. The Woodsum farm was typical of most farms in size, wealth, and physical resources.

As a group, these farmsteads graphically depict the incremental fashion by which most farms achieved their final connected organization. Nevertheless, this variety of stages should not conceal the fundamental difference between the two major periods of farm organization—the pre-1820 detached house and barn system and the post-1850 attached house and barn system. Perhaps the best example to illustrate the differences between these periods is the change in the Nevers-Bennett farm between 1885 and 1887, when the detached house and barn farmstead was converted into a single unified ensemble (see fig. 24).

The Nutting Farm

Between 1820 and 1830 the Nutting farmstead of Otisfield, Maine, was expanded and modernized according to the most current building and agricultural practices of the period. This included the construction of a new house attached to the old one, a large detached barn, and a granary. Just twenty years later, a farmer building a similarly scaled farmstead would probably have selected the connected house and barn arrangement rather than this detached arrangement. The Nutting farm is especially important to this study because it preserves so many of its original, early nineteenth-century buildings in the popular early nineteenth-century tradition of a detached house and barn (figs. 67, 68, 69).[1]

1795–1820

In 1795 Nathan Nutting of Groton, Massachusetts, purchased a 130-acre tract of land from Joseph Jones, the original settler. The original buildings on the present Nutting farm were probably log huts erected by the first settler before 1795. According to a family story, it was in one of these log buildings that Nathan and Rhoda Nutting stayed while erecting their center-chimney Cape Cod house soon after their arrival in 1795. The original log structure was located near an old well on the south side of the present house, and, although few nonfortification log structures have survived in New England, their frequent record in early accounts indicates the presence of a widely used temporary structure.[2] In plan, the Nuttings' new structure was a typical two-rooms-deep, center-chimney, Cape Cod house with three major rooms (see fig. 28A). The back room was the kitchen, and the southeastern room opposite the barnyard was the "best room" or parlor. A half-cellar with stacked boulder walls was dug under the eastern parlor side of the house with boulders supporting the central chimney. Similar partial cellars were typical of modest eighteenth-century structures in the region. Minimal classical vernacular details in the Federal style remain on both the interior and exterior and could have been added anytime until 1820.

Although there is no documentary evidence, there undoubtedly were barns on the site between 1795 and 1825, when the present major barn was constructed. A small 15-foot by 15-foot barn, now standing beside the granary, could have been an older

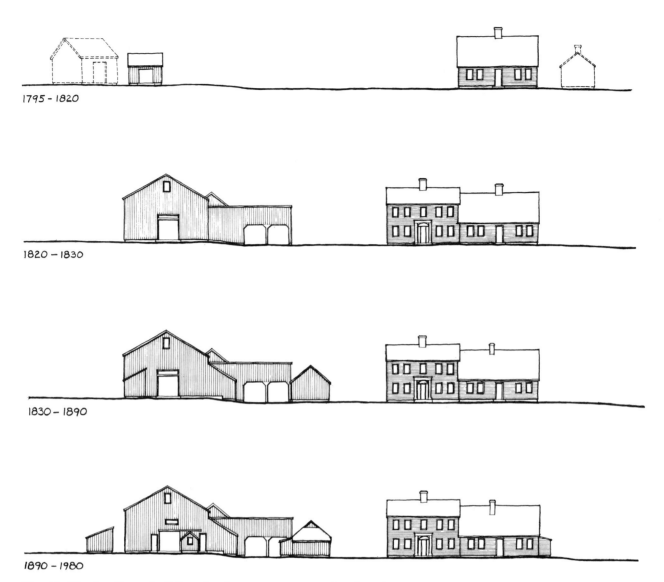

1795 - 1820

1820 - 1830

1830 - 1890

1890 - 1980

Fig. 68. Nutting Farm, building development, 1795 – 1980, elevations.

barn. A large English barn would have been the typical complement for the Cape Cod house of a prosperous farmer like Nathan Nutting. Several smaller outbuildings would also have been very likely. Although some of the early pre-1820 history of agricultural buildings is conjectural, the first thirty-year development of the Nutting farmstead seems to be typical of most late eighteenth- and early nineteenth-century farms with separated clusters of houses and barns.

1820–1830

The most significant phase of building development occurred within a ten-year period between 1820 and 1830. A major hall-and-parlor big house was extended northward from the original Cape Cod house and a large barn, vehicle shed, and granary were also constructed. The project was initiated by Nathan's son Lyman, who employed his younger brother Nathan Nutting, Jr., who had studied or been apprenticed as a builder

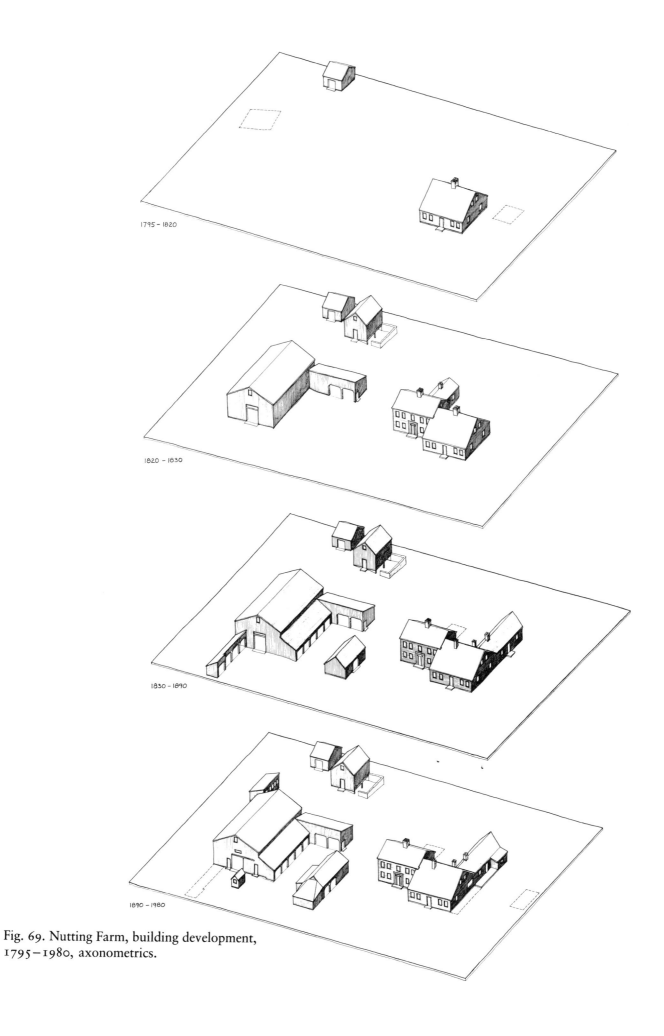

1795 – 1820

1820 – 1830

1830 – 1890

1890 – 1980

Fig. 69. Nutting Farm, building development,
1795–1980, axonometrics.

in Boston. The front facade of the new hall-and-parlor house is an excellent example of a two-story, five-bay, Federal style house. The front doorway is adorned by a broad, louvered fan with sidelights enframed by pilasters that support a complete Grecian Doric entablature (fig. 70).

On the interior, a semicircular stair with delicate curved stair brackets joins the hall-and-parlor rooms at the front doorway (fig. 71). The four principal rooms on both floors contain several variations of finely crafted Federal style molding and woodwork, perhaps indicating different construction dates. A one-story kitchen ell extended perpendicularly approximately 30 feet from the rear of the hall-and-parlor house and was probably built at the same time. Similar ells in one- and two-story forms were typical additions to this type of house. A cellar was dug under the southern two-thirds of the new house, where a finely cut granite slab arch supports the central fireplace. Traces of a milk room are also evident in this cellar.

The new house addition radically altered the shape and pattern of living in the original Cape Cod house. In the terms of the children's rhyme, a hall-and-parlor big house was added to an original Cape Cod little house. What is somewhat unusual about this development is that the little house was a larger Cape Cod house. Although most farmers initially built a smaller, single-room structure for their first frame house, the relative wealth of the Nutting family helps to explain this atypical development. The new big house addition produced a complex house plan with two kitchens, a typical pattern for nineteenth-century farms. The new kitchen in the one-story ell of the hall-and-parlor house was also supplemented by an alternative kitchen in the hall room of the new house. It was equipped with an oven and a wide fireplace mouth, but it shows little sign of extensive kitchen use and was probably needed only irregularly or during the coldest winter months.

The existence of two active kitchens in the same house usually indicates the presence of two families in the household. This was the case in the early 1820s when father Nathan and his wife, Rhoda, shared the house with their eldest living son, Lyman, and his wife and two children. The marriage of Lyman Nutting in 1818 and his rapidly expanding family probably precipitated the series of new construction projects, especially the building of a new kitchen. If the newly married couple followed the long-established tradition, they moved into the new addition, leaving the parents in the older portion of the house, to which they were more accustomed.

Nathan Nutting, Jr., probably also built the large New England barn and granary at about the same time as the hall-and-parlor house. All three structures have similar diamond-shaped, mortise-and-tenon ridge beams bearing identical hewn markings. Nathan Nutting's barn was not like most barns in the Otisfield area because his building was designed with a long central floor with a gable-end door, which differed substantially from the more common English barns with their door in the middle of the side wall. This barn was probably one of the first of its type built in the Otisfield area, and its introduction would almost certainly have resulted from carpenter Nathan Nutting's contact with new ideas and styles from the Boston area. The structural system in the Nutting barn is unusual in rural southwestern Maine because it employs a major-purlin, common-rafter roof framing system rarely found in Maine barns before 1880 (see fig. 32B).[3] An elaborate bracing system and an unusual rafter-girt connection also reveal the hand of a skilled master workman willing to experiment. Farmers in the surrounding area may have copied the new organization of the barn floor and its gable-end doorway,

Fig. 70. A Federal style doorway with a louvered fan and side lights. Nutting Farm.

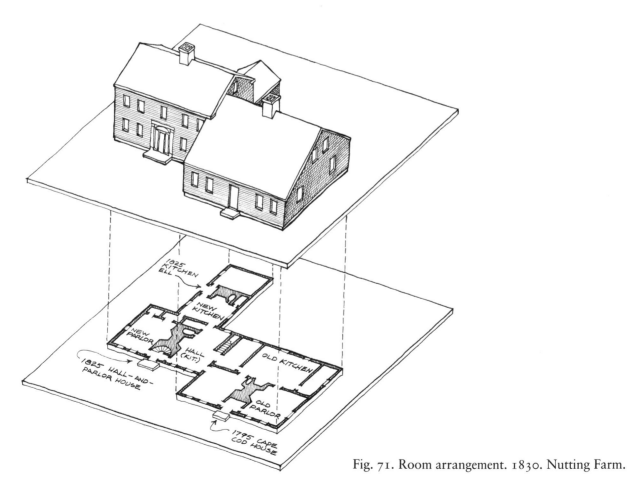

Fig. 71. Room arrangement. 1830. Nutting Farm.

but they did not copy its complex structural system, which they probably found excessively complicated.

The front facade of Nathan Nutting's barn demonstrates two construction characteristics of the early nineteenth-century: the low, $6/12$ pitch of the roof and the extreme offset of the door in the gable end.[4] As a general rule, barns built after the 1830s have steeper roof pitches (usually $8/12$ to $12/12$) and have more centrally located doors. Unlike many early nineteenth-century barns, however, the Nutting barn is aligned in a rectilinear relationship with the major house and the road. Many barns of this early period were not built in geometric alignment with the house or the road, but, as we might expect, Nathan Nutting probably influenced his family to employ another of the newest building developments of the period, which included the geometric alignment of all farmstead structures to each other and to the road. Thus the Nutting barn employed two new features that were to become standardized in the connected farmstead arrangement during the next thirty years: the rectilinear alignment of all buildings and the gable-door barn plan. Both new features, however, preceded the popularization of the connected farmstead arrangement, so that the new Nutting barn in the 1820s stands detached from the house.

The granary on the Nutting farm is really a multipurpose agricultural building accomplishing three principal functions in a small, compact, three-tiered arrangement (see fig. 52). A grain and general storage room was located in the second-floor attic, a chicken roost hung over the first floor, and a large granite-walled pig house filled the cellar. The grain storage area was vented by spaced vertical boards attached to the front gable, which appear to date from the original construction. During the 1820s the Nutting's granary with pig house below was an advanced agricultural building that followed the most current agricultural practices.[5] Twenty years later, however, the same type of building would be called a pig house, indicating a shift in emphasis to the importance of the pig for its manure and soil mixing ability. After 1840 declines in New England grain production, especially wheat, probably also made the older English designation *granary* obsolete.[6]

The absence of a cellar under the Nutting barn is another indication of its early nineteenth-century construction date. Large barns constructed after 1850 were usually set atop a full or partial cellar, which frequently contained a pig house and storage areas for manure, root crops, and vehicles. The location of Lyman Nutting's pigs in a separate building followed the older English tradition of multiple outbuilding construction, but later nineteenth-century farmers found it more convenient to house the pig below the barn.

Attached to the south side of the big barn was a four-bay, shed-roofed vehicle storage area, which extended perpendicularly from the barn toward the house. It was probably built soon after the barn. The 14-foot by 40-foot shed is made of timbers from a pre-1840 barn, and, if the usual custom was followed, these timbers came from the original barn. The structure is called the well shed because a well is sheltered in the southern end. The building first served as a farm wagon and general storage shed, then as a stable and ox house.

The large, finely crafted buildings that Nathan and Lyman Nutting constructed during a short period of the 1820s were not typical of most farmers. Although the Nuttings' income from agricultural products was above average, they acquired the wealth that made their rapid building expansion possible through the sale and harvesting of timber on large tracts of land in Cumberland County, Maine. The drawings in figures 68 and 69 show the Nutting farm as it probably looked in 1830, when it was a model for a prosperous, up-to-date farm of the period. It employed the detached house and barn arrangement that was the well-established, popular model for a farmstead in the early nineteenth century.

1830–1890

A third major phase of building construction transformed the Nutting farmstead between 1870 and 1880 but did not alter the basic detached house and barn arrangement. In 1875 Lyman's youngest son, Albert Franklin Nutting, initiated these changes: he added a kitchen ell to the back of the original Cape Cod house, massively remodeled the interior of that house, and removed the old kitchen-ell addition from the back of the hall-and-parlor house (fig. 72). In a commonly recurring pattern, he initiated these projects with his new wife, Martha, whom he had married the previous year. The new kitchen ell contained an advanced kitchen workroom with brass and iron set kettles placed into a masonry chimney along with washtubs near a south-facing window. By the 1870s this masonry unit of set kettles or boilers and stove had replaced the open-hearth fireplace and became a standard feature of a modern farm ell (see fig. 96B). The new ell also contained a woodshed, storage rooms, and a farm laborer's room upstairs. Albert Nutting remodeled the Cape Cod house by removing the original central chimney with its three fireplaces and replacing it with three separate stove chimneys. The original kitchen in the Cape Cod house was relocated at the southeastern corner, and a Victorian

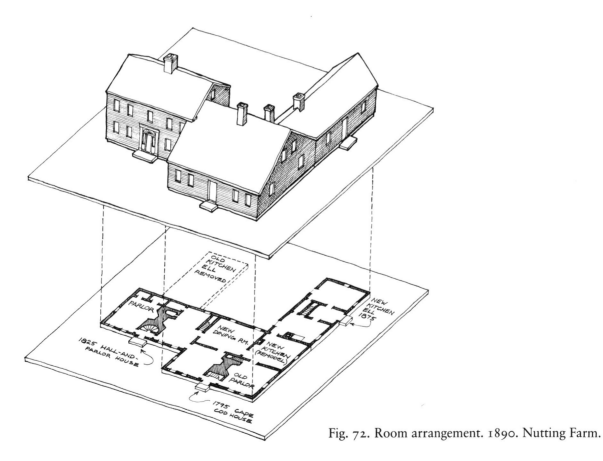

Fig. 72. Room arrangement. 1890. Nutting Farm.

dining room was inserted in its place. Martha and Albert's new dining room was a decided break with the older pattern of a kitchen-centered eating area, reflecting a more genteel pattern of farm living that was widely publicized, but irregularly adopted, in the rural areas of New England.[7]

One major goal of Albert and Martha's remodeling projects was to convert the farm from a two-kitchen dwelling back to a one-kitchen dwelling. The consolidation of the two kitchens became desirable when Lyman died and the old age of his wife, Charlotte, necessitated the merging of cooking facilities. Following well-established custom, the parents had continued to live in the portion of the house they had always occupied, so that Charlotte Nutting lived in the hall-and-parlor house, while Albert Franklin and his new wife, Martha, moved into the newly remodeled Cape Cod house.

It is interesting to speculate about why Albert Franklin and Martha did not construct their new kitchen ell between house and barn, which was a widely practiced procedure in 1875. They could, of course, simply not have appreciated the connected style and have chosen to build differently; but two other factors may have influenced their decision. The new ell off the back end of the Cape Cod house allowed the elderly parent, Charlotte Nutting, to continue to occupy the hall-and-parlor portion of the house and did not disrupt her pattern of living, as a connecting ell to the barn might have done. Second, since the large barnyard was previously situated on the south side of the barn, sanitary and convenience requirements for the connecting ell would have necessitated a re-formation of the barnyard on the opposite side of the barn. Therefore a connecting ell was possible, but it would have been extremely inconvenient. These considerations dictated that the appropriate placement for a new kitchen ell was on the opposite side of the house. Perhaps it was not stylishly correct according to the tastes of the times, but it worked best for this farm.

Between 1830 and 1870 a combined carriage house and stable was constructed between, and in front of, the house and the barn. Later, it was enlarged by the addition of a bay to facilitate the parking of larger carriages. The expansion probably occurred during the major house remodeling of the 1880s. During the middle of the century, a picket fence was constructed around the front yard and was rigorously maintained by yearly whitewashings until after 1880. In 1875 a sugar maple and a silver maple were set out to mark the marriage of Albert and Martha and their arrival in their new home. Family tradition suggests that Charlotte Nutting was chiefly responsible for the flowers and shrubs that lined the front yard fence. An elm tree and an English rose, planted in the front yard, were reportedly brought from Groton, Massachusetts, by Nathan Nutting in 1795. This rose is said to have been brought from England.

In a final phase of late nineteenth-century construction, a sheep shed was built off the front, west end of the barn. A manure shed was hung off the south side of the barn to protect valuable manure gathered from the cow tie-up area along the inside wall. This covered area also served as a shelter for livestock during inclement weather.

1890–1980

Construction projects and alterations have continued until the present. Most changes have resulted from the abandonment of farm production and from non-farm-related improvements, but these have not significantly altered its 1890 appearance. Following the end of sheep raising in the 1890s, the sheep shed was converted into an icehouse to assist in the cooling of bulk milk, which was becoming a major source of farm income in the late 1800s. A milk house for the storage of bulk milk was constructed on the end of the sheep barn–icehouse about 1900 and was subsequently relocated into another small building, which now stands in front of the main barn. Probably in 1910 Silas, a fourth-generation Nutting, built an octagonal corn silo inside the north middle bay of his large barn. He had the interior of this silo lathed and plastered to increase the airtightness of the container and to promote corn fermentation or ensilage. A hen house that once stood at the southern end of the main house was relocated at the back of the major barn in 1910. Silas Nutting constructed a "piazza" or porch off the south end of the Cape Cod house in the same year, and he probably moved the hen house because he considered it unsightly from the new porch. Since 1930 the sheep barn and its milk house addition have been taken down, the old carriage house has been expanded twice for automobile and tool storage, and the kitchen ell has been remodeled into a garage.

The farm is still maintained by the fifth generation, Mr. and Mrs. Albert Dean Nutting. Despite the major alterations of the 1870s, it retains much of its 1830 appearance and remains one of the best-preserved examples of a pre-1830 farmstead in New England.

The Bacon Farm

The old Bacon farm of North Yarmouth, Maine, stands on a prominent hilltop site on the road between North Yarmouth and Gray. During its two-hundred-year history, this farm was remodeled many times and gradually evolved from a detached house and barn arrangement into a fully connected house and barn arrangement (figs. 73, 74, 75).[8]

Fig. 73. Bacon Farm, North Yarmouth, Maine, early 1900s.

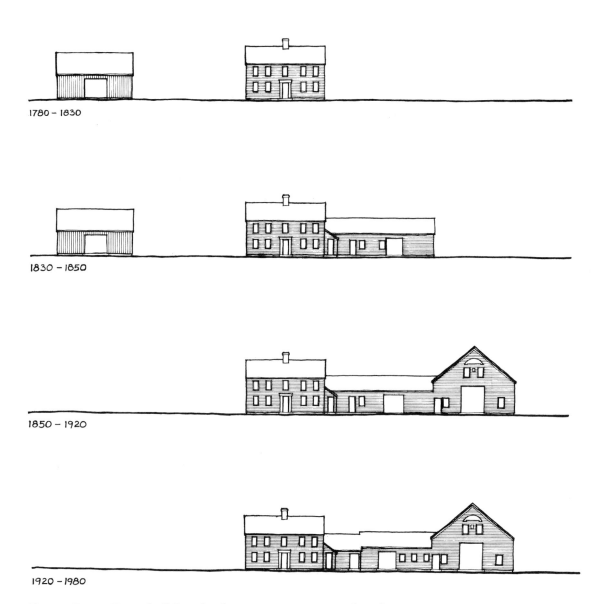

1780 – 1830

1830 – 1850

1850 – 1920

1920 – 1980

Fig. 74. Bacon Farm, building development, 1780–1980, elevations.

1780–1830

In 1795 Samuel Bacon purchased the property and probably the existing two-story house from Ammi Mitchell, who may have built the house in the 1780s. It was situated along the north side of the road, which traversed a south-facing hillside, as did all of the neighboring farms. Perhaps the builder of the Samuel Bacon house followed a customary siting procedure echoed by a farmer in 1873: "As a general rule the home should be located on the north side of the highway and if possible, on the south side of some sunney slope."⁹ By 1813, when tax records became more explicit, the house was appraised at six hundred dollars, which was an unusually high valuation for this period. It was a large (38-foot by 30-foot) two-story, center-chimney, two-rooms-deep house with

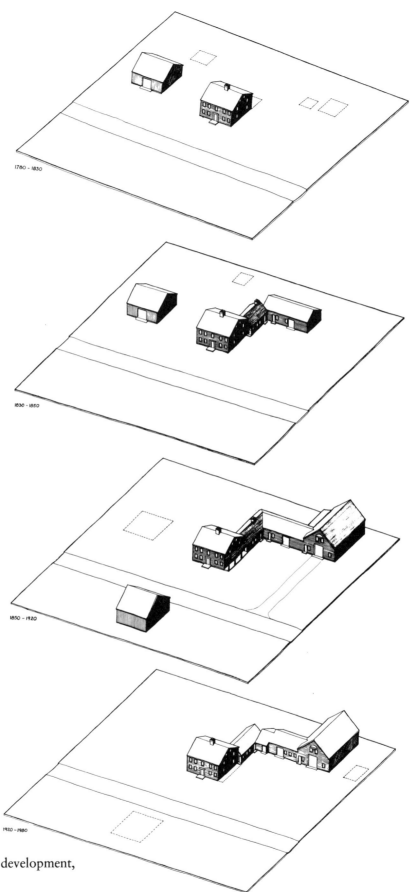

1780 - 1830

1830 - 1850

1850 - 1920

1920 - 1980

Fig. 75. Bacon Farm, building development,
1780–1980, axonometrics.

the kitchen located in the major back room (see fig. 28B). Like most pre-1850 houses, it contained interior finishes from several periods, principally a late Georgian phase and a Federal phase. The kitchen and portions of the southeast parlor contain the earliest Georgian detail, including four-panel doors with ovolo molding and hand-wrought nails and latches. The Federal style finish probably dates from a major period of remodeling between 1810 and 1825 and includes the staircase with its delicately tapered newel posts and squared balusters. The southwest parlor and the two upstairs front chambers contain Federal style mantels, chair rails, and door casings. Additional Federal period finish includes wallpaper in the second floor southwest bedroom, dated by an 1810 pattern, and the remains of freehand wall border painting found in the upstairs southeast chamber.

The cellar gives evidence of exceptional care in construction and finish. A massive stone and brick chimney arch (10 feet by 13 feet) supports the extensive chimney system of six fireplaces and flues and an unusual attic smoke oven. A double sill rings the foundation and is supported by a carefully fitted, two-foot-thick granite boulder wall. In the attic unusually long diagonal roof braces stabilized the roof-framing system. They show the hand of a skilled framer, as does most of the framing and woodwork throughout the entire house.

An early side door leads from the western side of the house to the site of the first major barn. The barn appears on an 1853 map and stood approximately 100 feet from the house. It had a high valuation in the 1813 tax records and might have been built in conjunction with the main house. The placement of this early detached barn on the north and west side of the house in the path of the winter wind occurs in other farmsteads along the same road. Perhaps these farmers followed a custom recommended by an agricultural writer in 1822: "Let your dwelling house and its appendages be to the leeward as it respects commonly prevailing winds (those in winter especially when fires are constant) of your barn and stock yard; and sufficiently distant from them to avoid accident by fire." [10]

Three more buildings completed the pre-1830 Bacon farmstead. In 1819 Samuel Bacon, Jr., was taxed for a slaughterhouse and a cooper (barrelmaking) shop. Although he was described as a cooper in 1806 soon after he inherited the property from his father, this was the first record of a specific outbuilding used for this purpose. A slaughterhouse was listed on the Bacon farm from 1819 until 1831, and it was probably located near the barn. In 1829 Samuel Bacon, Jr., was taxed for one-half ownership in a cider mill, which may have been located on his property, perhaps on the site of an old foundation at the back of his house. The location of all three buildings is unknown. They indicate an extensive but not unusual amount of home-industry activity, which supported the prosperous early nineteenth-century farm. In the late 1820s Samuel Bacon, Jr.'s farm had a detached house and barn and was a typical example of the building arrangement of a prosperous yeoman farmer at the end of the first quarter of the nineteenth century.

1830–1850

Samuel Bacon, Jr., expanded his cooper trade in the 1830s and reached a high point of wealth and building expansion during this period. At some time during the first half of the nineteenth century, he added a one-and-a-half-story kitchen ell to the back of his house. This probably occurred in 1831, when he was taxed for a wood house, which was a common designation for this multipurpose building. In plan it was a single-room kitchen with a large fireplace and a small room behind the fireplace. It was built as a major kitchen ell and either added another working kitchen to the house or made obsolete the older Georgian kitchen within the big house. This type of structure was a common remodeling addition to older eighteenth-century houses in the nineteenth century and signaled the beginning of the expansion of kitchen workrooms in the ell—an important component in the connected farmstead plan.

Between 1832 and 1836 Samuel Bacon built a long (47-foot by 20-foot) ell building off the end of his kitchen ell, probably to house his expanded cooper business (although it is possible that an unrecorded structure housed his trade). The building was unusually long and wide to have been an ell or carriage house of this period. The prosperity of farmer Bacon's cooper trade was similar to the fortunes of many small artisan producers in New England, who prospered in a remarkably versatile prefactory era between 1790 and 1850. That era was to end with the rise of a factory system, but while it lasted, it provided rural New England with a balance of industrial and agricultural production to sustain its small towns and farm areas.

1850–1920

Following Samuel Bacon's death in 1849, the cooper business was probably continued by his son-in-law, James Merrill, but it had declined significantly by 1855 and was no longer in existence by 1877. Although farm production increased, the overall value of the farm declined in the third quarter of the nineteenth century, perhaps indicating the critical loss of the nonfarm income from the cooper business. The large detached barn was removed or destroyed by fire before 1877, the year the farm was sold by the Bacon family and farmed by a series of tenants. At some point in the later nineteenth century, a new barn was constructed directly across the road from the main house, probably to replace the original barn.

In 1884 James Prince bought the farm and initiated a major period of building and remodeling. The major focus of his expansion program was the building of a five-bay barn in 1900. He connected the new structure to the old cooper shop and thus created a connected house and barn. The barn's roof framing employs a major-purlin and sawed common-rafter system, which by 1880 had begun to replace the ancient major-rafter, minor-purlin system. Despite some modern improvements, such as the use of wire nails, most of it maintained the basic construction system of a mortise-and-tenon barn of the mid-1800s. Inside, a circular silo was built into a central haymow bay along the east wall. It was lathed and plastered on the inside to promote the fodder ensilage process. A manure shed was also constructed along the barn's western wall.

The farm modernization program was completed in 1908 with the installation of an elaborate water pumping system, including a hydraulic ram, a water storage tank, and several miles of piping. A continuous water supply was always a problem on this hilltop site, and the demands of an enlarged dairy herd necessitated this expensive facility. The name "Walnut Hill Farm, 1900," was proudly placed in the center of the barn gable upon its completion. Many farms in the North Yarmouth area followed this late nineteenth-century practice, most likely inspired by gentlemen farmers or by farmers who wanted to create a desirable image to attract the important summer tourist trade.[11]

Sometime after 1880 the exterior of the major house was remodeled into what might be termed a Victorian farmstead. A bracketed door hood and double doors with rounded glass upper panels replaced the original late Georgian exterior casing and single front door. A porch built across the eastern facade of the big house emphasized the re-location of the dooryard from the western side of the house, facing the old barn, to the eastern side, facing the new one. A 1910 photograph shows two giant elm trees, which once stood between the house and the old barn on the western side of the house. They marked the old dooryard of the pre-1850 detached house and barn arrangement (fig. 76).

A fire probably caused the reconstruction of the rear portion of the kitchen ell, which before 1895 squared off the corner between the old cooper shop and the kitchen ell. The last neighborhood post office in North Yarmouth was located in this ell, and it continued to operate there until 1934. A hen house was constructed near the eastern side of the new barn, probably after 1910.

1920–1980

Farm production ceased in the 1950s, and most of the subsequent changes either elimi-nated old farm structures or converted them to modern domestic uses. The barn across the road from the house was removed before 1940, the manure shed and the hen house

Fig. 76. Bacon Farm (early 1900s) showing the site of the original barn (*far left*) with two large elms marking the original dooryard. The later barn and new dooryard are behind the house.

soon after. The porch and hood were removed in 1980. The entire ell from the original house to a point halfway into the old cooper shop was removed, and modern structures were reconstructed in approximately the same location. Today the farm is owned by the Gervais family and looks much as it did at the turn of the century. But there is little trace of the many changes that occurred during the previous hundred years.

The Nevers-Bennett Farm

The Nevers-Bennett farm, of Sweden, Maine, mentioned in the opening chapter, underwent two major periods of building development, one in the 1820s and one in the 1880s. These produced two very different farmstead arrangements, which dramatically illustrate the changes in New England farmstead organization in the nineteenth century (figs. 77, 78, 79).[12]

1820–1835

In 1820 Amos Parker, a farmer, purchased fifty acres of land where the Nevers-Bennett house now stands. The site may have contained minimal buildings, including a small house and barn. From mortgage deeds and an investigation of the existing house, it can be assumed that he built the two-story, center-chimney, two-rooms-deep Federal style house within four years of his purchase (see fig. 28B). Amos Parker was forced to mortgage his expensive property for large amounts several times during the next ten years. Unable to keep out of debt, he finally sold his (probably) partially completed house in 1833–35 to Samuel Nevers, who purchased it for his soon to be married son, Benjamin.

The large, 38-foot by 28-foot house shows many signs of an ambitious early beginning in the 1820s, a rapid, half-finished completion, and a major remodeling in the late 1830s. The foundation is probably one of the finest in the region, with smooth, cut

Fig. 77. Nevers-Bennett Farm, Sweden, Maine.

granite cellar walls and an extremely large (9-foot by 13-foot) three-pier, granite chimney support. The attic rafter frame is composed of common, butted rafters with a ridge board: a roof-framing system usually used in minor ell buildings. It shows the signs of quick construction techniques and is certainly not the framing system that is anticipated by the finely crafted cellar.

If major portions of the interior were finished by Amos Parker in the Federal style of the period, they were largely removed and replaced by Greek Revival and late Federal woodwork, probably between 1835 and 1840 when Benjamin Nevers moved into the house with his new bride, Charlotte Brigham. The exterior of the house is finished in the earlier Federal style with a louvered fan surmounting a sidelighted doorway (see fig. 77). In plan the house is two-rooms-deep with two parlor rooms to the front and a kitchen located in the middle back room.

An early genealogical history of Sweden, Maine, states that Benjamin Nevers, "built the house . . . where he always lived." [13] If built between 1835 and 1840, which seems highly unlikely, it would probably have been the last house of this type built in Maine. But if it is understood that the changes and additions that Benjamin Nevers initiated to his probably incomplete house contributed to a major remaking or finishing of the house, then the old record would not be entirely incorrect.

There is no record of early agricultural buildings, so it is not known when the large

Fig. 78. Nevers-Bennett Farm, building development, 1820–1980, elevations.

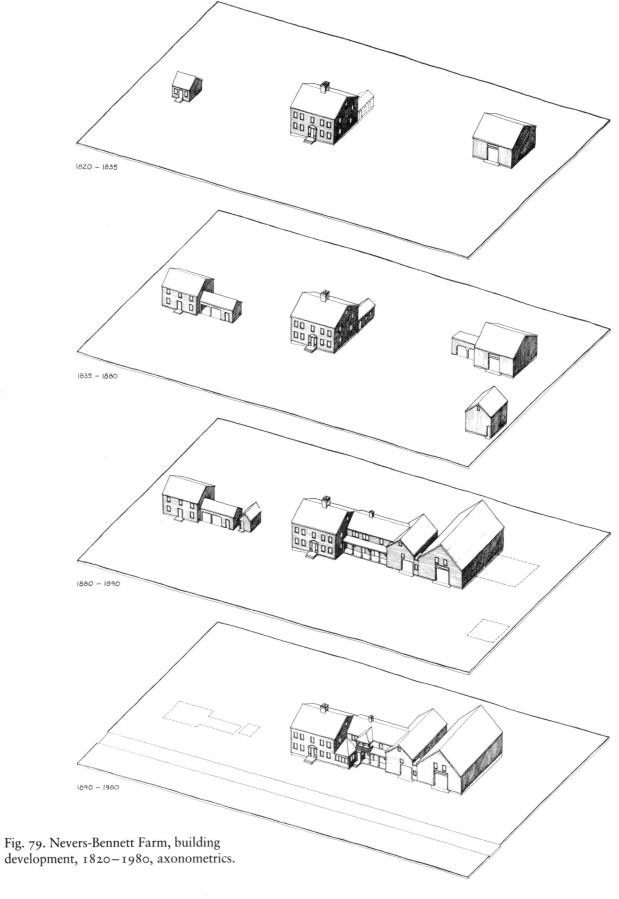

1820 – 1835

1835 – 1880

1880 – 1890

1890 – 1980

Fig. 79. Nevers-Bennett Farm, building
development, 1820–1980, axonometrics.

English barn shown in the 1860s photograph was constructed. It appears to be a large three-bays-wide barn with double strap-hinged doors, probably without a cellar. It was almost certainly built before 1840 because after that time a barn on one of the most prosperous farms in the Sweden area would not have been constructed in the older English style but in the newer gable-door fashion.

Amos Parker may have initiated his ambitious house-building scheme based on anticipated profits from his store, which he located beside his new residence along the road from Fryeburg to Paris, Maine. Samuel Nevers purchased the store along with the house, and Benjamin Nevers became proprietor of this store in 1833. Figure 24A shows the farmstead that Samuel Nevers purchased for his son Benjamin in 1833–35. A wood house or workroom-kitchen probably extended northward from the back of the big house.

1835–1880

With the financial backing of his father, Benjamin Nevers was able to remodel and expand his farmstead into one of the most prosperous farms in Sweden, Maine, during the middle of the nineteenth century. A photograph from the 1860s shows the farmstead with its full complement of buildings, probably added before the early 1850s (see fig. 24A). Attached to the end of the English barn was a three-bay vehicle shed, a frequent addition to an increasingly vehicularized New England farm after the middle of the century.

A carriage house or stable shown in the right foreground indicated the degree to which horses were replacing oxen as a primary source of animal labor and transportation for farm and particularly for domestic use. The house has a symmetrical white picket fence around the front yard. Two newly planted maple trees mark the outer boundary. Not shown in the photograph was Benjamin Nevers's store, which was probably expanded into a large, two-story building before 1850.

This configuration of buildings, probably completed in the 1850s, remained unchanged until 1884. Because of the old age and declining health of Benjamin Nevers, little building activity was initiated between 1860 and 1880.

1880–1900

Upon the death of Benjamin Nevers in 1883, the farm passed to his daughter, Charlotte Clarender, and her husband, Charles W. Bennett. Within the next five years, the Bennetts embarked upon a rapid period of farm modernization and building expansion. Figures 78 and 79 show the dramatic change in the farmstead that the Bennetts initiated in a series of three major building projects between 1885 and 1887. In 1885 a new 55-foot, two-story ell was built outward from the main house toward the old barn. It was planned to accommodate a kitchen, summer kitchen, woodshed, and a large shop in the standard connected farmhouse room arrangement. The upstairs was left unfinished and served as a general storage area and extra bedroom. In 1886 the carriage house was moved approximately 50 feet from its original position along the road into alignment and connected with the end of the kitchen ell. Its roof was removed and a new, steeper one added.

In 1887 another barn, from the farm of Cephus Haskell three miles away, was disassembled and reconstructed next to the relocated carriage house, forming a continuous building complex from house to barn. Charles Bennett obtained a relatively new barn, which contained a major-purlin, common-rafter system not usually found before 1860 in rural Maine. It was a large (40-foot by 50-foot) four-bay barn with a steep $^{12}/_{12}$ sloped roof. The old barn was probably disassembled during the reconstruction of the new barn, since it was described as being in bad repair when Charles Bennett began running the farm.

Charles Bennett located the barn next to his stable, producing a dramatic twin-gabled profile, in spite of the fact that this configuration was to allow a large snow accumulation between the two gables. Charles Bennett was surely not unaware of this possibility when he located the barn next to the carriage house, but the potential inconvenience was probably offset by the powerful arrangement of forms his "range" or line of buildings produced. At some time before 1890 the entire facade of house, ell, carriage house, and barn was clapboarded and painted white to produce the striking unified facade, still the sign of a prosperous Maine farmer in the late nineteenth century. The 1900 photograph shows Charles and Charlotte Bennett in the front yard of their handsome new farmstead (see fig. 24B). The Nevers's white picket fence is conspicuously absent from this scene, as the tightly constrained order of the old front yard was rejected for the more unified order of the late nineteenth-century connected farmstead.

The big house was also remodeled by the Bennetts with the introduction of stoves in most of the rooms and the replacement of the original twelve-over-eight lights by the popular Victorian standard—a two-over-two light. Completing this phase of construction, a unique two-story closet room was added to the western wall of the main house, providing storage closets for a house type now notorious for its lack of closet space. The old Nevers store was probably expanded at this time to include a vehicle storage shed and an icehouse for domestic and farm use.

1900–1980

A final period of farm expansion occurred during the first quarter of the twentieth century. The second floor of the kitchen ell was remodeled to accommodate the family of Ethelbert Bennett, son of Charles Bennett. A second-story summer porch was also added during this period, and a downstairs room in the kitchen ell served as the Sweden post office, with Charles Bennett as postmaster. The stable was expanded to the rear to accommodate more horse stalls. A hen house was built across the road from the main barn next to a corncrib that might have been built as early as 1890. The existing sugar maple trees were planted in 1920, and a downstairs sun porch was added in 1928.

The store went out of business in 1906, and the main store building was later moved 300 yards to the west to become Sweden's fire department building. The old kitchen workroom was removed in 1960. A series of nonfarmer owners has remodeled the interior of the big house several times, although much of the 1830s Greek Revival woodwork still remains. The central chimney and fireplace were removed in the 1950s, and the closet addition was removed in 1980. Today the Nevers-Bennett farm remains much as it was after Charles W. Bennett dramatically remodeled it in the 1880s, changing his farmstead from a detached house and barn arrangement into a fully connected complex.

The Woodsum Farm

The Woodsum Farm of Harrison, Maine, was typical of most small nineteenth-century farms in rural New England. For the three previous farms, adequate information exists to produce a relatively complete architectural history, and the record of building typified the basic patterns followed by most builders of connected farms. Yet each of the three previous farms amassed greater wealth than was typical of most farmers, and their buildings, reflecting their good fortune, were usually a little larger, a little more stylish, and built a little earlier than those built on most farms (figs. 80, 81, 82).[14]

The Woodsum farm, however, is more typical in scale, dates, wealth, style, and operation. It is also more typical because there are few references in the historical record about the buildings or the people who made them. No elaborate family genealogies document its inhabitants, newspaper accounts rarely mention the lives of the people who lived there, and commercial and industrial records list no major accounts. No letters, diaries, photographs, or written material have survived. Oral history provides few details because different families have lived on this farm and few survive. No personal artifacts, tools, furniture, or machinery of any kind are known to exist. In short, few of the sources used to reconstruct the history of the three previous farms can be used to determine the history of the Woodsum farm. Still, silent buildings can be cautiously interpreted. If we combine lessons learned from the three previous buildings with patterns developed from this research, the history of buildings like the Woodsums' can be recreated.

Fig. 80. Woodsum Farm, Harrison, Maine.

1835 – 1845

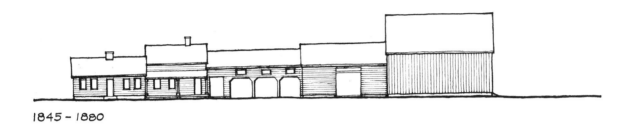

1845 – 1880

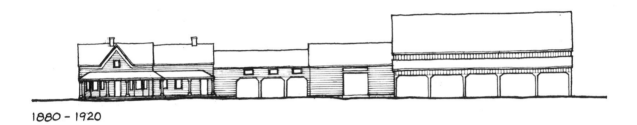

1880 – 1920

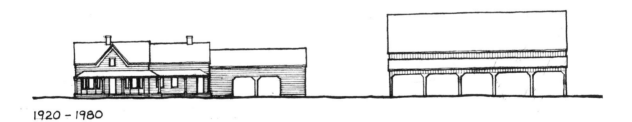

1920 – 1980

Fig. 81. Woodsum Farm, building development, 1835–1980, elevations.

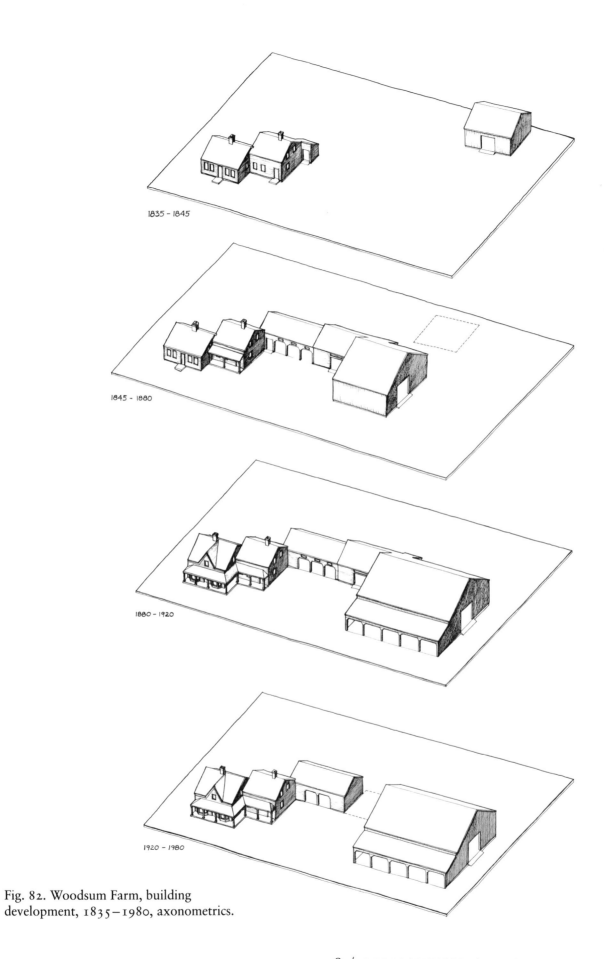

1835 – 1845

1845 – 1880

1880 – 1920

1920 – 1980

Fig. 82. Woodsum Farm, building
development, 1835–1980, axonometrics.

Benjamin and Abigail Woodsum built their farm along the road between Harrison and Norway, Maine. It had changed hands several times in speculative transactions before being acquired by them in 1836–38. The relatively late settlement date usually indicates a property not considered prime agricultural land and stripped of valuable timber. The farm site was near the home of John Woodsum, Benjamin's father, who assisted the young couple by cosigning one of the deeds to their property. Benjamin and Abigail Woodsum may have lived in the home of John Woodsum while their new home was being constructed between 1830 and 1840. With a relation's home close by, the young couple would not have needed to construct a temporary log hut, as might have been the case with earlier settlers. Therefore, their first house was probably the kitchen ell of the present house. This is one of the few stories handed down by a previous owner, and it is confirmed by on-site investigation.

This first house was a small, one-and-a-half-story, half-house, one of the most common forms in the early nineteenth century (see fig. 28A). The owners of the three previous farms constructed larger, more stylistically up-to-date houses during this period, but for the son of a common farmer in the 1830s this would have been the standard house form, and remained so until after 1850. The single major room was equipped with a large fireplace and probably an oven. Although stoves were introduced by prosperous farmers in the 1820s and 1830s, common farmers were only beginning to incorporate them into their houses, and even if a stove was planned for the new house, it probably would not have altered the fireplace construction because of the continuing strength of the fireplace tradition.

Since Benjamin Woodsum raised the crops and animals of a typical mid nineteenth-century farmer, he would also have constructed a barn. We can be certain that this was not the present barn on the property, and it probably was not located in its present position.[15] The old barn may have been located in the field in back of the present one. Although no physical evidence exists, the only other shred of oral history associated with this farm was supplied by a previous owner, who recalled a stone foundation removed from the pasture in back of the present barn. This could have been the location of an original barn because it is appropriately situated with regard to the typical detached barn arrangement of the early nineteenth century.

By 1845 the Woodsums probably constructed (or moved) an attached one-story, center-chimney, Cape Cod style house (now altered) to accommodate their four children (fig. 83). In plan it is a typical two-rooms-deep house with a small back room and two large front rooms. Although the fireplaces have been removed and the rooms greatly altered, it appears that neither of the three major rooms in the big house ever served as a kitchen. This would be consistent with the later date of the house, thus making the kitchen in the ell the only and original kitchen.

Most historical studies have assumed that the Cape Cod house was replaced by a variety of Greek Revival houses after the 1820s. This is sometimes true, especially in the case of prosperous farmers and city merchants, but average New England farmers continued to build and modify versions of the Cape Cod house well into the 1860s. It is not surprising to see Benjamin and Abigail Woodsum add a complete Cape Cod house to their ell in the 1840s. It appears that their new house was built next to the original location of the small one, but it is also possible that the smaller, older house was moved into a position adjacent to the new one during construction. The new Cape Cod house was equipped with three downstairs fireplaces, indicating that they were not entirely obsolete by the 1830s or 1840s (although stoves or fire frames may have been used in front of the fireplaces at this time). In the absence of other dating information, we know that Benjamin Woodsum mortgaged some of his land in 1845 for three hundred dollars. Perhaps this transaction helped to finance the new house addition or subsequent additions.

1845–1880

Sometime between 1845 and 1870, but probably after 1855, Benjamin and Abigail Woodsum enlarged their farmstead to its present size, including the long back house, stable, and barn. The centerpiece of this new expansion was undoubtedly the present barn. It is rare to find a barn of this type with sawed timbers and a bent construction system before 1840; most barns in this style were built after 1850. Some farmers were beginning to build full or partial cellars in the 1850s, but even if he had wanted one, Benjamin Woodsum was wise not to build one. Since the land has a high water table, a basement would have been filled with water for many months in the spring and would have been extremely impractical.

    The ell or back building that stretches out from the original house is composed of pieces from many different buildings to produce a four-bay structure that probably served as a kitchen workroom, wood house, vehicle shelter, and tool room. This ell was added to an older kitchen shed, which might have dated from the original house construction.

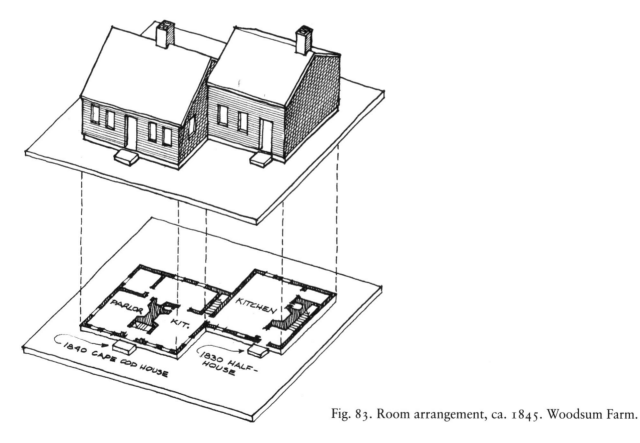

Fig. 83. Room arrangement, ca. 1845. Woodsum Farm.

The third major building was a stable or carriage house structure that survived in dilapidated condition until the 1940s, when it fell down. It was described as a three-bays-wide English barn with a door in the middle of the side wall, and its plan measurements (taken from the foundation, which still existed in 1978) showed it to be 30 feet long and 20 feet deep, which was a consistent English barn measurement. This structure could have been Benjamin Woodsum's original barn, which was moved into alignment with the house and new barn. Although the back building exists in dilapidated condition, the facade of the entire complex was once painted, clapboarded, and highlighted by small ornamental windows over the vehicle bay openings.

The dates and sequence of construction for the three connected agricultural buildings are not known, but it is tempting to attribute a major period of construction to 1855, when Benjamin Woodsum mortgaged his farm for $1,500. Between 1860 and 1870 the value of the farm rose from $1,800 to $3,000, which roughly corresponds to the mortgaged amount. During the same period, the farm reached a peak of wealth with crop acreage and farm production at an all-time high. This usually indicates a potential period for farmstead expansion.

A contributing factor to the Woodsum farm expansion project may have been a greatly enlarged production of hops. A large hop drying barn built between 1830 and 1860 is located about 300 yards south of the main house. This would have been a substantial investment for an individual farmer and was probably beyond the means of Benjamin Woodsum. Its construction may have been financed collectively by several farmers, as was often the case with cider mills, threshing machines, and saw- and gristmills. Since the hop industry flared and quickly vanished by 1880, this venture probably only temporarily increased the fortunes of the Woodsum family but could have provided them the margin to build the major barn buildings in the 1850s.[16]

1880–1920

Between 1865 and 1880 three Woodsum children left the farm. In their declining years, the senior Woodsums probably initiated little new construction. In 1879, one year after Benjamin's death, with no children remaining to continue the farm, Abigail Woodsum sold the farm to the White family, who introduced the next series of changes, re-forming the farm into the shape we see today.

The big house, or Cape Cod house, was significantly altered in a commonly repeated pattern (fig. 84). The front and back walls were raised 4 feet and the roof raised and steepened in a process often described as raising the roof. Similar projects were usually initiated to create more attic space; but the steepening of this roof by means of rafter extensions was also undertaken for its stylistic effect and matched the angle of the large Gothic style dormer inserted in the center of the roof. Delicate paired columns, in a style often labeled carpenter Gothic, supported porches added around the house. Brackets were added at the eaves of the main roof and porch. Double window bays and a double door were also added to the front facade. It is not known when the original central chimney was removed, but it could have been replaced with stove chimneys at this time. These exterior changes, occurring between 1870 and 1900, combined to produce what might be called a Victorian farmstead of the late 1800s.

Two additional bays were added to the original three-bay barn by a common pattern of agricultural expansion. This probably occurred during the major remodeling

Fig. 84. The front facade of the original one-story, center-chimney Cape Cod house with
raised and steepened roof, Gothic center gable, porches, and window bays. Woodsum Farm.

period of the 1880s. Since the two new bays were built in an identical manner to the
older ones, they were almost certainly added before 1900, after which different construction techniques would be expected. The cowshed, which stretches along the southern
side of the barn, was probably added after 1890, when dairy production became the
chief source of farm income.

1920–1980

Although farmed continuously until the present date, the condition of the farm has
declined. The back porch was taken down, and the stable and outhouse were removed
in the 1940s.

The four farms in this section have demonstrated the various ways connected farm
buildings developed. Each one shows different sequences of construction and usage that
influenced the making of most farms. Yet uniting these four farms was a group of consistent building and social patterns employed in their making, which are examined in the
next chapter.

5 Pattern in Building and Farming

No need to look around; all the farms around here are pretty much the same.

Richard Chadbourne

From a passing car, connected farms sometimes appear to be strangely composed and haphazardly strung together (fig. 85). Present residents have also commented on the apparent whimsy of the farmers' planning decisions. But when Richard Chadbourne described the farms in the Ingalls Hill neighborhood of Bridgton, Maine, he knew that, despite some difference in appearance, most farms were organized and operated similarly. The visual variety among farmsteads was the result of a building tradition that allowed individual farmers a range of design choices within a uniform pattern of overall farmstead layout. This chapter outlines the major recurring patterns of spatial organization and activity usage that characterized most connected farmsteads in the nineteenth century.

Fig. 85. A connected farm complex with multiple outbuildings and additions. Fryeburg, Maine.

The Arrangement of Buildings

Most connected farm buildings follow the organizational structure of the refrain, "Big house, little house, back house, barn." The distinguishing characteristic is that the big house and the barn are located at opposite ends of a string of connected buildings (fig. 86). Together they form either a straight or a staggered line of buildings in a flattened L- or U-shaped plan, usually aligned rectilinearly with the main road. The entire complex acted to shelter a south- or east-facing dooryard, protected from north and west winter winds by this line of connected buildings. More than 85 percent of the surveyed connected farms outside of town centers in Maine and eastern New Hampshire conform to the same organizational strategies of siting, linking, and connecting.

SITING THE BUILDINGS

Three farm planning principles guided most farmers' decisions for the layout of a connected farmstead (fig. 87). The first, most consistent consideration was that all buildings, particularly the house, be aligned at right angles to the major road with the principal facade of the house facing the road. This may seem like an obvious consideration today, since nearly all buildings assume this orientation, but builders in rural New England have not always sited structures this way. Before 1800 rural builders usually aligned the front facades and doorways of most houses and barns southward, without particular regard for the orientation to the road.[1] As late as 1830 an agricultural writer

Fig. 86. A typical connected farm arrangement with house (*upper left*) and barn (*lower right*) at the ends of a south-facing line of buildings defining a working dooryard (barn outbuildings at extreme lower right).

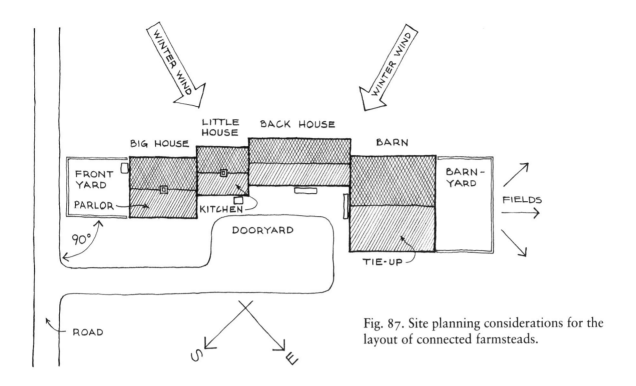

Fig. 87. Site planning considerations for the layout of connected farmsteads.

gave this advice to Maine farmers: "When the case will admit, the farm house, barn, etc., should front the south."[2] Today it is often possible to identify eighteenth-century houses and barns because of their now conspicuous nonalignment with the road. Where possible, buildings faced both south and the road, but southern orientation was the primary consideration. Between 1770 and 1830, most rural New England builders gradually came to favor an alignment in which the principal facades of new houses and barns, and particularly the formal front facade of the house, faced the major road without regard to southern exposure (fig. 88). This was a fundamental change in rural architectural planning and indicates that the rural population was relinquishing a nature-directed life-style in favor of a more road-directed, town-oriented way of life. It was almost as if the traditional building alignment of medieval origin was suddenly tugged out of its agrarian orientation by the increasing pull of economic and social influences of the town.[3] The swiftness and completeness of this conversion within a sixty-year period is one indication of the depth of this new town and commercial orientation for the rural population

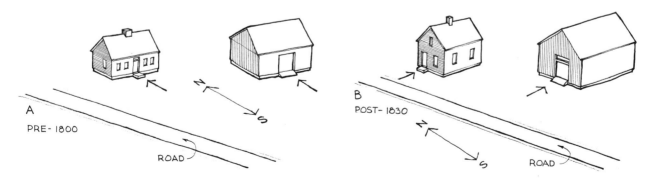

Fig. 88. Orientation for rural houses and barns: *A*, pre-1800, south-facing; *B*, post-1830, road-facing.

of New England. This change was to have important implications for the popularization of the connected building plan.

The second major siting consideration for connected farms was the provision for a southerly facing dooryard and kitchen ell. A southern or eastern exposure was important because farmers needed a dry, sunny work place for their many activities (see fig. 62). A distinct benefit of the connected farm arrangement was that the line of attached buildings sheltered the dooryard, and to a lesser extent the barnyard, from northern and western winter winds and from excessive snow accumulation. The wisdom of this planning strategy is particularly evident in the early spring. Piles of melting snow and pools of muddy water make the shaded north side of a typical connected complex impassable, while the dooryard and the barnyard on the southern side are dry for early springtime chores. Because of the region's short growing season, an early spring start has always been critical to the success of agricultural activities. The environmental advantages of a south- or east-facing dooryard generally improved the quality of domestic and farm life, and it still has much to recommend it, even to those who no longer farm.

The orientation of the dooryard also affected many architectural features of the connected farm. A comparison of the front and back sides of a typical farm vividly demonstrates the response to climatic considerations that guided the planning of these structures. The south or east side facing the dooryard is usually perforated with doors, windows, porches, dormers, and building additions, while the north or west side usually lacks these amenities and is relatively blank and unadorned. Inside the buildings, the major rooms are also directed toward the south-facing dooryard, except for the parlor, which was usually oriented toward the front yard and road.

The third basic siting principle was to locate the barn's animal tie-up bay and barnyard in a southerly orientation and in close proximity to fields, pastures, roads, and wells. The consideration of a southern exposure for animal yards and their housing was echoed in all periods and was summarized by Samuel Deane in 1790: "A cowhouse should be in the southerly part of the barn when it can be so ordered. The cattle will be less pinched with the cold northerly winds."[4] Most farmers in all periods have followed this strategy, which even Vitruvius recommended to his Roman readers.[5] In the most common arrangement, like the Sawyer-Black farm, the door of the New England barn faces east into the dooryard permitting the side with its cattle tie-up bay to face south (see figs. 4 and 5).

These three basic strategies developed alongside the new nineteenth-century practice of locating the kitchen in the ell instead of in the big house. The result was that the kitchen in the ell continued to maintain its traditional southern orientation while the big house was freed to align itself with the major road without particular regard for southern exposure (although where possible it was also aligned to the south). In the typical remodeling situation where a kitchen ell was added to a pre-1830 big house, there were usually only one or two ways to string the connected kitchen ell and barn outward from the main house to form a south- or east-facing dooryard and barnyard, and this direction was usually selected.

These three planning strategies were obvious to most farmers and combined to influence the placement of most connected farmsteads between 1820 and 1900. Figure 89 provides an outline of the various arrangements that were usually constructed following these basic guidelines. All three rules are perhaps so obvious to any New England

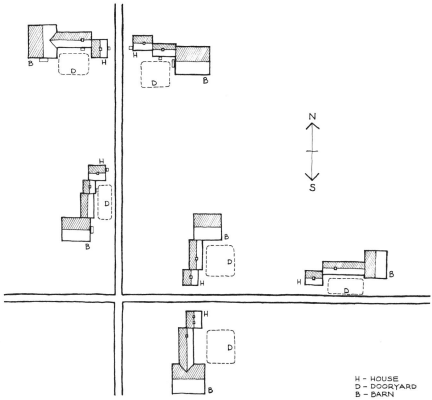

Fig. 89. Six common arrangements of connected farmsteads
in relation to compass and road orientation.

farmer, past or present, that they may hardly seem worthy of comment. And that is
precisely what these vernacular rules were: unarticulated, commonsense rules, ingrained
in usage and habit, which became a standard part of the farming and building traditions
of the region.[6]

Yet the layout and organization of many connected farms cannot be understood by
simply following these general rules. Three other factors greatly complicate this tidy
picture. First, the rules were not static but evolving in time. Much depended upon how
strictly a guideline was followed and the degree to which it came into competition with
previous rules or ideas. For example, the desire for a rectilinear alignment of the buildings, both to each other and to the road, gradually gained popularity in the late eighteenth and early nineteenth centuries and became accepted by most builders after the
1820s. But if a building was constructed between 1780 and 1820, the new consideration
might only partially influence siting decisions; often only the house and not the barn
would face the road, indicating a compromise between competing planning ideas
(fig. 90). After the 1820s, however, most builders and owners accepted the principle of
road orientation for all buildings, so that it became practically unthinkable, until the
present, to fail to align a building at right angles to an adjacent road and to other farm
buildings in the complex.[7]

Second, the planning rules that influenced connected farm layout and siting were
frequently applied to existing, nonconnected farmsteads of various ages and configura-

tions. These had usually been organized according to older vernacular rules. Consequently, the degree to which a new building idea could be implemented often depended upon the existing configuration of the farmstead. The frequent compromise between a new planning idea and an existing farmstead organization is evident in the case of the original Nevers homestead in Sweden, Maine. There, an earlier south-oriented house was joined to a later road-oriented barn by a connecting ell (now gone) producing a nonaligned and nonrectilinear plan.

A third, intangible factor was the effect of individual selection and choice by builders and owners in the planning decision-making process. Some farmers defied

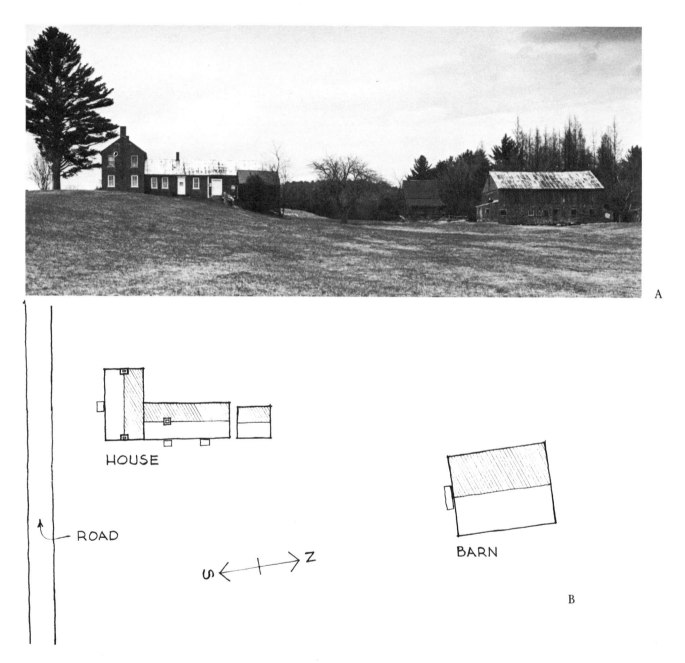

Fig. 90. A house aligned parallel with the road. The detached barn is oriented southward and not aligned with the house or road: *A*, view from the east; *B*, plan. Chase-Lowell Farm, Buckfield, Maine.

convention and made their building differently. For example, Tobias Walker of Kennebunk, Maine, whose building will be analyzed in Chapter 6, defied a customary planning convention by placing his dooryard on the north side of his house and barn. As we shall see, he had good reasons to do so, but his family still had to contend with a snowy and late-drying dooryard. Additional factors that influenced building arrangement in all periods include initial site selection, the location of roads, wells, and fields, site topography, and the size, wealth, and type of farming operation.

The siting of connected architecture in New England's towns followed some of the same patterns as farm examples, but beginning in the early colonial period, the constraints of earlier English precedent and lot size (caused by the high cost of land) dictated a perpendicular alignment of connected buildings with the road. In the towns of New England, perpendicular road alignment superseded the south-facing agrarian tradition.[8] During the first quarter of the nineteenth century, this linear arrangement became standardized in the immensely popular connected house and carriage house arrangement of the region's small towns, paralleling the development of the connected farm complex.

LINKING THE BUILDINGS

A farmer had considerable choice about the way buildings were joined together. Most structures could be joined to accentuate the uniformity or the nonuniformity of the connection (see fig. 6). In a uniform pattern of connection, separate buildings were aligned to minimize or disguise the building linkage, and in a nonuniform pattern of connection, individual structures were offset, exaggerating the building linkage. The more common practice of offset building connection is a distinctive characteristic of many connected farmsteads. Even to a sympathetic observer, the joining of individual buildings might sometimes appear to defy any organizational principles or rules, but the physical connection between most structures was not random.

From a practical standpoint, a staggered or offset building connection lessened the surface contact between two buildings joined together by allowing existing doors and windows to remain operable and thus minimizing the internal disruption to either building. This was an especially important consideration for New England farmers, who perfected a popular tradition of moving and realigning structures. A staggered building alignment also permitted the farmer to use each building independently and somewhat differently. This was an important overall consideration to the success of the connected farm plan because the presence of diverse, adjacent activities often required a degree of activity separation. Most farmers found it desirable, for example, to separate their kitchen workroom from the woodshed and their parlor from the kitchen; this separation could be reinforced by the offset of separate buildings joined together. The logic of this practice is apparent if each connected building is understood as a somewhat separately operating unit that joins other separate units. The uneven exterior appearance of many connected farms can seem overly complicated, but the unit is jagged only from a visual or formal perspective. Operationally, the stagger and offset of buildings worked extremely well to accommodate the New England farmer's mixed-farming, home-industry system, one that necessitated the adjacency of diverse activities requiring a degree of separation.

An offset or nonsymmetrical connected building alignment for farm buildings was an ancient English tradition brought to America.[9] But there is, perhaps, another, more subtle reason for the persistence of this characteristic. The novelty of surface treatment in individual buildings suggests a certain amount of individuality, zealousness, even bravado, on the part of some farmers who might have enjoyed the juxtaposition and clash of different building forms. There may even have been a degree of anti-city formality or an individual pride in breaking formal rules—in this case, the genteel, aesthetic rules of uniformity and order that were frequently employed in fashionable connected town houses. Whatever the reason for this frequent juxtaposition of forms, it is important to emphasize the significant role of the builders and owners in designing these buildings. Within every connected building complex there were usually several different ways of aligning or offsetting, unifying or contrasting, and finishing or not finishing the buildings so as to achieve the same operational results (for example, the decision to rotate the English barn in the connected complex; see figure 98).[10] There was a significant degree of choice and individual expression, therefore, in the organization of connected farms, which many farmers chose to exploit for a variety of practical, aesthetic, and personal reasons.

CONNECTING THE HOUSE AND BARN

The practice of linking house and barn with a connecting ell is one of the most striking features of connected farmsteads, and it is this characteristic that primarily influenced the way these buildings were used. Farmers chose the system primarily because it worked sufficiently well to house their mixed-farming, home-industry operation, and they could afford to do so because its adoption required only moderate adjustments to their previous building arrangement. What probably appealed to them most was the sensible organization of rooms in the ell to accommodate the diversity of activities required of their multiple-task operation. It was a system that proved remarkably efficient and adaptable to a range of daily and seasonal activities and to long-term change as well. The advantages were summarized in the cover article of Maine's most prestigious farm publication, *Abstract of the Returns from Agricultural Societies of Maine, 1857*: "This plan [of a connected farm building] is designed to meet the wants of farmers in Maine who have moderate sized farms devoted to the usual 'mixed husbandry'. . . . The well, cistern, wood-house, ice room and cellar, or any out building, may be reached with the fewest steps and the least possible exposure" (fig. 91).[11] Behind the praise for its convenient organization was admiration for the way it looked, but common farmers would certainly not have selected the new arrangement based upon its appearance unless it first met their basic requirements for living and working.

The connection of the barn to the extended ell was, of course, the most unusual aspect of this system. For farmers to select it, they had to overcome a substantial tradition against such practice. Since their initial settlement in the New World, New Englanders had separated their house from their barn as did all other American farmers.[12] Spatial separation reinforced a basic distinction between the place of people and the place of animals, as well as between the work activities in the house and in the barn.

When the largest portion of New England farmers connected their houses and barns in the nineteenth century, they appeared to alter their customary practice radically, but the connected arrangement is actually much closer to the typical American farm layout. While physically connected to convey an image of unity and balance, house and

Fig. 91. "View of Model Farm Buildings for a Maine Farmer," the cover
illustration for an article endorsing the connected farm building organization in 1857.

barn are actually quite distinct in function and operation (see fig. 7). The big house
epitomizes this separation by literally turning its major facade and its parlor room away
from the dooryard and barnyard, toward the front yard and road. Most activities in the
big house, particularly those occurring in the formal parlor, had little or nothing to do
with the activities in the ell or the barn. At the other end of the connected complex, the
barn engulfed most farm activities within its massive shell or channeled them into the
barnyard away from the house. Consequently, the traditional American separation between house and barn, or between people and animals, is maintained and strengthened.
Of course, Yankee farmers knew they were building in a nontraditional fashion, and
they had to defend their new scheme against the criticism of outsiders. In 1843 a
Connecticut farmer praised the connected farm building arrangement to skeptical readers of the Albany, New York, *Cultivator*, and defended it against the potential problem
of noise and smell from the barnyard: "it will be seen that the wood house and shop,
and lane [covered passage] intervene and prevent all unpleasant connection. . . . But,
after all, the farmer who is ashamed of his cattle yard, or its odors, had best set his
house from them a goodly distance indeed!"[13] Arguments such as this never persuaded
New York farmers or those from other areas of the country to build in the connected
plan, but many Yankee readers were certainly impressed by its logic.

The feeling of separation between connected house and barn is also reinforced by
the nonlinear, nonaxial linkage of different buildings, which contributes to a spatial
differentiation between buildings, and even between adjacent rooms in the complex.

Today people who have walked from house to barn in one of these complexes often comment with surprise at the many spatial changes and the surprising length of the journey, even though, upon outside inspection, the complex appears much smaller and more unified. This experience is primarily the result of the nonlinear passage through the multiple buildings.[14]

All these factors allowed the New England farmers who built connected farms to maintain the typical American distinction between house and barn while simultaneously connecting and unifying them. Overall the connected farm organization performed a delicate balancing act between the visual unification and the functional separation of the opposite poles of house and barn. It successfully accomplished both tasks, providing its users with a new, unified vision of a small family farm in New England.

The Working Ell

The key to understanding the way connected farm buildings functioned and why farmers made these structures can be found in the buildings of the ell—the little house and back house between the big house and barn. The ell was a highly refined architectural and technological solution to the difficult problem of sheltering New England's mixed-farming and home-industry operations. It can be thought of as a small but intensive farm-factory. This is an unusual term for a small-scale family farm center, but *farm-factory* emphasizes the intensity and variety of seasonal activities conducted within its multifunctional space.

Work activities in the ell were primarily undertaken by farm women (fig. 92). This work revolved around the kitchen, and most activities originated from, interacted with, or returned to the farm kitchen. The mid nineteenth-century kitchen and its adjacent rooms were the place for: butter and cheese making; crop processing and preserving; home-industry crafts, such as clothes making and quilting; handcrafted items, such as leather and wood items; soap and candle making; and the never-ending chores of washing, mending, cooking, and child care.[15] To accomplish these tasks, New England farmers had standardized the arrangement of linked workrooms in the ell to include: a kitchen, kitchen workroom (summer kitchen), wood house, and workshop or carriage house. A typical arrangement of rooms in the ell is shown in the Erastus True farm of North Yarmouth, Maine, built in 1842 (fig. 93). This type of linear room organization became so popular throughout the region that by 1867 an agricultural writer cautioned against the excesses of ell building and recommended a more compact plan "rather than buildings stretching off in a continuous line, as we too often see where ell upon ell is added to the main structure."[16] But New England farmers found great advantage in their "ell upon ell" system, and they continued to build these structures into the twentieth century.

The ell on the Marston-Lawrence farm in North Yarmouth, Maine, built in 1863, has an advanced ell plan for its period (fig. 94). Its rooms are larger and more specialized than the rooms of the Erastus True farm, but the basic organization is similar since both farms conducted the same type of agricultural operation. Both show the standard kitchen stove chimney of the mid-1800s, located between the kitchen and its workroom and including a brick oven and boilers. Together these rooms constituted the working

Fig. 92. The work of the ell. A woman emerges from a snowbound kitchen
ell, probably on her way to the well. Unlike the record of male farm work, few
photographs show women at their daily chores. South Paris, Maine, area, ca. 1890.

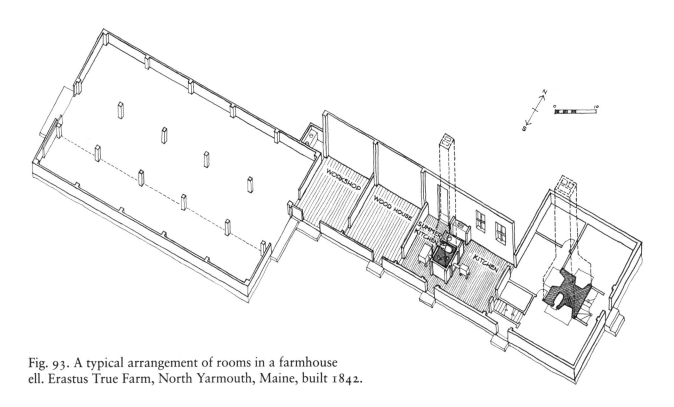

Fig. 93. A typical arrangement of rooms in a farmhouse
ell. Erastus True Farm, North Yarmouth, Maine, built 1842.

PATTERN IN BUILDING AND FARMING / 123

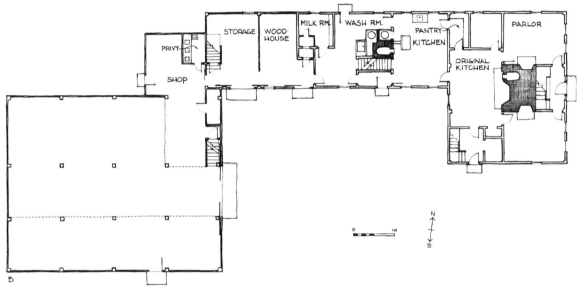

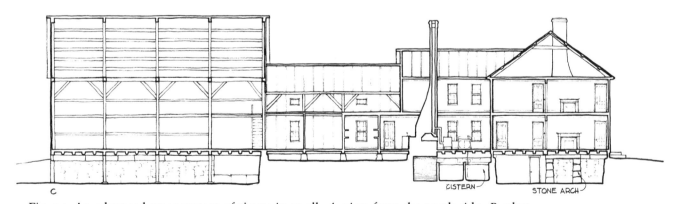

Fig. 94. An advanced arrangement of rooms in an ell: *A*, view from the north side; *B*, plan; *C*, section. Marston-Lawrence Farm, North Yarmouth, Maine. Ell and barn built 1862–1865.

heart of most connected farms during all periods. It was here that crops and raw materials from fields and barns were processed for home consumption or sale; home-industry tasks were carried on and the daily tasks of food preparation, washing, and child care were undertaken.

Surrounding the important first floor rooms of the ell was another system of service spaces. The sectional drawing of the Marston-Lawrence farm shows this secondary system, which included: the second floor of the ell for weaving, farm laborers' quarters, and grain and corn storage; the cistern underneath the kitchen for water storage; the milk room in the cellar of the main house for butter making; the fireplace cellar arch of the main house for perishable food storage; and the barn cellar for the pig house and manure and root crop storage. An icehouse for milk cooling was also located next to the barn. A nearby well and kitchen garden completed the system of spaces and facilities supporting the work activities of the ell.

Today the workrooms of the ell that still preserve their nineteenth-century appearance have a quaint, rustic character, but at one time they were the pride of modern, efficient farmers who made their ells a focal point for agricultural and domestic improvement. The ell was a place of applied technology and contained the latest labor-saving devices that a farmer could afford. A series of nineteenth-century technological improvements was directly associated with the development of the ell, but none was more significant than the introduction of the kitchen stove.

THE STOVE

The popular acceptance of the kitchen stove to replace the fireplace was one of the most important technological changes that facilitated the development of the connected farm ell (fig. 95). The stove revolutionized the New England farm kitchen and its work spaces during a thirty-year period between 1820 and 1850. Its rapid introduction significantly reduced the laborious task of open-hearth cooking and expanded the range of cooking

Fig. 95. The kitchen stove. A typical farm kitchen with cookstove, metal lined wooden sink (*left*), hand pump (*far left*) and doorway to the summer kitchen and woodshed. Berry House, Unity, Maine, ca. 1900.

possibilities.[17] The kitchen became a cleaner, safer place in which to live and work, and the never-ending chore of firewood production for multiple fireplaces was greatly reduced. The stove significantly increased the warmth of the entire house and profoundly affected the overall quality of family life. This transformation was accomplished in an amazingly short period, considering the magnitude of physical and social changes and the strength of the old English fireplace traditions.[18] The introduction of the stove represents one of the most significant improvements in the quality of life for any generation of American farmers. Perhaps only the changes associated with farm electrification provide an appropriate comparison.

The architectural changes that accompanied the introduction of the stove on the typical New England farm are apparent in a comparison of two kitchen chimneys from different periods (fig. 96). The first is a fireplace chimney from the Hamilton house, built in the 1790s; the second is a stove chimney from the Chase house remodeled in the 1840s. The Hamiltons' fireplace chimney is typical of the pre-1830 detached house and barn period; the Chases' stove chimney typifies the post-1850 connected farmstead era.

The introduction of the stove contributed to several other important changes in the spatial and operational organization of the kitchen and the ell. Although it is not usually associated with the major changes in building between 1820 and 1850, the impact of the stove on the new Greek Revival house forms and common farm building construction was extensive. When farmers began introducing stoves into their houses, they could have set up the new devices in the kitchens of their typical, pre-1830 center-chimney houses. It certainly was a financially compelling possibility. Yet they generally chose to build an attached ell to accommodate the new kitchen stove. The kitchen in an ell

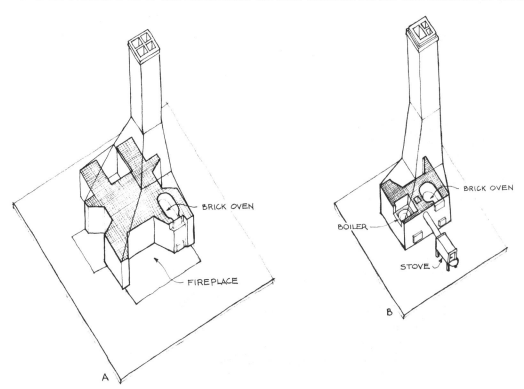

Fig. 96. Kitchen chimneys: *A*, typical pre-1830 fireplace chimney, Hamilton House, North Yarmouth, Maine, 1790; *B*, typical post-1850 stove chimney, Jacob Chase House, North Yarmouth, Maine (kitchen remodeled), 1840s.

attached to the major house had been employed in colonial New England, and continued to gain popularity during the early 1800s, but it was not a common tradition and was selected for most houses only after 1820.[19] The acceptance of the stove accelerated the change from the old colonial fireplace tradition of kitchen in the main house to the new nineteenth-century tradition of kitchen in the ell attached to the main house (fig. 97). The reason why so many colonial and pre-1830 houses in New England have their original big house kitchen fireplaces is that during the nineteenth century the construction of a new kitchen in the ell for the stove made the original fireplace obsolete but did not necessitate its destruction. In fact, it continued to be used as a second kitchen on many farms (see Chapter 4, The Nutting Farm, 1820–1830).[20]

The new kitchen area in the ell was also favored because it allowed greater flexibility and expansion than was possible within the constricted framework of the pre-1830 kitchen. The kitchen of the pre-1830 Hamilton house, for example, was set within the structural framework of the big house and could not easily be expanded (see

Fig. 97. Kitchen conversion. A late nineteenth-century stove has been inserted into a walled-up kitchen fireplace to make a Victorian sitting room. The kitchen was probably relocated in an ell to the right. Conner House, Unity, Maine, ca. 1905.

fig. 35 A). In contrast, the kitchen of the typical post-1830 house could easily be expanded into the rooms of the ell, and this factor contributed to the popularity of the connected farm organization. The stove also enabled New England builders to alter radically the traditional room organization and structural system of the house. For over two hundred years, the location of the massive central fireplace chimney had stiffly regimented the room arrangement of New England houses.[21] When the chimney was simplified from a massive fireplace complex to a small brick stack, it allowed builders a number of planning opportunities. The variety of room arrangements and chimney locations in the Greek Revival big house attests to the fundamental changes from the center-chimney system. The introduction of the stove also contributed to a change in the structural system of post-1830 houses. In earlier houses, the location of a massive fireplace core generated the basic module for room division and framing. Without the center chimney, New England builders were free to adopt a more standardized structural system close to the modern balloon-framing system.[22] The extent of these changes is evident when one compares the room arrangements and construction systems of the Hamilton and Staples houses (see fig. 35).

THE SET KETTLE

The introduction of the stove was associated with the set kettle, another major technological improvement to the kitchen ell of the post-1830 house. The set kettle, boiler, or wash boiler was a deep iron kettle set into an airtight masonry counter with a fire box below. It was a water-heating device used for cooking, washing, cleaning, and animal food preparation, and was often installed alongside the first stove in the kitchen ell of a connected farm (see fig. 96). The boiler was an eighteenth-century European invention introduced in the estate houses of the early 1800s. In the Rundlet-May house of 1807 at Portsmouth, New Hampshire, for example, the boilers stand beside the famous Rumford Roaster. It was Benjamin Thompson (Count Rumford) who made extensive studies of European boilers and kitchen cooking devices between 1797 and 1806.[23] Early nineteenth-century pattern books, such as Asher Benjamin's *American Builder's Companion* of 1806, pictured similar boilers, which contributed to their rapid popularization throughout New England.[24]

Set kettles were commonly built into the side or back of existing fireplaces in older, pre-1830 houses, often in the area between the kitchen and its adjacent workroom. In structures built after 1830 (such as the ells attached to the True and Marston-Lawrence houses), a large masonry unit commonly combined the set kettle with a brick bake oven and flues for stoves (see figs. 93 and 94 B). This combination was probably one of the most popular cooking and heating units for the kitchen ells of houses built between 1830 and 1880 (see fig. 96 B). Perhaps the inclusion of a brick oven in this postfireplace masonry unit is surprising, but the brick oven remained a popular kitchen amenity alongside the new stove until after 1880, when improved stove ovens finally replaced it.

The set kettle was also rendered obsolete after 1880 by the introduction of hot water heating devices attached to the stove. These containers were either mounted on the side of the stove or (later) stood next to it. The standing hot water tank, usually made of copper, filled domestic hot water needs on the farm well into the twentieth century until it was replaced by the electric hot water heater. Many inhabitants of connected farms still remember the standing copper hot water tank.

Although the stove and the boiler were probably the most significant nineteenth-century inventions, other technological changes also influenced the development of the kitchen ell. Water conveyance and storage devices were important additions to the working ell. The relentless chore of hauling water from outdoor wells was greatly simplified by handmade, then machine-made metal pumps. By 1850 the metal kitchen pump was the conspicuous mark of a prosperous farmer, although most did not obtain their first metal pump until after the Civil War.[25] Early pumps were mounted over the well or over the kitchen sink. Kitchen pumps were supplied by wells, gravity-feed systems, and water storage compartments or brick cisterns in house cellars. In many areas cisterns were fed by rainwater collected from the roofs and located beneath the kitchen (see fig. 94 C). Such devices were once common in areas with water supply difficulties such as Kennebunk and North Yarmouth, Maine.

Horizontal water conveyance in wooden pipes from springs or wells to the house had been attempted since the colonial period, but the method was not widely practiced.[26] Water piping did not become widespread until lead pipes were commercially available in the last quarter of the nineteenth century. After 1860, many prosperous farmers used the hydraulic ram, an early gravity-triggered water pumping device.[27] The windmill was a late nineteenth-century device used on some farms, supplying water until it was superseded by gasoline and electric pumps in the twentieth century. The list of technological improvements adding to the convenience and quality of life in the nineteenth-century farm home also included such items as the (foot pedal) sewing machine, mechanical churn, kerosene lamp, metal sink, and a variety of manufactured hand tools like the apple peeler—all labor-saving devices associated with the work of the ell.

Four technological changes symbolize the extent to which the domestic lives and the buildings of most rural New Englanders were radically transformed within a fifty-year period of the nineteenth century (1820–70): (1) the replacement of fireplace by stove, (2) the replacement of homemade cloth by manufactured cloth, (3) the replacement of hand-hauling well water by the metal pump, and (4) the replacement of hand tools by machine tools for farming and domestic work. Each major change helped to facilitate the transition of the New England farming system to greater productive and commercial capabilities; each assisted in developing the ell into a more commercially oriented farm-factory.

Typology of Connected Farms

The most common type of connected farmstead is an arrangement like that of the Sawyer-Black farm of Sweden, Maine (see figs. 4 and 5). This typical connected farm is composed of a one-story center-chimney big house, a one-room-deep kitchen, a three-bay back house, and a three-bays-wide, four-bays-deep New England barn. During the period when the connected building organization became popular, several important factors influenced variations, refinements, and extensions to the basic four-part arrangement: (1) the development and accentuation of the carriage house or stable within the back house area, (2) the increased size of farm buildings, (3) the influence of town examples, and (4) architectural style and construction developments.

One popular variation on the standard "big house, little house, back house, barn" arrangement produced a dramatic juxtaposition of barn and carriage house. This form was probably inspired by town and city examples, where a carriage house instead of a barn might terminate a building complex (see fig. 101). Most farmers had a distinct choice about whether to emphasize or minimize the carriage house, or stable, which was usually the last back building in the connected complex adjoining the barn. The majority deemphasized the carriage house by locating it within one bay of the back house. Still, all farmers had the option of emphasizing this structure by simply aligning its gable end toward the dooryard. The drawing in figure 98 depicts the dramatic visual change resulting from different orientations of an English barn moved and converted into an attached carriage house, a common practice of the period. The decision to differentiate the carriage house probably indicated the increased importance of the horse and carriage to the farmer, as well as the influence of town-generated architectural styles.

Greater mechanization and improved methods of agriculture on the New England farm between 1850 and 1890 increased crop yields and animal production for most farmers and, consequently, increased the overall need for storage and animal shelter space. The massive complexes of connected farm architecture that seem to stretch endlessly across the northern New England landscape were a product of that era and were usually built (or reached their present size) after 1870 (fig. 99). These farms often followed the same organizational structure as smaller, more common connected farms, except that the back buildings and barn(s) are larger, more numerous, and often highly specialized. Since connected farms of this size required substantial financial resources, they are usually found in agricultural areas that were prosperous during the second half of the nineteenth century. Two such areas were the River Road of Windham, Maine, and the Route 16 area north of Milton, New Hampshire, where connected farms of massive size still line the roadway.

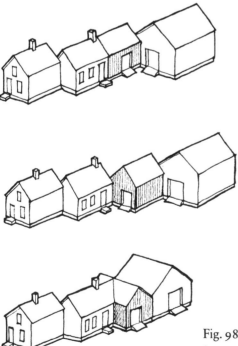

Fig. 98. Three arrangements for the placement of an English barn within the same connected building complex.

Fig. 99. A massive connected complex. North Bridgton, Maine.

Several interesting variations of the typical connected farm arrangement occurred when ells were built outward from both sides of the big house. Such ells were often constructed to accommodate an additional family (usually a married son). Sometimes a carriage house was built off one ell and a barn off the other, although working barns at either end of the complex were also constructed (fig. 100).

Throughout the nineteenth century many farmers did not choose to conform to the new connected house and barn organization, but instead built according to older traditions. One of the most common alternative organizations continued the older eighteenth-century tradition of building a detached house and barn. In many cases the barn was placed directly across the road from the house, to be nearer fields, water supply, and pastures.

Roughly paralleling the development of the connected farm building arrangement, town and city dwellers developed a connected complex, substituting a carriage house (or chaise house) for a barn (see fig. 101). This town tradition of house-to-carriage house connection was derived from an older colonial tradition that received renewed popularity with the building of connected manor houses in the early Federal period (see fig. 14). By 1830 the tradition of house-to-carriage house connection was commonly accepted in New England's small towns and influenced the rural adoption of the connected farm building arrangement.

Although town and farm connected building arrangements share many characteristics, there are significant differences. Connected farm buildings unite a house with a barn (for livestock and crop shelter); connected town buildings unite a house with a carriage house (for carriage and horse shelter). The primary distinction between these two large

Fig. 100. A farmstead with a major barn at either end of the connected complex. Bridgton, Maine.

overlapping categories of New England buildings is the presence or absence of a barn.

The distinction between a carriage house and a barn in nineteenth-century towns, however, is not always clear because many, perhaps most, town dwellers of that era kept cows and farm animals as well as horses, and raised some food for their own consumption. But in spite of similarities in use, the architecture that farmers made was consistently different from that of town dwellers. The carriage house or stable is usually smaller than the barn. It is also frequently identified by its distinctive offset door to one side of the gable end, while barns always locate their major door in the middle of two side bays. Most town carriage houses in New England employed a sawn, vertical stud construction system in a combination of balloon-frame and mortise-and-tenon techniques, which are usually products of the second half of the nineteenth century. Almost all barns are constructed in a heavy timber, mortise-and-tenon construction system regardless of their nineteenth-century date of construction.

The distinctive offset door to the carriage house of many connected town houses allowed the carriage to be parked on the opposite side of the door, with horse stabling accommodations usually located to the rear. This is the same pattern produced by relocating the original side-wall door of an old English barn into the gable end (see fig. 49). It is not known which idea came first: to convert the English barn into a carriage house or to offset a door in the gable end of a new type of building. Probably they were mutually reinforcing. The most popular form of connected town building was composed of three buildings: a Greek Revival big house, a short kitchen ell, and a carriage house. Built between 1830 and 1910, it is now one of the most common forms of rural housing in New England. Many small towns of this region contain a high density of these structures.[28]

Two different approaches to the making of connected farm buildings were well established by 1850 and continued to structure the possibilities for the farmstead organization during the next fifty years (see fig. 6). In one pattern, the overall arrangement of the connected farm was achieved incrementally by the addition of separate buildings, usually over a period of time. This strategy had the effect of exaggerating the individuality of each building in the connected complex and consequently might be termed a juxtapositional and incremental form of connected farm design. In the second pattern, the individual farm buildings were more uniformly made or uniformly joined together according to a strategy that emphasized visual order and unity. Generally the buildings on older, smaller, or poorer farms were built incrementally and are often differentiated from each other. Newer, larger, or wealthier farmsteads tended to be organized more uniformly and usually achieved a more consistent visual organization. Both an incremental-juxtapositional strategy and a uniform-formal strategy are planning extremes, between which most farmers concocted their particular farmstead designs based on a variety of factors including farm wealth, existing building arrangements, community traditions, and individual taste. Thus most farmstead arrangements combined aspects of both planning strategies.

Architectural Style

The chronological record of stylistic change is widely used to describe the history and development of architectural forms.[29] In the case of connected farms, however, the chronological progression of architectural styles is an inadequate means to assess historical development because the vernacular and classically derived ornamentation employed by most New England folk builders remained so uniform throughout the nineteenth century. A more significant stylistic gauge to the development of the connected farmstead plan was the evolution of the rules that guided the application of both these classical and vernacular traditions.[30]

During most of the nineteenth century, farmers made several consistent assumptions about how their buildings would look. One of the most common was that refinements in architectural style should be placed on the frontal or public side of their buildings, while the back and sides would be left unadorned or minimally finished (see fig. 86). This strategy, labeled frontality, is often dramatically evident at the corner of house or barn when the white clapboards and Grecian corner boards of the front facade suddenly change into a weather-blackened surface of vertical boards or shingles.[31] In 1838 a farm writer ridiculed this common practice: "for we have sometimes noticed buildings with the front and ends, which are most exposed to view, painted, while all other parts of it are left to rot down in the natural state."[32] But to many rural residents of New England, past and present, it was and still is assumed that the building face that meets the public should be finely finished while the rest should be unadorned. (Of course, this strategy is not confined to New England farmers but is one of the most consistent patterns guiding the adornment of monumental buildings, particularly urban examples.)[33]

Another closely related visual strategy was the practice of placing the finest stylistic refinements on the major house and diminishing these on successive buildings leading to the barn. This might be termed a strategy of dissipation and is one of the most popular aesthetic strategies for connected farms. For example, the architectural detail of the big house might be slightly diminished on the little house, and further diminished on the back house and barn (see fig. 6A). This diminishing of the elements of architectural style is representative of the majority of connected farms in New England.

By manipulating the two basic strategies of frontality and dissipation, the individual farmer had a wide range of visual aesthetic choices about the way the farmstead could look. Perhaps the overriding decision controlling these choices was the degree to which the entire building ensemble was to achieve a unformity or a diversity between house and barn.

The way that most farmers chose to extend the architectural detail of the house to the barn was to place domestic type windows in the barn's front gable end and to clapboard and paint the barn facade that faced the road. As a general rule, only wealthy farmers could afford to extend the complete architectural order and style of the main house to the entire building complex. These farmers were also more likely to emulate the architecturally unified carriage house examples of town inhabitants with whom they shared similar values. Farmers of modest means, however, were more likely to diminish, but not terminate, the architectural refinements of their big houses on the rest of their buildings. It was less expensive to do so, and it probably represented a more restrained emulation of what was considered to be a style of the town.

The aesthetic strategy of dissipation, no matter how diluted, represented a decisive break with previous vernacular farm traditions. Those who built connected farms changed their farms by extending the architectural style and order of the house to their barns. This was a truly radical development by New England farmers, and it is this characteristic, more than that of house and barn connection itself, that is one of the unique aspects of New England connected farm architecture.

Most farmers chose variations of the same classical style to articulate their houses and barns, yet this consistency is seldom acknowledged in New England's extensive architectural literature. Most studies have emphasized the record of stylistic change during the nineteenth century. By focusing upon a small minority of town houses, such as the ones in figure 101, architectural historians have mistakenly suggested that a series of changing period styles dominated the architectural development of rural nineteenth-century New England.[34] But houses like these represent only a small percentage of the architecture in rural New England.

Most farmers selected only modest and limited interpretations of the widely publicized period styles. Throughout the entire nineteenth century, the majority of New England's farmers confined their stylistic choices to a vernacular version of a classical architectural vocabulary derived from a combination of the immensely popular Federal

Fig. 101. Connected town houses in period styles of the nineteenth century:
A, Italianate, Bridgton, Maine, ca. 1850; B, Gothic, "Wedding Cake House,"
Kennebunk, Maine, 1856; C, shingle style, Bridgton, Maine, ca. 1900.

A

B

C

PATTERN IN BUILDING AND FARMING / 135

and Greek Revival styles (fig. 102). Two periods within this classical-vernacular tradition are an earlier Georgian and Federal period from the early 1700s until the 1830s and a later Greek Revival period from the 1830s until 1910, although there is considerable overlap between periods. In the early nineteenth century, New England builders had developed a classically derived vocabulary through exposure and emulation of Georgian and Federal style houses and through a number of carpentry pattern books whose architectural ornamentation they applied to a well-established body of vernacular building traditions.[35] In the later, Greek Revival period, many of the detailing strategies of the earlier classical period were continued and augmented by an expanded volume of popular carpentry pattern books.[36]

The influence of carpentry pattern books, such as Asher Benjamin's, has correctly been credited with the spread of the classical stylistic vocabulary in the first half of the nineteenth century. The content of these publications is, however, limited to selective carpentry details of architectural style. It is surprising just how little information an early nineteenth-century pattern book actually contains. A typical Federal or Greek Revival period house can certainly not be built from one of these publications. Authors like Asher Benjamin (a skilled builder himself) correctly assumed that local builders would bring a complete body of vernacular traditions to supplement the stylistic details that these publications did provide. The vast building traditions contained in even modest houses and barns did not originate in pattern books, but in an active body of folk building traditions carried in the minds of folk builders.[37]

By the mid nineteenth century, the tradition of what might be labeled a classical-vernacular style was the overwhelming selection for the articulation of most buildings in New England. This style was characterized by classically derived details employed according to vernacular rules in a consistently stark, minimal fashion. Between 1800 and 1850 this style was visually transformed by the popularization of white paint for houses, barns, churches, workshops, mills, stores, and assembly halls.[38] This unity of style is one of the most important visual components giving cohesion and architectural order to what we now appreciate as the New England village aesthetic.

It is within this well-established vernacular context that most nineteenth-century period styles make their selective appearance on the buildings of New England farmers. Many farmers did choose limited aspects of the fashionable town styles but applied them sparingly according to principles derived from vernacular building traditions.[39] Common stylistic changes to the exterior of connected farms included: the raising and steepening of roof gables and the addition of roof dormers in the Gothic fashion; the widening of roof overhangs with bracketed supports; the enlargement of windows and making of piazzas or porches in the Italianate fashion; the application of Grecian pilasters and entablature detail in the most elaborate Greek Revival fashion; the addition of bays, turrets, door hoods, and porches, and the application of "gingerbread" ornamentation in the later Victorian fashion; and individually inspired or eclectic combinations of all those styles (see fig. 40). Many of these changes were applied quite literally to an understructure of the classical-vernacular style.[40]

The architectural articulation of connected building interiors follows a uniform pattern of application for most farmsteads. The strategy of dissipation is intensified on the interior with maximum architectural detail devoted to the major rooms of the big house, especially the parlor (fig. 103). Detailed stylistic refinements were usually confined

Fig. 102. Typical classical-vernacular style. Kennebunk, Maine area, ca. 1880.

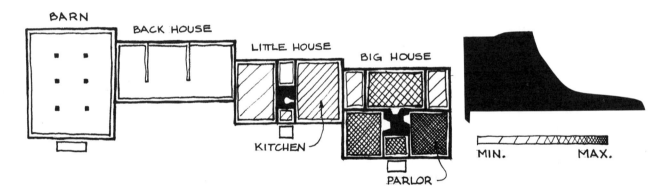

Fig. 103. Dissipation of architectural style within the interior rooms. The concentration of architectural detail is indicated by the relative density of the shading pattern.

to the big house and occasionally the kitchen, while the remainder of the complex was minimally finished in plaster sheathing for walls and ceilings and simple casings around windows and doors. Occasionally, heavy Victorian molding replaced earlier woodwork, but versions of the Federal and Greek Revival styles dominated big house interiors throughout the nineteenth century.

It must be emphasized that most New England farmers continuously displayed a cautious, reserved attitude toward stylish excesses in their building. Most were like Tobias Walker, who remodeled his farmstead many times, employing a sparse classical-vernacular vocabulary on the inside and the outside of his buildings to construct a severe but powerful aesthetic system. Walker was not a country bumpkin who blindly or crudely interpreted classical styles. He was well educated for his time, and he clearly knew of other architectural styles. Nevertheless, he chose to adorn his house and barn in the widely popular classical-vernacular style. Expressing a preference for unity, he chose to have his buildings look much like other houses in his farm neighborhood. Today, in spite of numerous assumptions and assertions to the contrary, most people still agree with Tobias Walker and build their houses accordingly.[41]

Construction Traditions

PERMANENCE AND CHANGE

In order for a building like the connected farmstead to achieve widespread acceptance, it had to be both selected by and available to many members of a society. A few determined builders in any society can frequently build with great liberty without regard to the physical and economic constraints that structure the buildings of most people.[42] For a building to achieve widespread popularity, however, it must usually obey construction traditions of tested stability and common usage and be genuinely appreciated by its builders and owners. One of the reasons the connected farmstead arrangement had such wide appeal was that it followed existing construction techniques available to most farmers.

Rural New England builders had developed many of their techniques from English traditions refined by over two hundred years' contact with conditions of the New World. Unlike builders in other northern regions of America, Yankee craftsmen maintained a relative homogeneity of English construction practices, which helps to explain the unity and strength of tradition within this region.[43] Building construction traditions within rural New England may be classified according to two contrasting strategies: the tradition of permanence, involving a high degree of building maintenance, reuse and preservation; and the tradition of change, involving the practices of building modification, alteration, and readaption. Both strategies influenced the development of the connected farm building arrangement.

The strategy of building permanence is often concealed under the facades of farm buildings that have been remodeled many times. One of the most consistent patterns of building usage for New England settlers of all periods was to save houses and barns by moving and reusing them. Another strategy of permanence was the English tradition of building incrementally and adding on to existing structures. This saving, making-do tradition reinforced the practice of reusing materials, particularly structural members, for new construction, and was nearly universally employed in rural New England. For example, the ells on 75 percent of the farms analyzed for this study were constructed from reused building materials. Although the same practice is employed by rural people worldwide, New Englanders elevated it to a refined and acceptable art at all economic levels and in all forms of construction.

The architectural tradition of permanence was balanced by a second, equally strong tradition of building change or impermanence. The buildings that were reused were not saved in a spirit of nostalgic preservationism, but were unceremoniously readapted in a

A

B

Fig. 104. The "raising" and conversion of a one-story house into a fashionable connected town house: A, the original house raised on cribbing and being prepared for the insertion of the new first floor; B, the converted house. Bethel, Maine, ca. 1890.

practical no-nonsense spirit of farm improvement and modernization. It was a common practice to convert a house to a barn, a kitchen to a shed, or a shed to a shop (although rarely a barn to a house). As the examples in this book will continue to show, massive interior and exterior reorganization was clearly the accepted societal norm for these farmers. Figure 104 shows the raising and conversion of a small one-story house into a fashionable town house in Bethel, Maine, before 1900. While this project seems extreme today, it was actually a common one for New England builders, who had developed the custom of massive building alteration and remodeling.

This well-established tradition of building movement was perhaps the most widespread method by which New England farmers continuously changed their farmsteads. This was not a common English tradition, and its widespread usage is a particularly American building phenomenon.[44] Building movement was practiced from the early colonial period continuously until the 1940s. The frequency of moving major domestic and agricultural buildings in eighteenth- and nineteenth-century New England is staggering. When the history of building movement in a particular New England town is accurately recorded, as in the towns of Fryeburg and Cornish, Maine, it appears as if the entire town was constantly being moved about.[45] This seems to be the norm for most towns in rural New England. For more than half of the documented farms in this survey, building movement was associated with the formation of the connected complex. However, the vast amount of building movement in New England and throughout America went unrecorded, probably because it was such a widely accepted practice that it evoked no special comment.[46]

To a modern observer the practice of building movement might seem unusual or even astounding, but New England farmers were particularly well prepared for this task. In their long experience with logging, they had perfected the art of moving heavy logs on skids and wagons with the aid of oxen and later horses. Most farmers who moved their buildings were, therefore, merely converting their normal wood-hauling technology to the movement of buildings. This process was simplified because houses and barns were not secured to, but merely rested upon, their stone foundations or cellars. It was a relatively easy operation to disengage a building from its support system by means of simple screw jacks. Long support timbers called shoes or skids were inserted underneath the structure and oxen or horse teams dragged or rolled the building to a new location (fig. 105). The absence of telephone lines and busy highways and a neighborhood tradition of mutual assistance also facilitated building movement. The ability to move buildings, however, did not mean that all people automatically moved their buildings. Nineteenth-century American farmers in other parts of the country had similar abilities, but they did not seem to move their buildings as frequently as did New Englanders.[47]

The tradition of moving buildings was absolutely essential to the widespread popularity of the connected farm concept. Most farmers did not have the resources to construct an entirely new string of buildings, but they could afford to move and realign their existing structures into the new connected arrangement. Thus the connected house and barn system was an accessible, affordable means of improving and modernizing existing farms.

The total record of change in New England building traditions presents a graphic picture of people committed to the idea of physically tinkering, retooling and altering the buildings in order to improve their physical surroundings. This is not the record of a people unwilling or unable to change, but the manifest imprint of a modern experimenting people well in keeping with the optimistic predictions of Thomas Jefferson and Alexis

Fig. 105. A converted schoolhouse moved by twenty teams of horses and oxen. The building was transported half a mile from a location at the far left of the photograph. Yarmouth, Maine, ca. 1900.

de Tocqueville in regard to the potential of the masses for individual improvement.[48]

The characteristics of permanence and change in the New England farmer's attitude toward building construction were not in opposition but actually complemented each other. Together they produced a Yankee compromise between an unnostalgic, adding-on type of permanence, and a tinkering, tradition-bound type of change. These overlapping attitudes allowed builders to retain those aspects of the tradition that worked or were highly regarded while radically altering or discarding other aspects. This is not just an issue of change or permanence in architectural style (although elements of style are involved), but a process of building reaching to the deepest levels of decision making about form, use, and construction. By studying this process through time, it is possible to develop a model for interpreting the buildings of New England farmers. Figure 106 demonstrates the ways that New England farmers both changed their buildings and kept them the same.[49] In this model, a component of a building has a purpose and a cultural meaning that was continuously added to and reinforced, or subtracted from and dis-

PERMANENCE AND CHANGE

Columns span the years: 1775 | 1800 | 1825 | 1850 | 1875 | 1900

BUILDING ORIENTATION
SOUTH FACING (S)
ROAD FACING (R)

	1775	1800	1825	1850	1875
BIG HOUSE	S →	S+R →	← R	← R	← R
KITCHEN ELL	—	← S	← S	← S	← S
BARN	← S	S	S+R →	← R	← R

YARD ARRANGEMENT
FORMAL, GENTEEL (F)
VERNACULAR, FUNCTIONAL (V)

	1775	1800	1825	1850	1875
FRONT YARD	V	V+F	V+F →	← F	F →
DOORYARD	V	V →	V+F	V+F	V+F
BARNYARD	← V	← V	← V	← V	V

BUILDING GROUPING
CONNECTED, UNIFIED (C)
DETACHED, DIFFERENTIATED (D)

	1775	1800	1825	1850	1875
BIG HOUSE	D	D+C	← C	← C	← C
KITCHEN ELL	—	← C	← C	← C	← C
BARN	D	D →	D+C →	← C	C

ARCHITECTURAL STYLE (EXT.)
CLASSICAL-VERNACULAR (C)
UNARTICULATED, FUNCTIONAL (U)

	1775	1800	1825	1850	1875
BIG HOUSE	C+U	C+U	← C	← C	← C
KITCHEN ELL	U	C+U	← C	← C	← C
BARN	U	U →	C+U	C+U →	C

BUILDING USAGE
WORK ACTIVITIES (W)
NONWORK ACTIVITIES (N)

	1775	1800	1825	1850	1875
BIG HOUSE	W →	W+N →	← N	← N	← N
KITCHEN ELL	—	← W	← W	← W	← W
BARN	← W	← W	← W	← W	← W

FRAMING SYSTEM
MORTISE-AND-TENON (M)
BALLOON FRAME (B)

	1775	1800	1825	1850	1875
BIG HOUSE	M →	M+B	M+B →	← B	← B
KITCHEN ELL	—	M+B	M+B →	← B	← B
BARN	← M	← M	M	M →	M+B →

HEATING – COOKING SYSTEM
FIREPLACE (F)
STOVE (S)

	1775	1800	1825	1850	1875
BIG HOUSE	F	F	F+S	← S	← S
KITCHEN ELL	F	F	← S	← S	← S
OUT BUILDINGS	F	F+S	← S	← S	← S

TECHNOLOGICAL IMPROVEMENTS
RAPID DEVELOPMENT (R)
SLOW DEVELOPMENT (S)

	1775	1800	1825	1850	1875
BIG HOUSE	S	S	S	S →	S →
KITCHEN ELL	—	S+R →	← R	← R	← R
BARN	S	S →	S+R	S+R	S+R →

ARCHITECTURAL STYLE (INT.)
FORMAL, HIGH STYLE (F)
FUNCTIONAL, MINIMAL (M)

	1775	1800	1825	1850	1875
BIG HOUSE	← F	← F	← F	← F	← F
KITCHEN ELL	M	M →	M+F	M+F	M+F
BARN	← M	← M	← M	← M	← M

Fig. 106. Interpreting permanence and change in the nineteenth-century connected farm building complex. Arrows pointing to the left indicate a tendency toward greater permanence. Arrows pointing to the right indicate a tendency toward greater change.

regarded. This helps to explain how certain elements such as the New England farm kitchen were constantly remodeled, while other features such as the parlor were maintained and preserved in spite of normal pressures to change and remodel. This diagram also helps to explain the rapid changes in certain areas of construction when a major set of building traditions was undermined and discarded, resulting in drastic reinterpretations of many aspects of the entire building system. This reshuffling phenomenon was evident when the sudden introduction of the stove swept away the entire tradition of masonry fireplace construction, with multiple ramifications on every level of the building construction system.

STRUCTURAL SYSTEM

Concealed within changing houses and barns on New England farms was a structural system that gave unity to most farm buildings. At the beginning of the nineteenth century, the heavy timber, mortise-and-tenon structural system was used for almost all houses and barns in New England (fig. 107). Before this time, regional builders had eliminated or absorbed a variety of competing structural and material systems including the vertical plank system, the French vertical post system, log fortification, stacked log cabin or log hovel systems, and especially stone and brick masonry systems, which were widely practiced in England.[50] In nineteenth-century New England, farmers modified their heavy timber system by introducing simplified techniques associated with the balloon frame, but they also continued many aspects of the old system.[51] They employed this combined system throughout the nineteenth century in various proportions for different types of buildings, although the newer balloon frame system gradually replaced the older mortise-and-tenon one.

Despite this gradual evolution in construction technique, most farm architecture can be classified into two distinct groups based upon the structural systems of house and barn, specifically the direction of the principal structural members in the walls. In houses the dominant direction of the structural members of the wall is vertical and requires horizontal sheathing. In barns it is horizontal and requires vertical sheathing (fig. 108). For the pre-1830 heavy timber, mortise-and-tenon house framing system, vertical wall posts, including the four major corner posts and smaller vertical posts or studs, were mortised into the upper plate and lower sill. These smaller studs were spaced to accommodate doors and windows or placed uniformly along blank walls. Siding was then applied horizontally and covered by clapboards or shingles. After the middle of the nineteenth century, when builders began to construct houses using the balloon-frame construction system, the custom of vertical structural members and horizontal sheathing remained unchanged.

Unlike the house frame, the barn frame relies on a series of major and minor horizontal members in its wall system. Although the vertical posts are critical components, it is the horizontal members that dominate the wall framing system. The use of vertical studs, so necessary for the placement of windows and doors in houses, is inconsequential in barns. Instead, a horizontal structural system is used to maximize the size of the structure. A distinct benefit of this system for barns is that exposed exterior siding must be applied vertically and allows precipitation to drain off. If the sheathing were applied horizontally, rain and moisture would collect in the joints or would require additional sheathing or clapboarding as used in houses. Since pre-1860 barns in New

Fig. 107. Rural framers preparing mortise-and-tenon joints in sawn structural members. The two workmen on the left hold mortise-drilling machines, Massachusetts, ca. 1900.

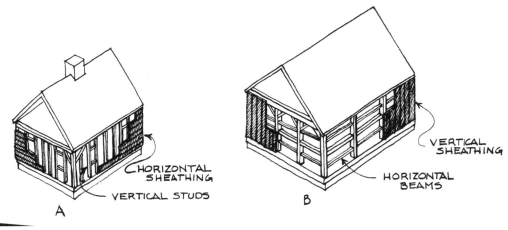

Fig. 108. Typical framing systems: A, houses with vertical studs and horizontal sheathing; B, barns with horizontal beams and vertical sheathing.

England have only infrequently been clad with shingles and clapboard (and then only on the public or front side), an additional layer of sheathing would have been a severe economic disadvantage.

Like any environmental determinant for explaining the meaning of architecture, however, the different structural systems in houses and barns cannot be attributed solely to moisture protection or structural convenience. This difference also reveals a desire to maintain a fundamental distinction between the house and barn. It is this distinction, nonetheless, that New Englanders were to challenge when they outwardly unified their houses and their barns during the nineteenth century.

One of the most consistent developments in the structural systems of New England farmers was the tendency toward simplification and standardization.[52] New England builders inherited an ancient construction system of English medieval origin, which they significantly modified during the eighteenth century and the first half of the nineteenth. They simplified many complex aspects of their mortise-and-tenon system, such as the gunstock post joint, and developed a standardized system of straight sawn members and uniform dimensions. Although the mortise-and-tenon system was never relinquished in nineteenth-century barns, many of the developments of the new balloon-frame system were integrated into regional housing and outbuilding practices. Farmers also continued to refine the module framing system for all buildings, which was a product of the same drive toward standardization and simplification in the construction system. A survey of the development of structural systems of houses and barns reveals that New England farmers adjusted and slightly altered, but did not fundamentally change, their barns, while they substantially transformed their houses. This fact will be analyzed to understand why they made connected farms.

Rhythms of Work

THE WORKING FARM

Repetitive cycles of work structured the lives and the buildings of New England farmers (fig. 109). The phrase *rhythms of work* contains two important concepts: *rhythms* underscores the cyclical nature of the farming enterprise, which was organized according to recurring daily, weekly and seasonal activities; and *work* underscores one of the essential beliefs of a farming people—that all aspects of life are given unity and meaning in work.[53]

The task of describing work on the farm is staggering simply because it includes almost everything that everyone did, all the time. Figure 110 has been compiled to show both the types of work and their continuous cycles on the nineteenth-century farm. The charts depict the cyclical rhythms of multiple activities that normally characterized a year's labor for many inhabitants of connected farms between 1840 and 1860. While they could describe many small, mixed-farming operations throughout America at mid-century, they also describe the model for progressive, prosperous farmers in New England. It was farmers such as these who chose the connected farm building system, as it was uniquely designed to accommodate their diverse range of seasonal activities.

Every day for a farm family began and ended with chores (fig. 111). For males these included animal maintenance tasks in the morning and evening. For females, they included the cyclical tasks of cooking, cleaning, washing, and child care, tasks which must stand between the concept of chores (daily maintenance activities) and seasonally timed work.

The midday dinner divided a typical farm work day. Activities or chores occurred "forenoon" or "afternoon." The two-part structure of the farm day is indicated in this typical diary passage from 1849: "AM. Clearing up old rubbish about the door yard, put ox sleds under cover, etc., PM. Rainy, filled vinegar casks with cider & sweetened water."[54] The noon dinner was usually the largest meal, just as it still is in many rural areas of America. Following late afternoon chores, supper reunited the family and generally ended male work, but female work continued, seemingly without end. Within

Fig. 109. Spring plowing. York, Maine, 1890s.

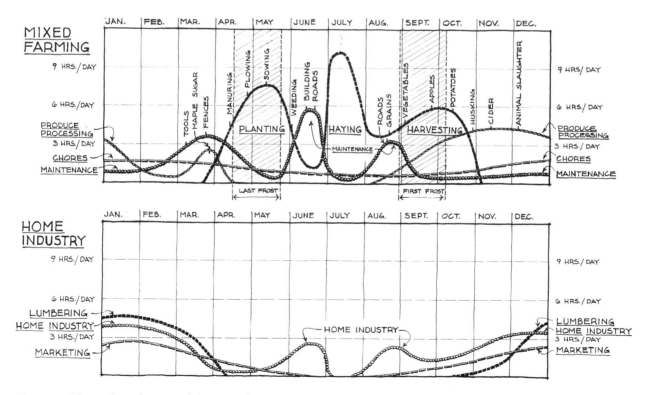

Fig. 110. The cycles of seasonal farm work.

Fig. 111. Bert Hamilton in the doorway of his shed cutting seed potatoes prior to planting. The hand-barrow, or wheelbarrow, and the sturdy ash-splint basket were commonly used for chores about the farm. North Yarmouth, Maine, ca. 1930.

Fig. 112. A farm couple. New England, ca. 1890.

this cycle of daily work, the kitchen took on paramount importance to the farm family. Mealtime was more than a means for nourishment: it provided a critical period of rest and gathering between labor. Like all periods of rest on the farm, it had its place within the cycles of work.

The weekly rhythm of farm life was punctuated by less work on the Sabbath. Most farmers, including those who did not attend church, welcomed this day of rest, although daily chores never ceased. Hard work, however, was not approved of on Sunday, and to disregard this would be to risk disapproval of a homogeneous farming community. But even this tradition was put aside in times of crisis, as when wet haystacks needed "opening" and people were forced to work "more than has been known for a number of years on Sunday." [55]

The cycle of the seasons was by far the most significant organizer of farm life. Figure 110 shows the annual work cycles of a farm during the middle of the nineteenth century. The seasonal chart is divided into mixed-farming and home-industry sections and vividly shows the summer (mixed-farming) and winter (home-industry) sides of the typical farmer's life. The chart was primarily compiled from the record of male work in the Walker diaries from Kennebunk, Maine. [56] A similar chart for female work could not be obtained from these accounts, but it would show home-industry activities taking place in the winter and spring and food processing activities concentrated in the summer and fall.

Winter work for males was usually divided between timbering and home-industry production. The marketing of wood, agricultural, and home-industry products was a time-consuming job, usually conducted in the winter by sled. Spring activities revolved around plowing and planting and were timed according to the drying of fields and the last frost. Spring activities were usually preceded by critical maintenance and preparation tasks such as fencing and vehicle and tool repair. Hay was the first harvested crop. It required a series of carefully timed stages, and because of its critical importance for the winter food of livestock, it literally consumed every waking hour for one to three weeks. The intensity of the haying season was balanced by periods of less concentrated work before and after. The fall harvesting period was timed according to the arrival of frost, with a distinct harvesting and process sequence for each crop. Food processing and storage tasks continued throughout the fall and into the winter.

In between the three peak periods of planting, haying, and harvesting, farmers integrated all the other activities of their mixed-farming, home-industry enterprise. In the spring between planting and haying, for example, they constructed most of their buildings. Eighty percent of the barn and house raising in the Alewive neighborhood of Kennebunk, Maine, occurred in late May or June, with most of the remainder in August after the haying season.[57]

The record of seasonal work presents a vivid picture of a farming population committed to a system of multiple enterprises in support of farm income. Unfortunately, the diversity of farm and nonfarm activities did not always reflect the value of those hours. In some nearly tragic ways, New England farmers had created the outlines of a system that was beginning to put increased labor into increasingly uneconomical tasks. Their mixed-farming, home-industry system was an inherently labor-intensive system and its principal disadvantages were that: the multiple outbuilding custom increased problems of building maintenance; mixed-farming practices for various crops and animals maximized multiple field use and the need for fencing maintenance; the rock-filled and infertile soil required labor-intensive methods of soil enrichment and stone removal; hilly terrain made road maintenance and marketing difficult; mixed-crop and animal farming required a diversity of increasingly expensive tools and machines and a variety of seasonal schedules to plant, harvest, and process different products; and home-industry activities such as logging and clothes making diverted considerable energy away from agricultural activities. All these factors were inevitable consequences of the mixed-farming, home-industry system, but, as we shall see, New England farmers had little alternative but to maintain these methods if they were to continue farming. Gradually, however, these factors made it more and more difficult for them to compete with more specialized producers in other parts of the country.

THE FARM FAMILY

The rhythms of farm work influenced the structure of the farm family. Its most important component was the working couple who shared continually overlapping activities in the operation of the typical farm (fig. 112). Together they formed a unit that might be described as a work-centered family composed of a dominant working male and a dominant working female. Usually they were a husband and wife, but in the instance of the death of one partner, which occurred frequently, the family could continue if the role of the missing member was quickly filled. For example, when a wife died, the farm could continue if the female work role was quickly assumed by another female, such as an unmarried sister or a hired woman, who would become the dominant working female. If this role was not filled, however, the family unit did not survive long (although, of course, there were exceptions).[58] If the husband or the dominant working male died, rapid replacement was crucial to the survival of the farm. Usually an older son would succeed the father, or the wife would quickly remarry. The need to replace either the male or female member in this work-centered family emphasizes the mutual dependence of both parties in the mixed-farming, home-industry production system.

The work-centered family passed ownership along male lines. By the early 1800s remnants of the the old English progenitor tradition of ownership succession had largely given way to a more paternalistic system in which the father usually maintained control of the farm until physically unable to do the major work. Frequently, the youngest son or oldest remaining son living on the farm was given control or ownership at this time and became the dominant working male. The transfer of control and ownership in male succession was, of course, not always trouble-free or absolute, but in general the senior male who continued to work and manage the farm maintained control.

The ideal family unit for most farm families in the nineteenth century was a nuclear family (with the anticipated addition of parents in old age).[59] But the factors of death and employment created a vastly more complex "typical family" (fig. 113). The ravages of early and sudden death from sickness, accident, or childbirth caused many families to gain members while other families were eliminated. It was common for households to gain related and nonrelated members including aged parents, orphaned young, widowed relatives, and neighbors. In general, the effects of sudden death created a much more fluid, changeable family unit. For example, the sudden appearance of a new wife and children within an existing family was a common occurrence (see Chapter 6, 1840–1850) as was the dispersal of children upon the death of both parents.

Employment situations, often dictated by the death of a family member, also influenced the organization of the typical New England farm family. Employment opportunities created two distinct kinds of family unit organization: families that gained members by hiring labor, and families that lost members when they were hired out for labor. Such employment lasted for short or seasonal periods but was a means for some to secure a permanent home. Farm wealth dictated this hiring-out process, which worked to sustain wealthier families and break down the unity of poorer families, who nevertheless gained critical farm income.[60]

The difficulty of establishing a new farmstead was another employment factor that structured the family. By the middle of the nineteenth century, young married couples in many established farming areas could not obtain a farm and often lived with their parents. The degree to which the two families shared accommodations was usually signaled by the presence of one or two kitchens in the same house. In a common pattern, the parents would retain control of the older big house with its older kitchen, and the younger family would use the new kitchen in the ell, although there was often considerable sharing between the two households (see Chapter 4, The Nutting Farm, 1830–1890). The multiple kitchen plan of many connected farmsteads solved this difficult planning

A

B

Fig. 113. Farm families: *A*, South Paris, Maine, area, ca. 1910; *B*, Bethel, Maine, area, ca. 1890.

PATTERN IN BUILDING AND FARMING / 149

problem and was another factor that contributed to the popularity of the connected building concept.

Male and female farmers worked together to run the mixed-farming, home-industry New England farm. How they worked together is crucial to understanding how a connected farmstead worked. Outwardly the roles were extremely rigid. The men worked in the fields and the barns, the women worked in the ell and the yards. Upon closer inspection, however, these roles become far more complex. Figure 114 shows a work role map of male and female activities in and around the connected farm arrangement. The areas of extreme role separation, like the kitchen and the fields, were generally adhered to, but must also be amended by accounts of women helping at haying and harvest times and males assisting in the kitchen.[61] The female and male work roles in the ell and the dooryard, however, involved a complex sharing and overlapping of activities. The kitchen garden, for example, was often plowed by the males, perhaps planted and maintained by both males and females, and harvested by females. This structure of distinct gender roles for shared activities seems to have characterized most overlapping work activities in and around New England farms including the connected farm.[62]

A revealing problem of gender work distinction developed after the mid-century, when many farmers began to improve the appearance of the dooryard and front yard. There was no precedent for who should care for this newly improved area. A newspaper article in 1829 accurately depicts the dilemma of maintenance for these yards: "one reason why so many door yards are neglected, is that it is a spot of doubtful jurisdiction, neither falling exactly under the scope of the word 'farm' which it is the man's to oversee, nor being properly in the house, where women reigns."[63] This dilemma was also created because the traditional maintenance of exterior plants and flower gardens was the work of women, but the cutting or mowing of the grass, which the front yard demanded, was a distinctively male occupation.

As the map of gender zones on the farm suggests, it is important not to overemphasize sharp distinctions between work roles. Unfortunately, most farm history sources are derived from male-dominated, pragmatically inspired accounts or interviews that have continually underestimated or neglected accounts of mutuality and sharing between partners. This is not to minimize the real work role distinctions that rigidly circumscribed most agricultural activities on the nineteenth-century New England farm, but the less articulated account of sharing does not break through the historical record easily. Yet when it does, it speaks of traditions not usually recorded, as in this diary entry: "Assisted wife in making soap."[64]

Neighborhoods

The world of the New England farmer extended beyond the boundaries of the individual farm and was structured by a larger context of social, political, and economic relationships. Perhaps the two most important units in that world were the farm neighborhood and the town. Although much has been written about the importance of the town, less is known about the farm neighborhood (fig. 115).[65] This is unfortunate because in terms of the day-to-day life of most farmers, the neighborhood was probably the most significant unit of societal organization next to the family.

A New England farm neighborhood usually comprised five to thirty farms, forming

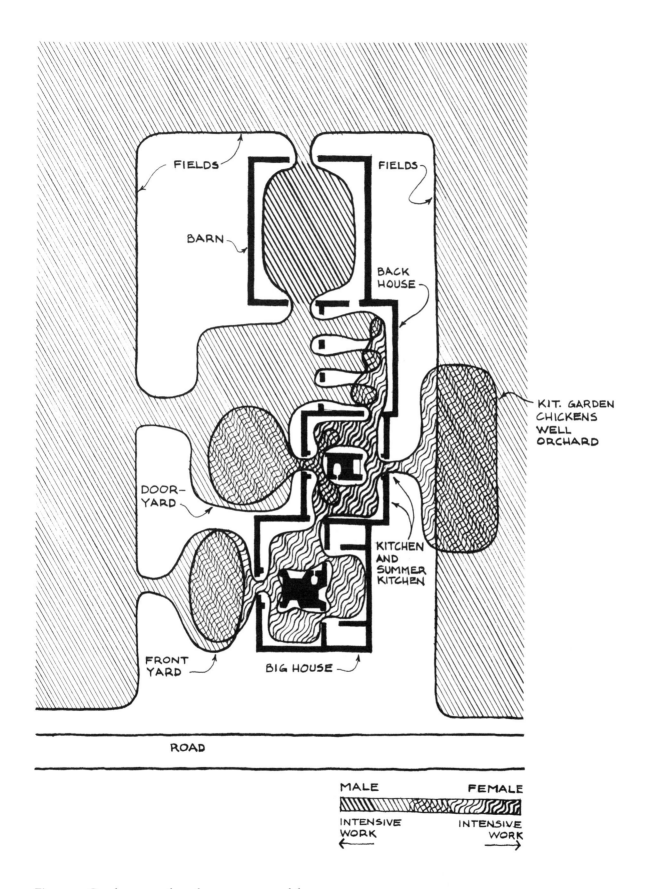

Fig. 114. Gender map of work on a connected farm.

Fig. 115. Conversing with neighbors, early 1900s. The dirt road leads to the old Doloff homestead in North Yarmouth, Maine, and remains virtually unchanged today.

a geographic district of culturally unified farmers operating independent farms within a traditionally defined system of social cooperation.[66] Two overlapping criteria gave organization to the New England farm neighborhood. One was geographic, such as a hillside or a grouping of farms along a road. The other was cultural, and can simply be described as people sharing a similar way of life. In practice, farmers reinforced these similarities by settling near relatives and friends or in similar socioeconomic neighborhoods, just as we do today. Geographic proximity, however, was the overriding criterion for neighborhood cooperation, and it acted to overcome a host of personal differences between farmers who found it to their mutual advantage to help each other.

The farm neighborhood facilitated cooperation, which was essential to the survival and well-being of each farm family. Shared activities included: education (district schools); work sharing (particularly the exchange of labor, animals, tools, and machinery); health care (assistance in sickness, birth, and death); services or craft specialization (blacksmith, herbalist, carpenter); disaster relief (sudden death, fire); celebrations and assemblies (barn raisings, sings, and huskings); road maintenance (construction, snow plowing, and repair); and general information sharing and socializing. Most of these activities, such as the road district, had a long precedent in English cultural tradition.[67] Although farmers in other areas of the country maintained cooperative practices, their widespread uniformity in New England must be attributed to the homogeneity of the English cultural traditions, which supported a close network of neighborhood mutuality.

The school district and the road district were neighborhood organizations legislated by the town government (fig. 116). A town's school district map for any period is one of the best sources for determining the outlines of a farm neighborhood system, because the frequent restructuring of its boundaries usually reflected shifting family alliances and changes in the neighborhood social organization.[68] The farm neighborhood exercised control over its school through elected representatives in cooperation with the town government. The one-room schoolhouse has been a conspicuous symbol of the New England neighborhood system since the colonial period.

The road district was a cooperative unit of farmers who maintained local roads (fig. 117). It often followed the same boundaries as the school district and was based upon precedents unaltered since the seventeenth century in England.[69] Each farmer was assessed a town road tax, which was usually paid in labor on the neighborhood road crew. In many rural areas this system continued through the Depression. "Breaking the roads" after each snowfall was another task of the road crew. The road district thus allowed each farmer to contribute equitably to the year-round maintenance of the town's roads. Many towns assessed a separate road tax, which each farmer could pay or work off.

The nonlegislated organization of a New England farm neighborhood is more fluid than a legislated school or road district, but the basic structure was maintained by farm families who desired its benefits. One of the most important aspects of the neighborhood organization was an elaborate system of work exchange, characterized by direct labor exchange, hiring out, apprenticeship, trading exchanges, and mutual assistance among farmers.[70] Practically every nineteenth-century farm diary records a huge volume of daily

Fig. 116. "Scholars" in front of their neighborhood school. Bethel, Maine, late 1800s.

Fig. 117. A neighborhood road crew stands beside a horse team and two ox teams hauling oxcarts (or dump carts). Wiscasset, Maine, area.

labor exchanges and indicates a highly developed tradition of work sharing, trading, and mutuality of very old English origin.[71]

Farm labor was frequently hired out for various agricultural, home-industry, and domestic service activities. The neighborhood network of hiring out labor to more prosperous neighbors allowed many farmers and their children to obtain scarce cash income and provided a means for many marginal farming operations to survive. The neighborhood hiring and labor exchange system was particularly helpful during the peak farming periods of planting, haying, or harvesting.

Each farm neighborhood also contained individuals who shared their particular craft or skills for cash or trade. These farmer-artisans cannot easily be separated from a larger network of town artisans and craftspeople, but each neighborhood of five to thirty farms might contain persons who specialized in carpentry, blacksmithing, butchering, clothes making, stonecutting, tanning, and healing (fig. 118).[72] The existence of these farmer-artisans was gradually threatened by the increasing productivity and economic advantages of town shops and factories during the middle of the nineteenth century, but many neighborhoods continued to provide these services into the twentieth century.

Another tradition of neighborhood work cooperation involved the use and sharing of agricultural machinery. The practices of hiring out, exchange, and group ownership were methods by which farmers cooperated to obtain valuable agricultural machines that they could not afford (or that were impractical to own individually). Perhaps the most commonly shared nineteenth-century machine was the horse-powered thresher usually owned by one or several farmers and hired out throughout a neighborhood (fig. 119). Beginning in the 1830s, this practice continued into the twentieth century.

Fig. 118. Neighborhood shops. A wagonmaker's shop located in the small
building next to the barn. Benson-Landon House, Kennebunk, Maine, ca. 1880.

Fig. 119. Horse-powered thresher. Wiscasset, Maine, area.

Other machines not commonly owned by individual farmers and often shared within a neighborhood were cider presses, mowers, and even specialized hop drying barns.

The neighborhood as a network of mutual health care assistance is well documented in farm diaries and in nearly every novel of rural New England. The tradition of family and friends "staying up" with sick or dying neighbors is a New England legend and was a vital part of the neighborhood mutuality system. Neighborhood assistance at birth and death was expected by all. It was also common to assist collectively an incapacitated neighbor at critical periods, such as haying, or to "take up a collection" to aid a stricken family.[73]

The neighborhood also gathered together for celebrations and special events. These were important social occasions for farm families and are prominently recalled in many town histories and stories of New England. Barn and house raisings with elaborate dinners, and huskings and sings were the most common events (fig. 120). Other opportunities for neighborhood and town celebration and socializing were holidays such as the Fourth of July, town meetings, and church-sponsored activities such as sings and camp meetings. In the second half of the nineteenth century, the traditional farm neighborhood adopted social organizational ideas and methods from the wider world. Consequently, an increasing number of communal activities were sponsored by the granges, lyceums, and numerous fraternal organizations.

The neighborhood cemetery is a vivid reminder of the extensive neighborhood organization that once existed throughout rural New England (fig. 121). A cemetery is perhaps a more fitting symbol for true neighborhood cohesion than a school district, because burial in neighborhood plots usually indicated a degree of cooperation or shared principles on the part of the neighbors who chose to be buried together. The neighborhood cemetery of New England stands between earlier English and colonial traditions of churchyard burial and a later nineteenth-century tradition of the town cemetery. Neighborhood cemeteries reached a peak of popularity between 1800 and 1850 and represent a powerful secular burial tradition originating in the religious conflicts of the eighteenth century.[74] The custom of a secular burial ground gained wide popularity in New England after the Revolutionary War and superseded a long history of religious burial in church burying grounds. The development of the town cemetery after 1850 gradually diminished the importance of the rural constituency for many reasons, but one factor was their promise of perpetual care. Although it is rarely noted, farmers at mid-century were already aware of rural cemetery abandonment. An example of this concern is eloquently expressed in Lura Beam's novel *A Maine Hamlet*, where an old farmer demands that his wife be buried in the town cemetery instead of the family burial ground near the farm.[75]

The key to understanding the New England farm neighborhood is its tradition of mutuality.[76] Perhaps the most subtle aspect of this tradition is the simultaneous presence of strong individual and collective characteristics. Although New England farmers continually cooperated in their neighborhoods, the reader should not assume that they functioned like a Shaker society or a modern commune. The legendary Yankee commitment to independence and individualism is not a fabrication but one of the most consistent character traits of these people in all periods. This commitment to individualism, however, must be understood in its eighteenth- and nineteenth-century context. Yankee individualism has always been set within the older English traditions of social

Fig. 120. Barn raising, northern Connecticut, early 1900s.

Fig. 121. Neighborhood cemetery. West Bridgton, Maine.

deference and consensus sharing.[77] One of the ways neighbors assisted each other and yet remained independent was summarized by an eighty-year-old farmer, Albert Mosher, of Gorham, Maine. When asked about the mechanics of neighborhood cooperation, he observed, "When you see your neighbor is in a hard place, you help him out." The surprise to city folks is that there is never a request for assistance. It is assumed and granted unspoken. This is, of course, the tradition of neighborhood mutuality. For hundreds of years, this prideful code has characterized New England farmers and perhaps most farmers throughout the United States. It is a system that unifies the extremes of individualism and cooperation. To farmers like Mosher, however, it is simply good sense and human decency: nothing more and nothing less.

III   Reasons for Making
        Connected Farm Buildings

6 Tobias Walker Moves His Shed

Route 35 winds westward out of Kennebunk, Maine, passing an assortment of pictur-esque old farms, simple wood-frame houses, and contemporary suburban homes. Young forests of mixed hardwood and white pine line the roadway, broken by occasional fields and pastures. It is a common scene in the lowland interior portions of Maine. Once this area supported a prosperous farming community called the Alewive neighborhood, but it is difficult to imagine the same terrain with open fields and productive farms. A few traces of the nineteenth-century New England farmers' presence remain: ancient trees rise in isolation out of young forests to mark the boundary of a forgotten field, mossy mounds beside the road indicate the remains of a collapsed farm shed, and young sumac clustered in a depression beside an old house tell of a vanished barn. Most of all, mute

Fig. 122. Tobias Walker Farm, Kennebunk, Maine, ca. 1930.

161

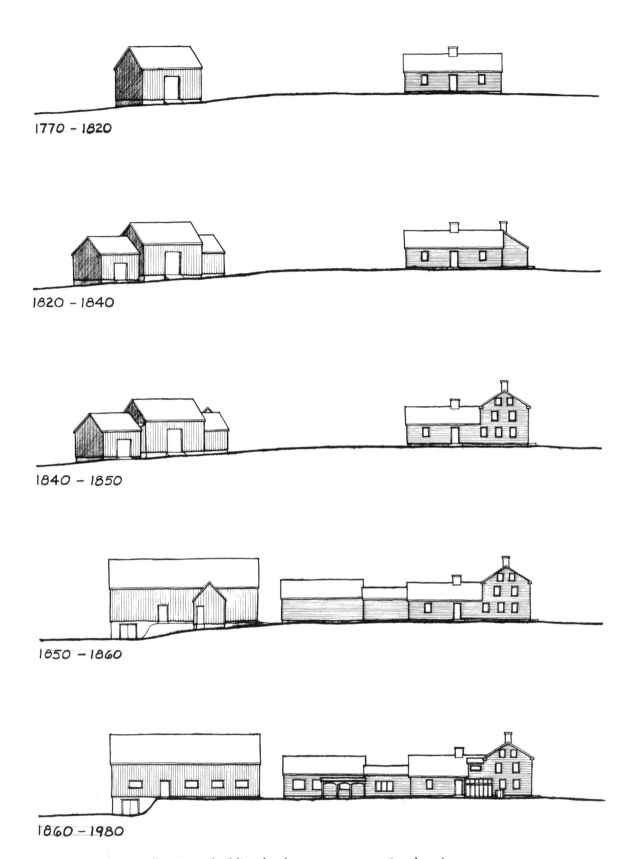

1770 - 1820

1820 - 1840

1840 - 1850

1850 - 1860

1860 - 1980

Fig. 123. Tobias Walker Farm, building development, 1770–1980, elevations.

rock walls stretch silently into thickening forests, testifying to the toil of generations to establish a farming way of life.

Occasionally, at a slight rise in the road, the thick tangle of young forest is broken by the rhythm of a row of huge sugar maple trees standing along the roadway. Invariably these trees mark the location of a long-abandoned farm. A nearby depression, now overgrown by thick trees, marks the cellar of the big house. A productive farm would have occupied this spot; now it is a darkened forest floor. It is a chilling scene even to those with no connection to these farms. It is also a bitter epitaph to the generations of farmers who toiled to make a life here.

The history of the buildings and the people who made the Alewive neighborhood could have gradually vanished into forests or faded into old legends, like the histories of thousands of similar farming neighborhoods in New England. Fortunately, however, the farm journals of the Walker family have preserved a considerable portion of the Alewive neighborhood's history. The journals of three members of the Walker family written between 1828 and 1893 record the daily activities of Tobias the father, his son Edwin, and Daniel, Edwin's son. The journal was begun by Tobias Walker on August 1, 1828, in his thirty-fourth year, and he continued making daily observations for more than thirty-seven years until his death on October 10, 1865. Edwin continued the journal without interruption for another twenty-six years until his own death on February 16, 1891. Daniel maintained entries for two more years, ending on June 27, 1893. Their combined record (referred to throughout this book as the Tobias Walker Diary) covers sixty-five years and provides an exceptional account of the development of a nineteenth-century connected farm complex (figs. 122, 123).[1]

The Tobias, Edwin, and Daniel Walker Farm

1660–1770

The original Walker farm site was part of a tract granted in 1660 to John Littlefield of Massachusetts, but it remained undeveloped until after the hostilities of Queen Anne's War. In 1753 and 1754 much of the area known today as the Alewive neighborhood of Kennebunk, Maine (at that time part of the town of Wells), was subdivided and sold in fifty-acre lots. Daniel Little bought the lot on which the Walker farm is now situated, but quickly sold it to Waldo Emerson who sold it again to the first permanent white settler, Gibben Wakefield, in 1761. It was Gibben Wakefield who "erected buildings thereon, a short distance from the highway."[2]

There is no record of the type of buildings that Wakefield erected, but if he followed a pattern similar to that of many early settlers, he might have constructed a modest house and separate barn. Wakefield's land and buildings were sold to Jeremiah Miller, who stayed for a few years before selling to Eliphalet Walker (Tobias's father) sometime before 1776. The pattern of short-term land tenure for many early settlers such as Wakefield and Miller was influenced by a plentiful land supply and short-term agricultural practices that quickly depleted the soil. A fluid, speculative economy offered lucrative but unreliable employment in logging, trading, and seafaring, and also contributed to short farm tenancy. While most settlers were primarily farmers and might have cherished a goal of creating a stable social and economic community (as local historical accounts take great pains to emphasize), the boom-and-bust cycles of the eighteenth- and early nineteenth-century New England frontier economy reinforced long-term traditions of mobility, land speculation, and short-term, mixed-farming agricultural methods.[3] All these customs were challenged and reformulated later in the nineteenth century, when longer-term, more stable farming practices were established.

1770–1820 (FIGURE 124)

Eliphalet Walker probably arrived on the site in 1770 following his marriage to Margaret Miller. The Kennebunk town history describes Eliphalet Walker as the farmer "by whom the old buildings were removed and new ones erected in a better location."[4] It is not known whether he took down the old buildings immediately or waited until his new ones were erected. Most farmers seem to have kept buildings inherited from previous settlers for as long as practical, unless they were wealthy and could afford to build new buildings immediately. Eliphalet Walker's decision to "remove" the buildings of a previous owner and construct new ones in a better location is consistent with many pioneer settlement accounts in which initial site selection was later modified to accommodate alterations in the location of wells, roadways, and fields.[5] Therefore, the old buildings were probably moved to a new location or disassembled and reused for new construction.[6]

Eliphalet Walker selected a new farm building site at the highest elevation of his property, and although his new site was to cause problems with well water supply, it probably satisfied other important requirements, including proximity to the road and fields. Eliphalet Walker undoubtedly sensed the future rewards of a fine situation or a commanding view from his dooryard when he located the site for his farmstead looking

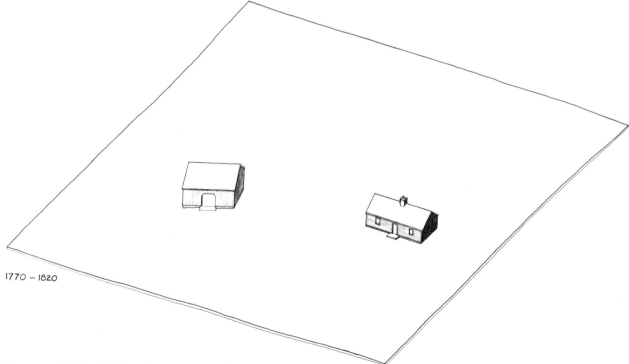

1770 – 1820

Fig. 124. Tobias Walker Farm, 1770–1820, axonometric.

south into the gently sloping valley of the Alewive Brook. The consistent selection of the farm building sites adjacent to the road and at the high point of a farmer's land holdings cannot be attributed solely to functional considerations but must include the desire for a dominant view.

The old site of Gibben Wakefield's building is not precisely known, but it is quite possible that it was located 200 feet to the south of Eliphalet's new house near a well that Tobias Walker would call the "old well." Before 1800 Eliphalet located a leather tanning shop near a bog to the west of his barns, where he probably used the water to wash hides. Described as a tanner, he probably employed assistants or apprentices, as his son Tobias was to do.[7] He was also a full-time farmer, as is evident from tax descriptions and the lands and buildings that his son Tobias inherited in 1824. Eliphalet and his son also began a shoemaking business on their property in 1817, using the leather from their tanning trade. Although the construction date of their shop is not mentioned in the journal, a 15-foot by 26-foot shoemaking shop existed in 1829 and it was probably constructed after 1817.

The house that Eliphalet Walker built between 1770 and 1790 was a low, single-story, center-chimney, hall-and-parlor type house (18 feet by 35 feet), which in 1980 was the oldest building on the site. It has been extensively altered, but its parlor still retains an early window with six-over-six lights and sliding interior shutters and handsome Georgian paneling with wide fluted pilasters flanking the fireplace. It cannot be determined precisely whether the barn that is first mentioned in Tobias Walker's diary was built by his father Eliphalet after 1770 or was one of Gibben Wakefield's original buildings. The larger English barn that is first described by Tobias Walker in 1834 was probably constructed by his father after 1800. Most early settlement barns before 1800 were small, often only 20 feet by 15 feet, and were replaced by the then standard English type barn, typically about 30 feet long and 20 feet wide, but often much larger. Tobias Walker's barn was probably built in the eighteenth century, because in 1829 and 1831 Tobias recorded extensive repairs to it: "laying the cow house floor," "stripped the foreside of the barn for shingling and had to put on some new roof boards," "shingling the back side of the barn," and "put on saddle boards [fascia boards] on the barn."[8] These typical barn repair practices, conducted in twenty- to sixty-year cycles, involved maintenance to the exterior sheathing, flooring, and foundation.

1820–1840 (FIGURE 125)

At the time of Eliphalet's death in 1824, Tobias Walker inherited a prosperous farm. There were three groups of buildings on the property: a house with a small shed; a barn with at least one small outbuilding; and a tannery with a bark house, tanning building, and shoemaking shop. Additional, unrecorded sheds or outbuildings related to the three major building groups were also likely.

At the time of his father's death, Tobias Walker probably began construction of a kitchen-ell addition to the northeast corner of the original one-story hall-and-parlor house (fig. 126). It is also possible that he made major repairs to an existing building. The kitchen ell measured 20 feet by 24 feet and contained a single large kitchen room with an open-hearth fireplace and brick oven, with two smaller storage rooms behind the fireplace. The new building added a second kitchen to the original house. Tobias Walker was departing from the colonial tradition of kitchen in the main house in favor of a newer pattern

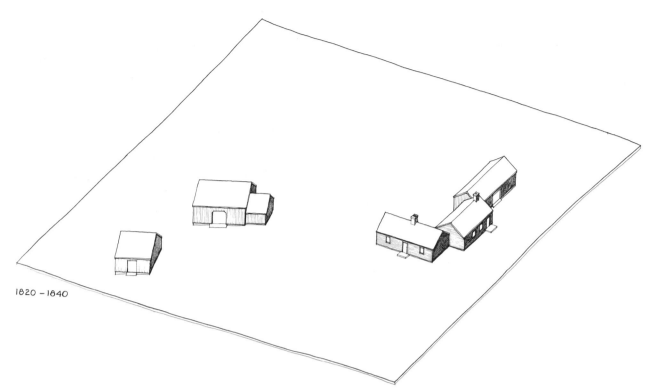

Fig. 125. Tobias Walker Farm, 1820–1840, axonometric.

of kitchen in a connected building. Although why he expanded his house is not certain, it did occur at the time his wife and father died and two widowed sisters and an unmarried brother came to live in the house. Perhaps the reorganization of his family necessitated the reorganization of the house, although it is also possible that the new kitchen was intended for his wife before her death in 1823. The cellar below the kitchen ell contains a stone marked with the date 1826. It is possible that this kitchen addition was

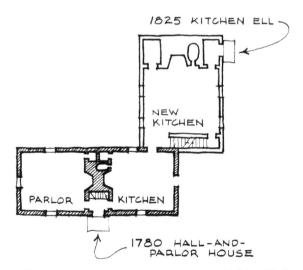

Fig. 126. Room arrangement, 1825. Tobias Walker Farm.

built or substantially remodeled as late as 1827. When Tobias Walker began his diary in 1828, he recorded what was probably a finishing touch to this cellar: "John Waterhouse [a neighbor] was here building cellarway for outer cellar door. Jere[miah] Lord was here finishing milk cellar and hanging doors."[9] The Walkers' new ell structure was a complete kitchen area above ground, but below ground it was a farm processing center for dairy products and a storage area for a variety of perishable field crops intended for domestic consumption and commercial sale. The outer cellar doors were constructed to provide an efficient exterior entrance for milk delivery as well as for storing the large quantities of potatoes, beans, and Indian corn that the Walker family continuously produced over the next seventy-five years.

Tobias Walker's next major project was to construct a multipurpose building adjacent to his new kitchen ell (fig. 127). In 1829, with the assistance of several laborers, he began cutting and hewing the major sill and plate timbers for a building he frequently referred to as the wood house. Two years later, on May 26, 1831, Tobias, with the assistance of master framer Jeremiah Lord and several neighborhood carpenters, "commenced framing a building for a wood house, chaise house and work tool shop." On the next day he "finished framing the building in the fore noon and raised it without our oxen before 2 o'clock."[10] Most agricultural buildings were constructed in a four-part process, as indicated by these accounts.[11] The first stage of material gathering and preparation could take several years, as a farmer cut and hewed timber or brought it to a mill for cutting. This phase could be hired out, but most frequently it was done by a farmer with supervision from a builder. The second phase, called framing, was the process by which timbers were cut to their exact lengths and shaped for mortise-and-tenon connectors. This phase was most frequently hired out to a master builder with a small crew of workmen. Because Tobias's wood house was a simple building, it took the crew of six men only a day and a half to complete the framing operation. The third

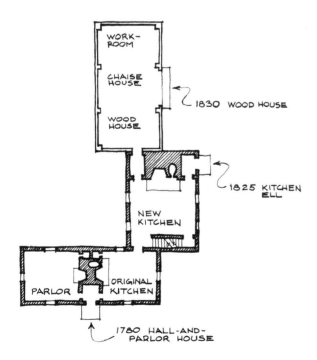

Fig. 127. Room arrangement, 1835. Tobias Walker Farm.

phase was the raising, which they completed in less than two hours. During this period, a derrick with a block and tackle hoist pulled by oxen was sometimes employed to facilitate the raising of the heavy beams. But Tobias indicates that this method was unnecessary, possibly because the building was small enough to be raised by hand. The fourth and final stage involved sheathing, roofing, and finished carpentry items, including doors, windows, and hardware.

The new wood house was placed adjacent to, and probably touching, the northwest corner of his new kitchen ell, chiefly to facilitate the storage of domestic firewood. The building was 18 feet by 34 feet, larger than most of his neighbors would construct for similar purposes, but consistent with the developing good fortunes of Tobias Walker. The building was subdivided into three unequal bays, which he identified by the activity that was conducted in each: wood house, for the storage of cut and split firewood; chaise house, for the storage of the horse carriage; and a workroom, for tool storage and repair.[12] This multipurpose utility building was similar to many three-bay storage buildings attached to houses and barns during this period. The irregular internal bay spacing was probably Tobias Walker's personal preference, an indication of the flexible internal subdivision within the nineteenth-century ell buildings.

The designation of a particular portion of the structure as a chaise house for horse-drawn carriages was a clear indication of wealth and status for a farmer in the 1830s. The ownership of a chaise for nonutilitarian purposes was a luxury that few farmers were willing or able to afford until the mid to late 1800s.[13] Most farmers would have owned a multipurpose farm wagon used primarily for marketing activities. Three years later Tobias "was stripping boards from the old barn and began to frame a shed for a stable on the south side of the barn."[14] This was a further indication of his increasing reliance on the horse for farm and domestic use. When horses became more widely employed, most farmers would house them in a bay of the major barn. Unlike farmers in other areas of the country, Tobias Walker and many of his neighbors did not replace their oxen with horses at this time but continued to employ both oxen and horses throughout the nineteenth century.[15] Tobias's oxen were especially important for winter wood hauling, as evidenced by the construction of a separate ox house near the barn in 1834.[16]

In May 1838 Tobias Walker gave several clear indications that he was becoming more concerned with the formal appearance of his farm: "Set out three fir trees at the end of the house, was building fence . . . Jere. Lord was here building the picket fence from the door [yard] to barn yard."[17] This appears to be the first occurrence of ornamental trees and ornate fencing on this farm and is consistent with theories discussed in Chapter 3 suggesting that, during the second quarter of the nineteenth century, a heightened awareness of formal aesthetic relationships began to influence the decisions of average farmers about the arrangement and appearance of their farms.

1840–1850 (FIGURE 128)

In 1840 a hog house or hog sty was erected near the barn.[18] It was a small but substantial frame structure, probably 12 feet by 16 feet, located near the back of the major English barn. The practice of making separate animal houses was derived from English farming traditions, but Tobias Walker's design was probably influenced by articles he had read in farm newspapers.[19] Tobias's own description on the day of construction indicates the

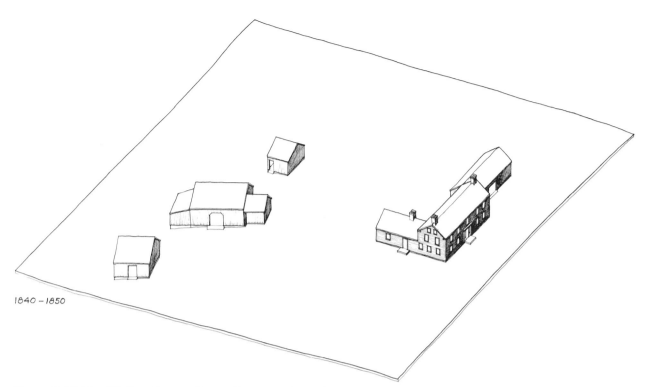

Fig. 128. Tobias Walker Farm, 1840–1850, axonometric.

progressive agricultural spirit of his project: "Mr. Waterhouse here, raised the building for to make dressing [manure] in, with the help of the hogs."[20] Tobias followed this widely recommended method each year by hauling light sandy soil to his barn yard, having the pigs mix it with manure, and then transporting it back to the fields. This labor-intensive practice was continued by Tobias Walker and his son Edwin for forty years.[21]

In 1842 Tobias began a major house remodeling project by adding a second story to his kitchen ell (fig. 129). It was more than a typical kitchen expansion project because it completely reorganized the house, changing the orientation of the farm in the direction of the road and converting the kitchen ell into the major big house. Tobias Walker undertook this extensive remodeling project in the spring of 1842 for his second wife, Mary, whom he married in October of that year. An extensive addition also provided living space for his wife's four daughters.

The new design dramatically transformed the existing residence. The one-story kitchen ell became a two-story big house, and the original hall-and-parlor house became an ell attached to the newer two-story addition. One of the principal results of this project was that the facade of the major dwelling shifted from the traditional south-facing alignment of the original hall-and-parlor house facade to a road-facing alignment of the two-story Greek Revival house. This pattern of building is consistent with many other examples in the early nineteenth century as orientation to the road became more desirable for the major facade of the principal big house.

The new house addition literally engulfed the original kitchen ell and converted its

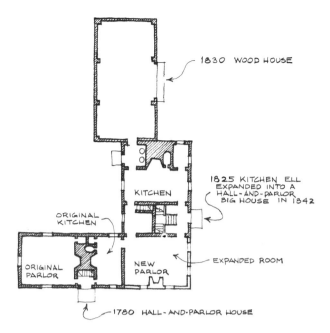

1830 WOOD HOUSE

1825 KITCHEN ELL
EXPANDED INTO A
HALL-AND-PARLOR
BIG HOUSE IN 1842

KITCHEN

ORIGINAL
KITCHEN

EXPANDED ROOM

ORIGINAL
PARLOR

NEW
PARLOR

1780 HALL-AND-PARLOR HOUSE

Fig. 129. Room arrangement, 1845.
Tobias Walker Farm.

simple one-story eastern facade into a 42-foot-long, Greek Revival big house (fig. 130).
The resultant L-shaped plan of main house and ell was an extremely popular form in
many segments of late eighteenth- and early nineteenth-century New England society.
Tobias Walker was certainly familiar with this type of building arrangement because he
passed several grand houses in this style on his frequent trips to Kennebunkport.[22]

The overall room organization of the new addition is similar to the hall-and-parlor
plan with end-wall chimneys and two major rooms on both floors separated by a central
stairway. However, the existing building necessitated adjustments to this typical organization. The new parlor room in the southeast corner had to be carved out of a portion
of the kitchen in the original hall-and-parlor house and the second kitchen had to be
disguised behind the stylistic two-story facade of the remodeled ell.

The new house addition followed the popular Greek Revival style. The casing of the
front door followed a version of Asher Benjamin's Greek Revival architectural details.[23]
The interior of the new addition was completely remodeled in a constrained version of
the style. The new front stairway was given a unique double landing or "good morning"
stair such as Tobias Walker's neighbor Seth Emmons had just installed in his house.[24] By
far the most consistent pattern of change within a farm neighborhood was the adaption
of a new style, machine, or method derived from an experimenting neighbor. Of course,
not all new styles or experimentations were copied; many were ignored and rejected.
Walker's remodeling project, employing five skilled carpenters and several laborers, was
beyond the financial means of most farmers. On September 27, 1842 he made this summary entry: "There has been 211½ days work (besides what our own family has done
on the house) by carpenters and joiners since we commenced hewing the timber."[25]

From journal entries such as this over a forty-year period, it is possible to discern
several recurring patterns of building and labor relationships at the middle of the nineteenth century. The distinction between the owner's role and the builder's is significant.
It is only partially correct to say that Tobias Walker and most of his farming neighbors
built their own houses and barns. In almost all cases, the most critical aspects of the

building process—the measurements, structural organization, and finished carpentry details, in short, all of the most vital traditions of building—were performed by skilled craftsmen called joiners, master builders, or carpenters, and not by the average farmer.[26] This does not minimize the role of the typical farmer, who, in many cases, supplied most of the labor. Most farmers probably called in the assistance of a master carpenter only during critical periods of construction, such as the measuring and cutting of the mortise-and-tenon joints after the major timbers were hewn or sawn, or for finished carpentry and interior woodwork.

Although there were differences in skill and experience among individual carpenters, there was a major distinction between these skilled semiprofessionals (in most cases also part-time farmers) and the ordinary laborers or farmers who might be employed for shingling, excavation, or sheathing work. There also seems to have been a distinction between professional framers, who were often barn builders, and finishers (or joiners) who were often house builders.[27] Although one master workman might oversee an entire project, occasionally the work was divided into two parts, with the framer constructing a roughly livable house and a skilled finisher or joiner hired later to apply the finishing carpentry work. The work of the masons, stonecutters, and painters or plasterers was typically separate from the work of the carpenters and was frequently hired out separately. This practice of differentiating craft skills became even more widespread toward the end of the nineteenth century.

Fig. 130. Two-story addition (*right*) added on top of half of the original one-story, hall-and-parlor house (*left*). Tobias Walker Farm.

Most farm journals were written by male farmers and concentrate on the agricultural work outside domestic buildings. Tobias Walker did, however, provide a few glimpses of the life inside the buildings. One of the most important nineteenth-century domestic improvements on the farm is recorded on April 27, 1840: "Moved the stove from the kitchen to the portch [porch]."[28] In 1840 Tobias was employing the soon to be common seasonal practice of moving the kitchen stove to an adjacent room so that the kitchen might remain cooler in the summer. The porch that Tobias describes was not an open structure but an enclosed shed or workroom attached to the back of his kitchen. This is the room that modern inhabitants now label the summer kitchen, although the term does not seem to date from the nineteenth century, and it was never used in Tobias Walker's diary. There is no way of knowing if this was the first domestic stove because no earlier purchases are recorded. Eleven years previously, however, Tobias had set up a stove in his shoemaking shop, so it is possible that his family had used an earlier stove in the house. In the same year that the kitchen stove is first mentioned, a hired mason "bricked up the fireplace in the kitchen and sat [set] up a Port [Portland] stove."[29] This entry records one of the most common nineteenth-century practices—the final act of replacing a fireplace with a stove.

Boilers or set kettles were introduced into the Walker house in 1843.[30] They were placed in the side of the kitchen fireplace just outside the "porch" workroom. Before this date Tobias had installed boilers in his shoemaking shop. Like the stove, the boilers were first tested or applied in the craft shop before introduction into the house. It is not known whether this was a common pattern. In 1845 the original house was also extensively remodeled, and another double-landing stairway, clothes presses or closets, and plastering and shingling were added.

1850–1860 (FIGURE 131)

In the spring of 1850 Tobias Walker entered a series of surprising accounts in his diary: "Hauled two stickes of timber from the pasture for shoes to move the wood house on," and soon after, "Preparing the ground and getting in readiness for moving the wood and work house."[31] Twenty years previously, Tobias had helped construct this building, which was attached to the northwest corner of his new big house. Now he was preparing to move it. On April 11, 1850 he wrote: "Joseph Waterhouse, William Ross and Jesse Taylor [neighborhood carpenters] here putting shoes under the wood house to move it [to] the other side of the house. P.M. Moved the building over next to the barn yard. Had forty oxen [to pull the wood house]."[32] As an isolated incident, the moving of a large building from one side of the house to the other might seem like an unusual event, especially when the building's purpose remained unaltered. But Tobias had a grand plan. I would call it a unifying, organizing, and connecting plan, but Tobias Walker might have described it simply as a commonsense way of organizing his farm so that his wood house would now be aligned more efficiently between his house and barn. There was, however, more to Tobias's plan than moving the wood house, because in the same year he was also planning to remove his old barns and construct a larger modern barn in their place (fig. 132).

Tobias's decision to move the existing wood house to the other side of his house was, I think, motivated by a desire to form an aligned building group in the new popular

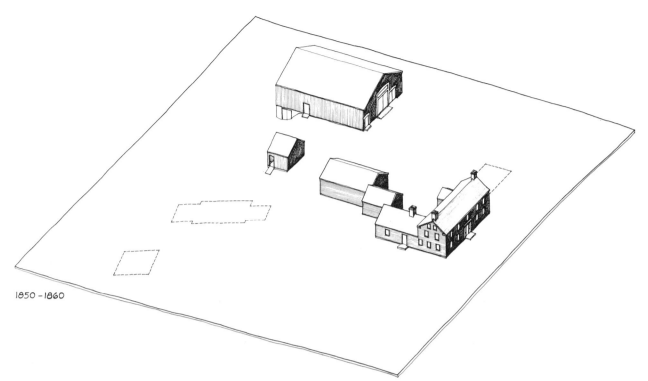

1850-1860

Fig. 131. Tobias Walker Farm, 1850–1860, axonometric.

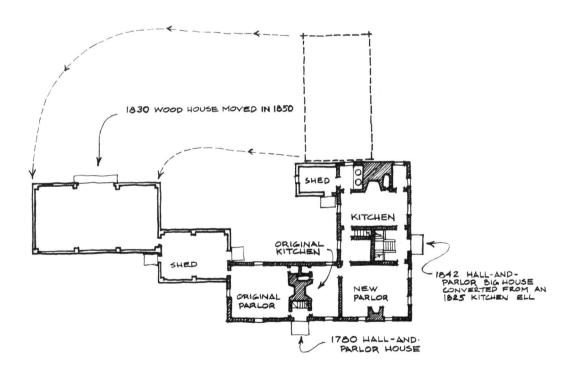

1830 WOOD HOUSE MOVED IN 1850

SHED

KITCHEN

ORIGINAL
KITCHEN

SHED

1842 HALL-AND-
PARLOR BIG HOUSE
CONVERTED FROM AN
1825 KITCHEN ELL

ORIGINAL
PARLOR

NEW
PARLOR

1780 HALL-AND-
PARLOR HOUSE

Fig. 132. Room and building arrangement, 1855. Tobias Walker Farm.

fashion of the connected house and barn. He never indicated why he moved his wood house, but planning decisions for most people are infrequently written or talked about and are often assumed in a consensus fashion by people who share a set of similar cultural values, such as those shared by Tobias Walker and his neighbors in the Alewive district.[33]

This does not mean that Tobias Walker merely followed a standardized collective formula without thinking; he had many options. One was to leave his wood house in its original location and construct a new barn near the old barn in the traditional detached house and barn plan. Another option, following the new style of connected house and barn, was to leave his wood house in its original position and construct his new barn in alignment and connection with the wood house and the house, thus forming a closely connected building group. This practice was cautiously recommended by some of New England's leading agricultural newspapers of the period.[34] Had he aligned his buildings in this way, he would have saved himself the considerable trouble of moving the wood house. But this arrangement would have situated his barn near the roadway and seriously handicapped the barn's function and expansion potential in the future. He therefore chose to reorient his farmstead by moving the wood house and constructing a new barn in a closely adjoining building plan. The result had the undesirable characteristic of a north-facing dooryard, but it was the best solution of several possible alternatives employing the connected farm organization.

The new barn was begun in 1850 and took three years to complete. Its builders employed many of the most advanced ideas and techniques of barn building available in New England during the middle of the nineteenth century.[35] In a popular expression of the period, it was a "commodious" barn, five bays long, three bays wide with a central drive in the gable end. The new long-floor barn had been employed in the Alewive neighborhood at least since 1832, and by 1850 it was rapidly replacing the old English barn.[36] Tobias Walker, now in his fifty-sixth year, hired a well-known master workman, and on November 29, 1850 he wrote that "Rufus Smith helped me begin to cut timber for a frame for a barn 62 ft. long, 38 ft. wide and 15 ft. posts".[37] During the next year, Tobias and his son Edwin prepared to build their barn by cutting and transporting pine and hemlock logs to local sawmills to be cut into beams and boards according to the specifications of Rufus Smith. A few of the longest timbers in the sills and plate were not sawn but hand hewn near the barn site, perhaps because transportation difficulties or mill capacity made it easier or cheaper to square the longest beams using the older hewing methods. By the fall of 1851 most of the boarding was "stuck up" (stacked for drying), and about half of the major timbers were square sawn or hewn and stacked near the barn site. Cutting and hauling the framing timber continued throughout the next winter, as did the local milling of shingles, braces, and clapboards in the spring.

Final preparation for the barn building did not begin in earnest until after the spring planting of 1853. On May 31, 1852 Tobias "took down the old barn," which was located close to the new barn site.[38] It was a decision that reflected confidence in his building ability because, if for any reason he could not erect his new barn by the summer, he would be in a difficult position in the fall. But apparently he was confident. After dismantling the old barn, he moved the ten-year-old pigsty to a position more convenient to the future barnyard.

Preparation for making the barn cellar had begun the previous winter with the hauling of rough cut stone for the cellar walls. On June 2, 1851 a crew of laborers began "to dig a cellar for a new barn."[39] All progressive agriculturalists of this period recommended a full barn cellar, particularly to contain valuable cattle manure and also for the storage of root crops and farm vehicles.[40] Undoubtedly this was his plan, but Tobias experienced great difficulty in clearing the ledge rock from the top of his little knoll: "Digging for a cellar, ledgy and very hard digging, almost discouraging."[41] At this point he could have shifted the location of his barn in order to obtain a full cellar. With the land sloping away to the north and west, there were several positions that could easily have yielded a full barn cellar if that was all he desired. But that would have necessitated moving the barn out of alignment with the house. He settled instead for a cramped one-third cellar along the barn's south side, although I think he probably moved the barn further away from the house than he originally intended in order to obtain even this minimal cellar. This is why, I suspect, the barn is not connected to the wood house like that of his son William, who had moved and connected his barn to his back house during the previous summer.

On June 7, 1852 a team of professional carpenters under the direction of Rufus Smith began the operation of framing, or cutting the mortises and tenons into the precut and sawn pieces already assembled on the site. The framing operation took eight men four days to complete, and on the morning of June 11 they "hauled the timber, from where it was framed to [the] place for raising." Before noon the wooden sills were set in place and after the midday dinner they "raised the barn frame."[42]

Tobias Walker probably had a large gathering of neighbors to help him raise his barn, but not all barn raisings were accompanied by elaborate community dinners and festivities. Frequently houses or barns were raised with small crews of five to ten neighborhood men in quick, matter-of-fact fashion as described by Tobias when he raised his wood house. The raising of a large barn by a prominent farmer such as Tobias Walker, however, frequently warranted the often recorded dinner and celebration. Rough finishing of the barn proceeded in rapid succession with a full crew completing exterior sheathing, clapboarding, and roof shingling in about a month, just in time for all hands to begin mowing hay on July 13, 1852.[43]

During the next year, the barn was properly finished with the addition of doors, windows, scaffolding, barnyard fencing, interior partitions, and weather vane. On September 26, 1853 Tobias recorded the completion of his barn: "Finished painting the barn."[44] Tobias had clapboarded the two-thirds of the barn visible from the road and then painted it white with small touches of red and yellow trim. The size and expense of this barn clearly distinguished Tobias Walker as a prosperous farmer in his neighborhood, but the clapboarding, and the white paint in particular, indicated that he was a modern, progressive mid nineteenth-century farmer. The dazzling whiteness of his new barn stood in stark contrast to his previous one and the weather-blackened form of most barns in the Alewive neighborhood. While he was not the first in his neighborhood to build such a large and finely detailed barn, Tobias Walker was engaged in a decidedly progressive act that was to contribute to a reorganization of a large portion of New England's rural landscape. Most farmers were to take a more modest and less costly part in this reorganization process.

The positioning of Tobias Walker's new barn was the key element in a plan that realigned and reversed the previous spatial order of his farmstead. Prior to 1850 the farm functioned in a separate house and barn arrangement. After the changes of the early 1850s, it functioned as a unified string of buildings that formed a north-facing dooryard and thus minimized the older south-facing dooryard of the original Eliphalet Walker house. Two more changes reinforced the formal, unified organization of this layout. In the busy spring of 1851, Tobias and his son Edwin found enough time to begin "building a post and picket fence in front of the house."[45] In conjunction with the front yard improvement, Tobias listed repairs to a "roller for leveling ground," which was probably employed in the leveling and scraping of the front yard or the dooryard and was a common improvement for the environment of the house and ell.[46]

Another project completed in the spring of 1851 was the sale and removal of the old shoemaking shop. Tobias Walker had ended his shoemaking business in 1842: "have concluded to draw the shoemaking business to a close, and the hands [employees] have quit today. . . . I have been in the shoemaking business more or less for twenty-five years."[47] Since 1817 Tobias had made shoes from the leather from his tanning trade, but he could no longer compete with the shoe factories of the towns and cities of New England.[48] Farmer-artisan Tobias Walker was one small casualty duplicated thousands of times in New England in a process we know today as the growth of the industrial-manufacturing system in America. The old shop building had stood vacant and in disrepair since 1842. On April 25, 1851 Tobias Walker "hauled shoes [long sturdy timbers that were used as supports or skids during building movement] to put under the shop for Washington Emerson. I agreed to let [him] have the old shoe shop [26 feet by 15 feet] for $40.00. He moves it on to the Alfred Road."[49] The building was moved five miles with the assistance of thirty teams or pairs of oxen. Building movement of this kind was extremely common throughout the nineteenth century and was one of the principal methods by which farmers with little income could reorganize and improve their farms. Most farmers freely contributed their ox teams in this collective neighborhood enterprise, although a wealthy farmer might pay each driver, usually a younger son or hired hand, a small amount for his services.[50]

In two final reorganization projects, a small outbuilding, possibly the old ox house or a sheep barn, was moved away from the barnyard, and the old bark house, once used to store bark for the tanning business, was totally gutted, repaired, and made into a general storage shed and woodshed. Tobias Walker ended his tanning business in 1844 because he could no longer compete against larger commercial operations. Thereafter he took his hides to the Shaker community at Alfred, Maine, which conducted a large-scale tanning operation.

In conjunction with the expansion and rearrangement of the agricultural buildings, a series of internal modifications drastically altered the traditional patterns of domestic life for the Walker family. Perhaps the most significant household improvement was a change in the method of water supply. In the fall of 1851, a brick cistern (water storage tank) was constructed underneath the newest kitchen. It was rectangular, "6 ft. long, 5 ft. wide, and 5½ ft. deep, 1234 gal.," and was fed by a wooden gutter system that drained the house roofs.[51] A hand pump was then installed to draw water from the cistern to a sink, probably located in the porch, milk room, or sink room as it was alternately called. This was the method widely recommended in the agricultural journals of the period.[52] This workroom was probably remodeled in 1853 and equipped with a new sink and drain, closets, a window, and shelves. Other recorded alterations of this period include typical domestic remodeling projects such as wallpapering and wood graining in the kitchen, oilcloth carpeting for the main entry and stairway, two coats of paint for most of the downstairs parlor rooms, and graining of doors and woodwork throughout the house. In one of the major room use changes of the period, the original kitchen in the hall-and-parlor house was reactivated and enlarged to accommodate Edwin Walker's new wife, Frances. Tobias was later to call this "Edwin's kitchen." This followed a typical pattern—a two-kitchen household with parents using the older one and the new couple using the newer, remodeled one.

All the changes of the early 1850s drastically altered the exterior form of the farmstead according to the progressive farm planning ideas and fashionable tastes of the period, but the basic operation of the farm and its interior room organization remained essentially unchanged, except for mechanical improvements like the cistern and the pump, which were added in a piecemeal, localized fashion. After 1855 there were few substantive changes to the Walker buildings and methods of farming. The organization of the Walker farm is therefore similar to others in the connected farm arrangement, which reached a plateau of stability following a relatively short period of change and reorganization. The final assessment of this process of stabilization as to whether it was the result of a failure to modernize old ways or the best possible alternative in an increasingly difficult economic context will be analyzed in the last chapter.

1860–1980 (FIGURE 133)

In the fifteen years before Tobias Walker's death in 1865, his son Edwin began to manage the operation of the farm. Tobias gave one-half of his holdings to his son Edwin in 1848 (officially recorded in 1854).[53] From the diary we learn that farm decision making gradually shifted to Edwin as he assumed more and more of the work load. Upon his

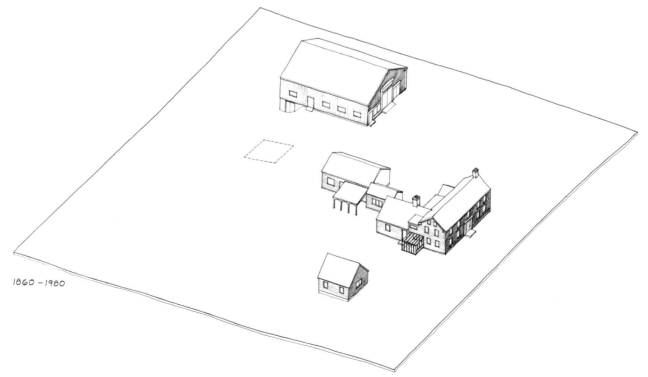

1860 - 1980

Fig. 133. Tobias Walker Farm, 1860–1980, axonometric.

father's death, Edwin continued the family journal without noticeable interruption. His entries show that he maintained the farm and buildings in good condition, regularly replacing roofing shingles and clapboarding, and painting, as well as making frequent interior decorating changes. In 1863 he replaced his twenty-year-old hog house with a larger structure on the same location.[54] The building was designed to house the hogs in the basement with the major floor used for storage. The newest kitchen and the workroom were again remodeled in 1879 with cupboards, new doors, and flooring. A new sheet lead sink had been added ten years before.

In 1875 Edwin converted the old bark house into an icehouse by installing double walls filled with sawdust for insulation in the commonly recommended fashion.[55] During the next winter Edwin and his neighbors gathered ice together and filled their icehouses. By the time Daniel had taken over in 1892, the demand for pigs was declining and his egg business was increasing because of Kennebunk's expanding tourist trade. He therefore moved the pig house to its present location south of the original dwelling house and converted its major floor to a hen house and the basement to a more conveniently located icehouse. The bark house containing the old icehouse was probably removed at this time. In 1891 Edwin Walker died, and his son Daniel continued the farm and the family journal.

On Tuesday, June 27, 1893 Daniel Walker made this entry into his journal: "Went to the village with butter. Got 10 bushels of corn of Edm. Warren at 5–8 cts/bushel. Got a rake and a scyth and ——— for haying."[56] On the surface it was just another matter-of-fact farm journal entry like the ones his father and grandfather had made all their lives. Together the three Walkers had kept a daily record for almost sixty-five years. It took a certain kind of Yankee persistence to record the events of 23,691 consecutive days.

For some reason, this typical account of a summer day in 1893 was Daniel Walker's last entry. The journal abruptly ends without a hint as to the reason. There is no noticeable disinterest or trailing off in the previous entries nor any hint of approaching hard times. Daniel continued to work the farm for thirty-three years before selling it in 1926. It will probably never be known why he ended the diary. He may have developed bad eyesight or some other unrecorded ailment, although the evidence seems to indicate he did not. But if the themes in this book are correct, he had abundant reason to stop. He probably stopped writing because the motivation that had always sustained its effort had been abandoned.

Thousands of similar journals, account books, diaries, and weather records were written during the nineteenth century in an era of improvement. Most of these accounts were far simpler than the Walkers' diaries, but they all partook of the same sustaining spirit of optimism, perfectibility, and progress. Most important, it was an attitude popularly shared and reinforced by most farmers. Yet a spirit so doggedly perfectionistic had little recourse once the prospects for improvement suffered irreversible setbacks, as they gradually did for most farmers by the beginning of the twentieth century. Many left for southern New England factories or the West. Those who stayed continued to farm but with diminishing expectations for the future. When this improving spirit finally dimmed on the New England farm, one of the casualties was the farm journal.

7   Why Tobias Walker Moved His Shed

Like thousands of other New England farmers, Tobias Walker reorganized his buildings into the connected house and barn plan (fig. 134). It was an enormous project in relation to his resources, but it was only one of many building and farm improvement projects that he engaged in all his life. Most of his neighbors conducted similar building projects as well. So deeply ingrained was this spirit of improvement that it would be practically unthinkable for farmers such as Tobias Walker to analyze the reasons for their commitment to improvement. Yet there were powerful factors motivating these farmers. One of the most significant was the changed condition of nineteenth-century New England agriculture.

Had he been asked, Tobias Walker could have described the vast changes between the farm of his youth in the early 1800s and his newly remodeled farm at the middle of the century. He probably could have recalled his father's wooden tools and slow ox-powered methods, which he was replacing with manufactured tools and horse-powered machines. He had witnessed a series of agricultural and social changes that had profoundly altered his life and separated his world from the one his father had known.

Fig. 134. Connected farm building, Bethel, Maine.

179

Tobias Walker undoubtedly approved of all these changes because he incorporated them into his life with apparent enthusiasm. But he might also have been aware that this rate of change was not a matter simply of personal choice, but one of survival.

In 1855, while proudly looking upon his newly organized farm, he may or may not have associated his new building plan with the relentless pace of social and agricultural change. In retrospect, however, it appears that the popular movement in New England farm reform was overwhelmingly motivated by the need to readapt the farm life-style in the face of intensive agricultural and manufacturing competition that threatened the survival of the region's rural society. Many farmers accepted the idea of a physical renewal for their farmsteads in an attempt to accommodate an increasingly commercial operation and to reverse the continual setbacks to their rural life-style and economy, particularly the devastating effects of emigration from the region.

The connected farm building plan was particularly well suited to a more commercially oriented farm and home-industry production. It was selected by farmers like Tobias Walker because it allowed them to accommodate the changes of increased commercialization in a building system easily incorporated into their existing farms. What is so intriguing about the way farmers such as Tobias Walker rearranged their farms is the forcefulness with which they applied a progressive-looking facade of farm improvement to their traditionally ordered farms. Sensing the impinging obsolescence of their customary methods, they chose to modernize the efficiency of their farming operation—the way it worked—in the face of intensive competition. But they maintained the fundamental components of their older farming operation—what it produced—because it could not be changed according to agriculture's mechanized and capitalized future. New England farmers selected the connected farm building arrangement as the best, and, in their minds, the most advanced type of building to modernize while simultaneously maintaining their traditional mixed-farming, home-industry operation.

In retrospect, this nineteenth-century New England farm reform movement only helped to prolong old-fashioned methods of agriculture into the twentieth century. But this should not detract from its achievement while it flourished during the nineteenth century. Connected farm buildings were the manifestation of a powerful will to succeed by farming, and in that goal, New England farmers were extremely successful, for a while.

This explanation of why Tobias Walker reorganized his farm is a beginning for architectural analysis. But the complete task of establishing why a particular building seemed appropriate to a particular individual or group at a particular time and place is far more difficult. It requires that the building be placed within a historical context that explains the choices and constraints that shaped the way it was made. This necessitates that a building be seen in the context of the many competing forms and ideas that existed at the same time. Perhaps the most effective way to approach this problem of architectural development is to identify the plurality of ideas that surrounded the making of any piece of architecture, and to ask the difficult cultural question, What choices did they have? as a way of enlarging upon the more easily documented architectural question, What choices did they make? The preceding six chapters have been devoted primarily to an explanation of the building choices that New England farmers actually made in the formation of their connected farms. In this concluding chapter this framework will be broadened by examining the many possible choices available to them. This requires that connected farm buildings be placed within a wider context of the conditions, places, and ideas that surrounded the physical act of their construction and gave meaning to their making.

The context for connected farms is described in three parts. The first section provides a chronological record of the major ideas that shaped popular opinion about the connected farm building arrangement. This might be termed a context of attitudes toward the connected farms as they developed. The evolution of the connected style is seen here through the eyes of New England's agricultural journalists, who followed its emergence in articles describing buildings of this period. The second section examines a context of place and conditions in which the connected farms were built. This might be termed a context of actuality, including historical, environmental, agricultural, and economic factors. Its purpose is to define the opportunities and constraints to building created by the rhythm of events, the environment, and conditions of the outside world. The third section examines a context of ideas that exerted influence upon farmers and motivated them to consider the connected farm building arrangement. Six major currents of nineteenth-century thought are juxtaposed against the specific action of one farmer, Tobias Walker. The goal is to evaluate the influence of each idea upon him and to determine how it might have coaxed or motivated him to reorganize his farm. In the concluding section, a summary is given of the reasons why farmers like Tobias Walker made connected farms.

Changing Attitudes Toward Farm Building

The development and popularization of the connected farm building organization can be followed in numerous articles from newspapers and agricultural journals describing farm building practices in New England. Although the basic arrangement was never widely sanctioned by leading agricultural writers, articles citing the advantages of the connected arrangement began to be published after 1850. During the first half of the century, however, New England's agriculturalists frequently differed in their opinions on the proper placement of buildings on a farmstead. This section begins with articles that describe farm building practices in the early 1800s and follows the controversial emergence of the connected farm building organization as the merits of the new systems were debated and compared with other farm arrangements of the period.

THE OLD ORDER

Agricultural writers of the early nineteenth century rarely described the common building practices of the period. They probably assumed that their farming audience followed widely known building procedures and needed little architectural or planning advice. In 1824 a writer for the *Yankee Farmer* probably assumed his audience would understand his analysis of a new type of barn door when he described the structure as "a barn of ordinary size and the main part of it built in the usual shape, but a good deal neater and tighter."[1] In one of the finest American agricultural dictionaries of the late eighteenth century, Samuel Deane provides only generalized information about the building practices and spatial arrangement of farm buildings.[2] Since Deane's book and other agricultural literature of the period explore emerging topics in such great detail, the absence of farm architectural information seems to indicate that a well-established body of vernacular building traditions guided the making of most farms and needed little explanation for the early nineteenth-century reader. It was these undocumented vernacular traditions that influenced farmers, such as Tobias Walker's father, to organize their farms according to time-tested procedures, such as a south-facing orientation for his separate house and barn.

Although little information about popular farm building practices was published before the first quarter of the nineteenth century, a great deal began to be published during the next thirty years. After 1820, as new farm planning systems began to be advocated, traditional building practices drew extensive criticism in the agricultural journals. Subsequent controversies about the arrangement of farm buildings developed because new styles collided with older, traditional customs. Because of the relative absence of debate before 1820 and the emergence of considerable criticism of the older building traditions after 1820, that date marks the beginning of a new era of farm planning in New England.

BARN CENTRALIZATION

One of the first major building reforms advocated by early nineteenth-century agricultural writers was the adoption of a single large barn to replace smaller, clustered barns. The customary English practice of multiple barn construction came under increasing attack as a wasteful, unsightly practice. This criticism is outlined by a Massachusetts observer in 1824: "Most farmers I saw had two or three small barns, and some two or three large ones. Nothing appears more detrimental to their interests. Superfluous buildings are nothing but a tax upon farmers, the cost of repairs being very great. . . . I would rather see the [hay] stacks stand thick around the barn, than to see more than one barn; and I am convinced that a barn 50 feet by 30 feet . . . would be sufficient for most of our largest farmers."[3] The author then recommended a barn that combined the various functions of animal and crop storage into a larger, centralized structure. Other writers recommended a similar strategy, praising the widely publicized Pennsylvania German barn as a model for a centralized, efficient barn.[4]

The idea of centralizing farm functions in a larger barn was, however, not entirely new to early nineteenth-century New England farmers. During the colonial period they had simplified their multiple barn system by combining the hay barn with the cattle barn to produce a larger English barn type.[5] The advice to build larger, centralized barns, therefore, might have only reinforced an existing pattern of development. Still, most farmers continued to employ multiple barns and outbuildings, as is evident from the constant criticism of this custom during the next fifty years.

By the 1850s the practice of constructing small barn clusters had become a conspicuous symbol of the old, unscientific farming methods. Progressive agriculturalists heaped blistering criticism upon the traditional ways: "I would have a barn, not half a dozen barns, and twice as many rickety sheds, of all shapes and sizes, arranged in gross confusion, as if they had been pitched together by the frolic of the elements. For shame on such barns as are seen in some parts of our country. If the cattle should get lost among them, I should not suppose they could find themselves." And before recommending a large single barn, the same author added, "If my predecessor had left a score of old crazy barns and sheds, some new and others old, some standing up, others tumbling down, and others looking for all the world as if they wanted to follow, I should be glad to get rid of them as soon as would be prudent."[6]

The attack on the custom of clustering small barns was usually coupled with an appeal to build barn cellars for root crop and manure storage. The cellar was an essential component in the new centralized barn plan and was continually recommended by agriculturalists throughout the nineteenth century.[7] Tighter, neater barns were also recommended for the protection of animals in the winter and for their physical beauty. The relationship between animal health and warmer, draft-free barns was emphasized in this typical passage: "Much improvement is seen on every hand over the old style, consisting of a wooden frame standing on a few wooden blocks or cobble stones, covered with single boards, with a generous crack at each joint for ventilation, rendering the inside rather the colder side."[8]

Despite their often satirical and antiplebian nature, articles such as these clearly and accurately describe the clustered, small barn arrangement that was the popular custom in the early nineteenth century. It was such an arrangement of multiple barns that Tobias Walker inherited from his father in the 1820s, and it was this old system that he and many of his neighbors were to reorganize into a modern connected building system during the next sixty years.

HOUSE AND BARN IN CLOSE PROXIMITY

In the early 1820s agricultural writers began to recommend several different strategies for the siting and arrangement of farm buildings. Previously, they seldom discussed the siting of house or barn, probably because the existing practices were so uniform and well established. After 1820, however, farmers received conflicting advice concerning the placement of their farm buildings, probably indicating that new ideas were beginning to challenge the older vernacular building practices.

Early nineteenth-century writers generally agreed about the relative importance of the house. Most recommended it be placed in close proximity to and facing the road, although the older practice of a south-facing orientation was still recommended.[9] There was, however, increasing disagreement concerning the relative position of the house and the barn. In 1822 a writer recommended that the customary distance be kept between house and barn: "Let your dwelling house and its appendages be leeward . . . of your barn and stockyard; and sufficiently distant from them to avoid accidents by fire."[10] One year later another writer also recommended distancing house and barn but provided a glimpse of a developing trend in the building arrangement of many farmers: "It is a common practice and with many a general rule to build a farmhouse adjoining, and perhaps in contact with sheds, barns, and other outhouses."[11] The author of this widely quoted article did not recommend this practice and cited the fire danger and sanitary disadvantages of such a system, but he implied that closely sited houses and barns were beginning to be built at this time. His descriptive phrase, "adjoining and perhaps in contact" is significant, because thirty years later this was not the way many mid nineteenth-century writers would describe the deliberately and forcefully combined house and barn arrangements of that period. The author was accurately describing a fluid planning situation in which several competing farm building arrangements vied for primacy in New England. Because the connected farm organization was never officially approved by New England's agriculturalists until after it had gained wide popularity, I think this author was describing an emerging grass roots building style that may have borrowed simultaneously from gentlemen farmers and vernacular traditions.

The description *adjoining and perhaps in contact* takes on additional force when applied to the development of any of the connected farmsteads previously documented, as, for example, the 1830 plan of the Nutting farmstead (see fig. 69). This farm accurately represents the spirit of the quotation, especially in comparison to its earlier building arrangement, where the house and barn were located at a much greater distance from each other.

CONNECTING HOUSE AND BARN

In 1839 an article concerning farm building arrangement appeared in the popular newspaper, *Maine Farmer*. It cautiously reversed the previous criticism of the closely adjoining or connecting building practice and outlined the basic organizational strategy for the soon to be popular connected farm arrangement.

> The domicile must be considered the most important building in the group, as it is designed for our comfort and convenience and should occupy an eligible situation near the road. This must be considered the starting point near which all other buildings should be located. The barn is the next building of importance and should be placed just so far from the house as a convenience requires and no further. . . . Perhaps the smaller buildings such as the wood-house, granary, piggery, etc. might be placed on a line between the house and barn, so that if we have business at either of these places we might do it while on the road and not have to stand out in a new direction to find them. These things can all be arranged to our liking if we begin right and have a plan of our premises so that when we are ready to erect a building we shall know where to set it, and shall not have to remove one to make room for another. I do not suppose that those whose stakes are set down for life, will take the trouble to make a stir among their buildings if they do not stand in range or at right angles with each other, but perhaps some young man who has a clear field and a clear mind, may profit by these hints if he has occasion to take the subject into consideration.[12]

This passage summarizes the essential characteristics of the connected farm building arrangement, which were to become standardized in thousands of farms during the next fifty years. The recommendation for the linear arrangement of connected support buildings between house and barn was an essential concept that farmers needed to accept in order to see the value of the connected building system. The quotation also freezes the development of the connected farm building arrangement in a period of transition. The previously objectionable idea of a closely sited or connected building arrangement is subtly transformed into an acceptable idea of thrift and practical good sense. The author of this article, however, never actively supports the fully connected system, because that in itself would have been a radical departure from building precedents and the recommendations of most agricultural writers of the period. The author, however, does create a solid, pragmatic case for its eventual acceptance by consistently underlining the functional advantages of the new system. Behind the homespun style of the article, he attempts to neutralize the traditional practice of separating and differentiating house and barn by emphasizing the efficiency of the new connected system.

A comparison with other articles of the period indicates that a highly cultivated journalistic style structured the author's seemingly casual observations. In this case, the author and reader share a knowledge of the current building practices and both are well aware that some buildings are already being constructed in the adjoining and connected fashion. The only point in question is whether or not the new building practices are to be widely accepted. In other words, this article was actually a finely balanced debate concerning the merits of a newly developing farm planning system. Such a debate would have been inconceivable twenty years earlier or later, because the building context would not have justified such a questioning, balanced discussion.

In conclusion, the author takes his knowledgeable audience aside and admits that most older, established farmers are not likely to reorganize their farms according to the new principles he has just outlined. He was well aware that the existing buildings on most farms did not conform to the new plan, which required that all buildings "stand in range [in a line] and at right angles with each other." These two criteria, linearity and rectilinearity, are essential planning characteristics of the connected farmstead system and ones that are distinctly absent from the eighteenth-century vernacular system. Their acceptance by New England farmers, consciously or unconsciously, was essential to the development of the new connected planning system. Both ideas were probably assumed by Tobias Walker, for they structured his many building projects, but they were not assumed by his father, who was influenced by traditional ideas and produced a very different type of farm building arrangement. Thus the twin concepts of linear range and a rectilinear alignment that guided Tobias had to displace the well-established vernacular traditions that had guided Eliphalet. While the acceptance of rectilinearity and linearity represented a distinct break from the past, the most unusual idea about the connected scheme was that there should be a balance and unity between house and barn.

BALANCE AND UNITY

The alignment of farm buildings in range or close formation is not a radical or unusual concept. It was a common characteristic of many farming areas worldwide, particularly in England, where there is a long history of closely aligned and connected farm building systems.[13] The decision to unify the connected house and barn visually by applying the architectural style of the house to the barn was, however, a fundamental departure from the common American practice. New England farmers had long been exposed to this practice in colonial estate houses with extended wings. The immediate source of the idea of balance between house and barn, however, was the example of New England's gentlemen farmers and merchants who had followed the example of grand estate houses and developed a unified building arrangement linking the main house to the carriage house and barn. It was this genteel, town-influenced example that provided average farmers with a model for farmstead reform when they reorganized their farms, beginning in the early nineteenth century.

The logic behind the farmer's decision to give the same architectural style, scale, and unity to connected house and barn is summarized in an 1858 article, published at a time when the connected and unified arrangement was already becoming widely popular: "There should be also a fitness in a set of farm buildings; a palace for a house and a hovel for a barn, or an expensive barn coupled with a diminutive, ill-arranged house, would be a manifest incongruity. Nor is this all. A cultivated taste requires that all the appointments, out buildings, grounds, shade and fruit trees, flower and vegetable gardens, should be arranged as to please the eye."[14] The idea of balance and unity between house and barn is the most critical planning idea separating the making of New England connected farmsteads from previous tradition and from other American farms. New England farmers not only connected their houses to their barns but also broke all traditional farming and building rules by applying the architectural detail of the house to the previously unadorned barns. It is this characteristic that so fundamentally separated Tobias Walker's new buildings from those of his father. His huge white barn was adorned in the same Greek Revival style as his house, and it could not have provided a more striking contrast to the weather-blackened cluster of his father's barns.

ACCEPTANCE OF THE NEW ARRANGEMENT

By 1850 farmers in many prosperous regions of New England were reorganizing their farmsteads in the connected farm arrangement. Articles depicting this plan were widely published in New England. For example, a lengthy description appeared in the annual report of the Agricultural Societies of Maine, 1857, and included a frontal elevation and extensive plans (see fig. 91).[15] Similar articles showing connected arrangements also appeared in agricultural journals throughout America but were not selected by farmers in other parts of the country; only a few are known to have been built outside New England. It certainly did not become a popular style in any other region.

The progressive New England agriculturalists who chose to publish articles on connected farms were, therefore, always cautious about their praise of this building practice, since they were well aware that it was not followed in other parts of the nation. Regional writers gave tacit, cautious approval and published articles about these farms without strong endorsement. After 1860 connected farm buildings were infrequently mentioned in articles that analyzed farm building practices in New England, even though they continued to be one of the most popular plans until the First World War.

This building development summary will give the reader a sense of the new ideas and attitudes that were popularized in the connected farm building organization. What is still lacking is an environmental and historical context within which to set this fragile package of attitudes and to help to explain this development within a milieu of competing choices and existing conditions.

The Context of Place and Conditions

Connected farmsteads were constructed within a context of environmental and historical conditions that structured the choices available to most farmers. Three overlapping contexts are examined: historical, environmental, and agrarian. The intent is to explain how the opportunities and constraints of context acted to shape the New England connected farm.

The severity of the problems that New England farmers faced may surprise some readers. The climate, the land, and pace of historical events worked against their long-term success. Yet connected farm buildings were built by farmers who adapted themselves to these constraints in a determined effort to succeed at farming.

THE HISTORICAL CONTEXT

While some events affected all New Englanders alike, others affected farmers differently from city dwellers. The opening of the Erie Canal, for example, affected everyone in the region, but particularly farmers, because it marked the beginning of intensive western agricultural competition. On the other hand, while the rise of the New England shipping and fishing industries brought prosperity to the cities, it had only a minimal, in some cases negative, effect on the prospects of most rural residents. The period between 1820 and 1860 wrought the greatest change in the lives and fortunes of the rural population. During this time American industrialization and its accompanying capitalized marketing system would irrevocably change farm life, replacing wooden tools and medieval farming techniques with iron tools and horse-drawn machines. Localized systems of farm production, home industry, and marketing gradually gave way to new scientifically based, agricultural techniques, a large-scale factory manufacturing system, and a marketing network expanded and dominated by the railroad. A collective spirit of progress shared by farmers and city dwellers alike sanctioned the improvements of the era.

Although these transformations took place gradually throughout the century, by the end of the Civil War, a major reformulation of social and economic values had occurred. In retrospect it appears that the traditional, preindustrial, agrarian society of rural New England (pre-1760 to 1860) entered a critical period of changing conditions and attitudes (1820–60) and emerged profoundly altered, and yet unaltered (1820–1900). In an even broader interpretation, the turmoil that engulfed these farmers in the early nineteenth century can be seen as the last in a series of rural revolutions from which New England farmers emerged as a modern people.

THE ENVIRONMENTAL AND GEOGRAPHICAL CONTEXT

The popular explanation for the reason New Englanders connected their houses and barns emphasizes the need for a covered barn passageway to protect the farmer from snowy, inclement weather. It has a compelling environmental logic but is insufficient to explain the comparatively recent popularity of this building practice and the reasons it was not adopted in areas with more severe winter climates. Environmental conditions did, however, contribute to the making of connected farms.

New England's climate is not ideally suited for most types of farming. A short growing season of 100 to 160 frost-free days is all that a farmer can generally expect.[16] Recent climatic studies have also shown that late eighteenth- and nineteenth-century weather patterns were extremely erratic, causing repeated crop losses as unexpected early fall and late spring frosts cut into harvest yields.[17] Summer weather patterns were also relatively cool and damp, especially when compared to the warmer, more stable patterns in other areas, such as the farming regions of the northern and central plains with similarly short growing seasons.

A short growing season with erratic weather fluctuations is not an insurmountable obstacle to agricultural success, but added to this was the problem of soil infertility. Most of New England's soils are largely glacial till: a loose mixture of sand, clay, and broken rock deposited by glacial action of a relatively recent origin.[18] New England settlers found that most of their soils contained a low percentage of organic matter. Consequently it was only marginally suited for the production of most marketable crops. Most of the region's land also contained large amounts of granite boulders, which necessitated laborious extraction. The few areas of New England that provided adequate farming soils were widely scattered along the intervale plains of the major river valleys. The Connecticut River Valley, Aroostook County, Maine, and the Lake Champlain Valley are the major agricultural regions of New England, but smaller, isolated intervale plains such as the ones near Fryeburg and Farmington, Maine, are more typical of the best farming areas in the region. Flat, fertile land constitutes an extremely small portion of the settled farmland of New England, and these are the areas that today still support the last major agricultural districts.[19]

During the early pioneer period, a thin surface layer of fertile soil encouraged an overextension of pioneer farm settlement into areas of marginal agricultural value and probably contributed to a general overconfidence in the long-range agricultural prospects for the region. The rapid depletion of this soil quickly forced early settlers to adopt short-term land tenancy practices and to develop nonfarm sources of income such as logging and fishing.[20] Generally these practices retarded more permanent land renewal and fertilizing practices, although it can be persuasively argued that the basic problem of soil infertility made long-term agricultural practices improbable no matter what practices were adopted or when they were implemented.

A short, erratic growing season and soil infertility (with the inability to increase fertility except by prohibitively costly methods) were crucial limitations to New England's agricultural development. Both factors reinforced the traditional practices of mixed-farming, home-industry agriculture where multiple-crop, animal, and home-manufactured products were produced in small quantities. In turn, this method of farming influenced farmers to seek a building system to accommodate these diverse functions. The multipurpose ell in the connected farm building arrangement was particularly well suited to this task.

The terrain of large portions of New England was also unfavorable to farming. Most settled areas contain low, rolling hills cut by small, winding streams. Consequently farmers were continually plagued by an inadequate transportation network, including a lack of sufficient or well-maintained roads, canals, and railroads. The hilly country of New England was, however, economically viable for farmers during the early settlement period (1700–1800 in the south, 1760–1820 in the north). Nearby markets for farm produce were available for the small quantities of eighteenth-century agricultural products despite transportation problems and soil depletion.[21] There were even some advantages to rugged interior farmlands, such as water power and timber. Gradually, however, the environmental disadvantages of the major interior regions took a depressing toll: poor roads, early frosts, thin soils, and inaccessible markets meant that these areas would become increasingly disadvantaged with regard to the development of nineteenth-century agriculture.

A critical long-range disadvantage of New England's topography was that the choppy, rolling hills, and rock-strewn terrain tended to retard the introduction of horse-drawn farm machinery. Small, discontinuous, rocky fields were ill suited to the flourishing of horse-drawn machine agriculture, and this irrevocably solidified New England's secondary status in agricultural production after 1860. (Other factors also retarded the introduction of modern technological agricultural methods in New England, and these will be discussed shortly.)[22]

The one distinct advantage of the region's hilly topography was that water power for mills was easily obtainable. New Englanders quickly and consistently exploited this advantage for mill and small shop production.[23] The growth of many home-industry activities was facilitated by the availability of small neighborhood grist- and sawmills and by the development of small-town factories. But even this initial advantage was short lived. In the industrial era of steam power after 1850, the widely scattered towns that were established near water power sites could not consolidate or compete against the larger, centralized factory system.[24]

The geographic difficulties of New England's farmers are surprising considering its close proximity to eastern population centers and European trade routes. The region's location was often cited as a distinct advantage for the growth of its agricultural interests.[25] This advantage was brilliantly exploited by New Englanders with the unprecedented development of their maritime industries and foreign trade, but the advantages of their location were not exploited by farmers. In fact, the very success of maritime, commercial, and industrial activities was criticized by agriculturalists as contributing to short-term, part-time farming practices.[26] The development of transportation networks to the western states (canals, rivers, roads, and railroads), however, was the most devastating blow to New England farmers, who constantly found their products undersold by western products even within their own New England region.

The environmental and geographic odds against the success of farming seem awesome today. New England farmers landed on one of the most inhospitable farming terrains on the eastern seaboard. It is within this harsh environmental context, then, that the development of the connected farm building organization can be seen as an appropriate response to the restricted agricultural opportunities presented farmers. Thus the connected organization responded extremely well to the half-farming, half-home-industry production necessitated by the limitations of the New England environment.

THE AGRARIAN CONTEXT

Clarence Day's leading agricultural history of Maine documents a process of agricultural improvement in which animal power and old-fashioned methods were replaced by machine power and modern technological farming methods.[27] However, in back of the technical record of agricultural modernization is the human record of the majority who farmed. It becomes abundantly clear from this history that farming gradually failed as a way of life for a majority of New England's rural population. From a progressive-technological perspective, New England's agriculture was slowly modernized during the nineteenth century with substantive economic and social improvements to smaller numbers of farmers.[28] From a cultural perspective, the majority of farmers entered a long, protracted struggle during the eighteenth and nineteenth centuries, but the viability of this way of life slowly diminished, until by 1940 it was no longer possible for most people to make a living by farming. These perspectives reveal different interpretations about the history of New England farming and, taken together, help explain why nineteenth-century farmers developed the connected farm building arrangement.

Western Competition. Western agricultural competition was the most important contextual factor to affect the development of nineteenth-century New England agriculture and its rural culture. Between 1825 and 1880 the productive superiority of America's western farmers restructured and narrowed the possibilities for New England's agriculture.[29] The triumph of western agricultural production coupled with an increasingly industrialized economy that supported western productivity dwarfed all other social, environmental, and cultural influences affecting nineteenth-century New England agricultural development.

The list of agricultural products that were undersold by western competition includes every major cash crop produced in New England. In a depressing succession of production declines, farmers found that they could not profitably compete in national markets for the production of wheat, beef, sheep, pork, hops, cheese, butter, apples, or potatoes (outside Aroostook County), or, into the twentieth century, corn, eggs, sugar beets, and sweet corn.[30] As I write, chickens are being added to this list. Each of these products was once the major source of income in many areas.

There were, however, many temporary reversals in these general trends. Sheep production, for example, rose and fell many times in the nineteenth century before becoming unprofitable for most farmers by 1900.[31] Most farm products were produced in limited quantities for regional markets throughout the nineteenth and twentieth centuries, and at times these markets proved very successful.[32] A few speciality items were quite profitable in various areas, for example, the tobacco farms of the lower Connecticut Valley. In addition, there were individual farmers who continued to produce successfully crops or animals that could not generally be produced by most farmers. But the overall record for New England agriculture is abundantly clear: each major product was, sooner or later, outproduced by other agricultural areas of the country until it was no longer profitable to produce these items in large quantities. The major exception to this rule was the steady rise and importance of dairy products, which gradually became the leading source of income for most farmers by the twentieth century.[33]

During the nineteenth century New England farmers did not passively accept the results of western competition but reacted quickly and consistently to develop new crops and techniques, such as pressed hay for Boston markets and a world-famous sweet corn canning industry. Consequently the history of New England's agricultural productivity is simultaneously the record of declines and the elimination of major agricultural and home-industry products, and the record of a determined effort to readapt and diversify in response to these changes. The connected farm building arrangement was just one of the most striking and visible examples of this concerted effort to adapt to these changing conditions. The organization of the connected farm allowed farmers to absorb the vagaries of agricultural and home-industry production in a flexible, adaptive spatial framework.

The record of changing crops and farm production must also be qualified by the fact that a few staples (including hay, corn, potatoes, dairy products, and apples) constituted the bulk of most farm production in any period in the nineteenth century.[34] The important distinction with regard to New England's staple products is that, while they were major cash crops, each product could not sustain prolonged production or be developed as a single source of income. Consequently these staples were constantly changed according to fluctuating market opportunities dictated by other areas of the country. As nineteenth-century agricultural writers constantly lamented, New England farmers (except in Aroostook County) never developed a single cash staple that could command a national market, although they repeatedly tried to do so.[35] The production record of most farms demonstrates both long-range shifts in major cash crop production and the diversification of farm production into a variety of farm and nonfarm sources of income. The emergence of dairying, however, gradually stabilized production toward the end of the nineteenth century.

Mixed Farming. As the name implies, mixed farming is an agricultural system for producing a variety of crops and animal products.[36] The system characterized most of New England's farms throughout the nineteenth century. It is the opposite of a single-source or one-crop system and relies on many marketable products to sustain farm income. In 1870 a Maine agricultural writer summarized the farming system of most nineteenth-century New England farmers: "We have no great staple crop like the wheat and corn of the West, or the cotton, sugar and rice of the South. Our soil, climate, and social condition compels us to pursue a mixed husbandry, to gain a variety of farm products, and these are varied according to the locality in which the farmer resides and the requirements of the markets, and whether these are near or distant from the farm."[37]

The diverse agricultural products of the early nineteenth-century farm were intended for both market and home consumption. Wheat, beef, and potatoes were the most common products, and they also provided the major dietary staples. Other major cash crops and animal products included hay, wool, flax, maple sugar, beans, butter, and apples. The production of such a large variety of agricultural products required a high degree of diversification and specialization in tools, buildings, planting and harvesting methods, and marketing techniques. While these were the normal characteristics of colonial and the early nineteenth-century farming, the system of mixed farming began to reveal its disadvantages after 1830, when it came into direct competition with the less diversified agricultural regions of the country. Farmers in other areas engaged in similar practices, but the variety of their production was becoming more structured by market opportunities. In the Ohio Valley, for example, farmers concentrated on a cycle of raising corn, grain, and hogs to establish the nation's leading center for pork production by the middle of the nineteenth century.[38] In New England, however, the diverse products of most farms required a host of separate tools, operations, and skills, and necessitated nonsequential, overlapping operations. When labor was cheap and outside necessities few, a farmer could work a little harder, press the children into service, hire a neighbor, cut back, and somehow survive. But the inherent difficulties in this minimal-cash, labor-intensive system took an increasingly heavy toll. For many reasons, however, New Englanders had little choice but to continue the mixed-farming system. Their harsh environment and western competition made diverse farm production their only realistic agricultural possibility. Consequently, when they modernized their farms in the nineteenth century, they chose the architectural arrangement of connected buildings because it was best suited to the improvement of their mixed-farming system.

When New England farmers could establish a single cash crop, they did so. In fact, the Yankee farmers who settled in Aroostook County, Maine, during the second half of the nineteenth century were sharply criticized for growing nothing but potatoes.[39] But for various reasons, farmers in most of New England could not establish a single, sustaining source of farm income. Although leading agriculturalists continually recommended the advantages of single-crop farming, most farmers followed the advice of a Maine writer who warned his readers: "Specialities are pretty in theory, but bad in practice."[40] This was not just antiquated advice, because New England farmers had witnessed many failures to achieve a single cash crop. The most spectacular was the widely publicized effort to grow silk in New England. Although today it is difficult to believe that a substantial effort was undertaken to grow the mulberry trees whose leaves feed the silk worm, substantial private and public funds were poured into this risky undertaking. It was even widely predicted in 1836 that silk would become "the cotton of the North."[41] Unfortunately, repeated efforts of this kind left New England farmers without a consistent cash crop. It is within this context of diversified agriculture that the multifunctioning connected farm ell made so much sense to New England's farmers. It was a building system designed to accommodate a variety of different overlapping, nonsequential farm and home-industry activities on the relatively small scale of a New England farm.

Home Industry. The custom of home-industry or nonagricultural production was as much a part of the typical New England farm as animal and crop production. In fact, a New England farmer might very well argue with the term *nonagricultural production* and insist that no distinction should be made between agricultural and nonagricultural products, since both sources of income were essential to the survival of the farm. Lumbering and occupations associated with wood products were consistently the largest single source of vital outside income to support the New England farm.[42] A majority of eighteenth-, nineteenth-, and twentieth-century New England farmers could even be called summer farmers and winter woodsmen, so important was the cash generated by lumbering activities. Timber products included lumber, cordwood, bark (for tanning), firewood, shingles, and a wide variety of hand-made wooden products such as furniture, tools, barrels, and boxes. The cash from logging was one of the principal reasons why these farmers attempted to maximize acreage, instead of increasing soil fertility on less acreage as continually recommended by the progressive agricultural press.[43] It simply made good economic sense for most farmers to have a timber resource in support of farm income. Up until the present, this tradition of farming and logging characterized the small-scale mixed production of many New England farmers. Recently a Maine farmer summarized his father's farming operation this way: "My father in the fifties milked about 20 cows to make a living. He also worked in the woods. He used horses both on the farm and in the woods. If the farm got poor, he sold off a few cows and worked a bit harder in the woods; if the farm got better, he brought on a few cows."[44] This description could stand for many of the nineteenth-century farmers who made connected farms.

In the early 1800s a greater percentage of home-industry production shifted from home consumption to commercial sale. Home industries, including the making of potash, candles, clothes, and cloth items, were frequently carried out by women in the kitchen and rooms of the ell alongside the production of crop and animal products such as butter and cheese.[45] By the the mid-1800s home-industry production continued to supply domestic needs but was becoming a more vital source of farm income and included the making of shoes, clothing, barrels, leather products, and tools. During the second half of the nineteenth century, home-industry production was often supplemented by the practice of "jobbing out" handcrafted components of products like shoes, wood items, and garments to farm families for later assembly at mills and factories.[46]

The home-industry production system was an indispensable component of the mixed-farming system. It becomes painfully evident that the people who were finally most successful at farming did not generate their primary source of income from agriculture. Most successful farmers developed critical nonagricultural sources of income, as for example, Tobias Walker's successful shoe and tanning businesses (see Chapter 6, 1770–1820), and Nathan Nutting's timber sales (see Chapter 4, The Nutting Farm,

1795–1820).[47] Without these varied nonagricultural sources of income, there would have been few of the connected farms this book portrays.

The opportunities and constraints of the New England farmer's context can also be compared to the plight of all small-scale nineteenth-century American farmers under similar pressure to adopt commercial farming methods. One of the dubious distinctions of New England farmers was that they were among the first groups of American farmers to be fundamentally challenged by the newly emerging industrial-capital system, which gradually defined the limits and structured the possibilities for all American farmers.[48] What is so remarkable about these farmers is the sustained vigor with which they met these challenges. Throughout the nineteenth century, New England farmers actively responded to the demands of their increasingly market-oriented economy and incorporated many aspects of the new system into their mixed-farming, home-industry traditions. They did not cling to outmoded methods but continually experimented, readapted, and retooled their farms within an increasingly harsh economic context. Simultaneously, they also acted forcefully to maintain their neighborhood work-sharing and mutuality customs.

The effort to preserve some aspects of their older traditions, particularly their social customs, should not, however, be romanticized or mistaken for antiquarianism. These were the same farmers who tore out and discarded their fireplaces, well sweeps, eight-over-eight windows, spinning wheels, and ancient wooden farm tools for more modern conveniences and thereby reaped some of the most universally cherished benefits of an expanding industrial economy. They consistently transformed their environment to eliminate a series of relentlessly debilitating chores that had structured and limited their lives. The steel tipped plow, stove, iron pump, reaper, almanac, and manufactured cloth are fitting symbols for the profound transformation they accomplished.

Still, rural New Englanders never fully integrated their lives with all the tenets of the commercial agricultural system. They desired the benefits of each new labor-saving device but they were also aware that each new purchase committed them to a system of economic exchange that their traditional farming operation and cultural organization was ill prepared to sustain. Perhaps it was inevitable that their commitment to some of the old ways would fail. Some, of course, would say that it was sheer ignorance and stupidity that made them cling to their older customs, but many drew a line at the point where their traditions of neighborhood cooperation and mutuality became incompatible with the direction of modern, commercial agriculture. Unlike visionaries, such as Thoreau or Ruskin, who could safely criticize the evils of industrialization while still receiving its many benefits, New England farmers eagerly sought these advantages yet also attempted to preserve aspects of their traditional culture that were highly vulnerable to the pressures of industrialism. Unlike Thoreau and Ruskin, who were able to find safety in retreat and solitude, New England farmers confronted the full impact of industrialization with their farms and their way of life. Despite the struggle of many generations, the demographic history of New England farming records that they were slowly and silently decimated on their rocky hillsides. Today one cannot help wondering whether, if only their environmental prospects had been more hospitable or if only their soils had been a little more fertile, these New England farmers might have reached a different compromise with the modern world from the one they finally obtained.

A Context of Ideas

Connected farm buildings were developed within a context of environmental and historic conditions that structured the choices and imposed constraints upon the farmers who made them. Another kind of context also influenced farmers. It was an abstract context of ideas that acted to shape attitudes and mold opinions about these buildings.[49] The purpose of this last section is to explain why a particular group of ideas appealed strongly enough to motivate New England farmers to reorganize their buildings in the connected building plan.

Establishing a linkage between a particular idea and its power to motivate people to build is a challenging problem of architectural analysis.[50] It will be approached by juxtaposing the actions of one farmer, Tobias Walker, against a background of potentially influential ideas that existed both within and without his nineteenth-century rural culture. Six major ideas have been selected because they have reverberated through this text and they seem to be the essential ideas associated with the adoption of the connected building organization. These concepts have also been described by various historians of New England as major currents of nineteenth-century thought. If these six ideas were influential to his building projects, we will have a deeper motivational explanation for the question, Why did Tobias Walker move his woodshed from one side of his house to the other?

THE IMPROVING SPIRIT

On September 4, 1869 Edwin Walker, Tobias's son, made this entry in his farm journal: "[At] work hauling large rocks from the field, some of them large ones that my father and grandfather have mowed and ploughed around nearly a century."[51] Edwin could have left the rocks alone and continued to plow his field as his father and grandfather had done, but in ways that now seem typical of many New England farmers, he was powerfully motivated to clean, straighten, reorganize, and finally to improve his farm. This improving spirit accurately characterized the Walkers' unending toil to better their farm. In the "Report of the Committee on General Farm Improvements," a Maine farmer summarizes this spirit: "The old ruts in which our fathers teamed so sturdily and persistently, are being carefully examined. . . . Improvement is now the order of the day; improved stock, improved buildings, improved implements, improved orchards, gardens, mowing, pastures, improved everything."[52]

This will to improve had its most powerful source in a Puritan work ethic and its sanction of individual toil toward collective improvement.[53] But there was also a strong Enlightenment component, which emphasized a rational faith in perfectibility and progress for its own sake.[54] Tobias Walker and his family continually exemplified this improving spirit in a cycle of building projects, as amply recorded in their daily journals. In fact, this commitment to improvement and perfectibility should be seen as a quasi-religious belief that permeated all levels of private and public life, becoming the assumed and unquestionable goal of all activity.[55] Of course, most farm remodeling projects in other regions had the objective of improvement. What makes it such a significant issue in New England is the dramatic and uniform way in which a majority of farmers like Tobias Walker improved their farms during a relatively short period of time.

At the beginning of the nineteenth century, the Puritan sanction of hard work and self-improvement was vitalized by evangelical reform movements, particularly educational and social reforms.[56] Tobias Walker was directly influenced by this spirit of improvement, as evidenced in his decision to give up liquor, read widely in newspapers, attend lyceums and lectures, intensify religious activities, purchase labor-saving farm and household machinery, and conduct a series of building and agricultural improvements. But there were limits to what a New England farmer such as Tobias Walker could improve. One of the things he could not alter was the basic system of mixed-farming, home-industry agriculture that was rigorously structured by the harsh constraints of New England's physical and economic context. These were givens he had to accept if he was to continue farming, but this did not stop him from applying his perfecting instincts to those portions of his farming operation that he could improve. Tobias Walker chose the connected farmstead organization and moved his wood house into alignment with house and barn because he considered it to be a distinct improvement to the physical shape and efficiency of his existing farm operation. But he continued to operate a traditional, and increasingly outmoded, system of agricultural production, which he could not improve upon. It is this dual aspect of intensive improvement of what could be changed and retention of what could not be changed that helps to explain the unique development of the connected farm organization in New England.

Farmers in other areas of the country also improved their farms, but they were not so constrained by the demands of the mixed-farming, home-industry system as were New England farmers. The essential difference in the improvements that Tobias Walker made was that he improved a traditionally ordered, mixed-farming, home-industry operation to produce a connected farm plan. Farmers in other areas of America, however, improved more commercially oriented farming operations to produce different, unconnected farm plans.[57] Although Tobias Walker produced different results from farmers in other regions, the primary motivation behind his building projects was farm improvement. The connected farm arrangement is a product of that extraordinary effort to make a success of mixed-farming, home-industry agriculture.

THE INVENTIVE TRADITION

The record of Tobias Walker's prodigious building activities would have evoked little comment from his neighbors. Within the limits of his competence and the extent of his resources, he conducted the typical building projects of many New England farmers who built connected farmsteads during the nineteenth century. When he moved his woodshed and reorganized his farm, he certainly did not think his alteration was unique. The customs of building movement, addition, and remodeling were deeply ingrained attitudes toward construction that characterized New England's rural architecture in all periods. Tobias Walker was the inheritor of this fully developed tradition of construction experimentation, and he freely applied it to the improvement and modernization of his farm.

Early European observers of the American people, and of New Englanders in particular, have frequently commented on their close relationship with tools and machines and their inventive, experimental attitude toward change.[58] Tobias Walker reflected this attitude in multiple construction projects where he repeatedly modified and reorganized his farm with an apparent ease and an American love of inventiveness and change. This inventive spirit is best known through the remarkable accomplishments of New Englanders such as Benjamin Franklin, Samuel Colt, Eli Whitney, and Rufus Porter, but each one rose out of a solid popular tradition of tool and technological inventiveness.[59] Today rural New Englanders are still justifiably characterized as a tinkering, jack-of-all-trades, inventive people, but the historical antecedents of these characteristics are far more profound.

At the beginning of the nineteenth century, the deeply rooted traditions of technological inventiveness acquired a new meaning in association with industrialization and nationalism. In *Civilizing the Machine*, John Kasson has used the term *Republican technology* to describe the unique blend of nationalism and machine appreciation that motivated nineteenth-century Americans to "glorify machines not simply as functional objects but as signs and symbols of the future America."[60] John Kouwenhoven has attempted to define this unique American relationship with tools and technological methods as "the folk arts of the first people in history who, disinherited of a great cultural tradition, found themselves living under democratic institutions in an expanding machine economy," which he labeled a "democratic technological vernacular."[61] Kouwenhoven's principal argument is that the tools and methods of technology are as American as apple pie, and that they characterize a uniquely American form of its dominant popular culture. The ambitious record of Tobias Walker's building projects certainly marks him as a consistent practitioner of this popular culture. When he began his major farmstead reorganization project in 1850, only the connected scheme was new; the traditions of building movement, alteration, and remodeling, which he employed so freely, were old and well established.

In order to understand fully why Tobias Walker moved his wood house, one must understand the spirit of tinkering, experimentation, and inventiveness that characterized his relationship with building. Instead of picturing his buildings as permanent, we must substitute a picture of their alteration as the normal, acceptable mode for what was supposed to happen to a structure in nineteenth-century rural New England. Tobias Walker had this spirit of building inventiveness, and when a new fashion of uniformly connected architecture came along, he merely applied his routine building procedures to the making of that new form.

THE CLASSICAL IMAGE

Many of the building projects Tobias Walker initiated had a classical inspiration. The wooden copies of Greek and Roman columns that graced his front doorway, fireplaces, and barns were most likely derived from classical pattern books. The uniform, whitened mass of his buildings communicated a popular image of antiquity, and the connected building organization vaguely suggested Palladian copies of Roman villa architecture. The extent of classical influence in rural, small-town New England is surprising to many who would expect it to be confined to wealthy houses in major cities. But antiquity, or at least the popular image of it, had an extraordinary appeal for many Americans throughout the nineteenth century.

The classical movement in America, however, extended far beyond the appreciation of architectural style. The appeal of classicism permeated every level of society and welded together diverse and conflicting forces such as Protestantism, pastoralism, and agrarianism. But its primary appeal to Americans was nationalistic.[62] The image of Greece and Rome became a symbol of progress, and virtue and was contrasted with the real and imagined decadence of European oligarchies and their urban industrialism.[63]

Americans selectively edited the classical source for its anticity message and, in the Jeffersonian pastoral tradition, produced a classical image that sanctioned America's agrarian simplicity.[64] Agricultural writers in New England and throughout America seized this classical image to justify the labor and virtues of the soil, and they would continue to evoke classical imagery in defense of agriculture until long after the Civil War.[65] In all its varied forms, the classical tradition was one of the most significant, widespread, and long-lasting influences to affect rural New Englanders in the nineteenth century.

Collectively New Englanders translated this classical image into a remarkably unified and long-lasting architectural and environmental aesthetic whose best-known product was the New England village. During the first half of the nineteenth century, this white, uniform, sparsely classical aesthetic became a popular symbol for improvement and progress for all levels of society. It replaced a darker, far less uniform popular aesthetic of medieval origin. The emergence of this new style was consistently noted by New Englanders at the middle of the nineteenth century, as in this frequently quoted address to New England farmers: "Instead of them [the old style], has sprung up a new order of building, neat, if not ornamental, useful, if not showy, and partaking no less of comfort than of good taste. The eye no longer, or much more seldom meets the old, half finished, square house of the better class of farmers in the last century, with its unpainted exterior or flaming red or dingy yellow; without garden, yard shrub or flower, hard upon the high road with no ornament."[66] Of course, such sweeping observations must be qualified. For most farmers this emergence was considerably less dramatic and more gradual. Ultimately, however, most New England farmers did select aspects of this classical aesthetic when they remodeled their farms and built in the connected building organization.

Tobias Walker was certainly a practitioner of this classically inspired aesthetic. When he applied his inventing traditions to the reorganization of his farm in 1850, he selected a classical image for improvement. What appealed to him was not only the Greek Revival style with which he chose to adorn his house and his barn, but also the classical idea of visual order and unity that linked his house and barn in a uniform, whitened mass. Tobias Walker had seen this unified building style in the houses of a few of Kennebunk's wealthy merchants, such as William Lord, whose house he passed nearly every week.[67] Of course, he also passed other styles and forms of building that he did not choose to copy. The classically detailed, connected buildings of Mr. Lord's estate probably appealed to him because they were a stylish symbol of progressive farming in New England, while still being close enough to his existing arrangement to permit emulation.

Farmers outside of New England also established architecture with strong classical overtones and elaborate agricultural buildings, but they did not build connected farmsteads.[68] Unlike Tobias Walker, they did not live near Federal estate houses with classical wings. They also did not seem to have relished the classical ideal of aesthetic unity for so long a period or to have felt so compelled to implement farmstead reform as New England farmers did. But the most significant influence of classicism on the connected farmstead arrangement was the adornment of the barn, following the house, in a severe classical style. This was a radical departure from popular agricultural precedents, and it was this practice that was distinctly borrowed from the houses of New England's wealthy manorial estates. In 1852 Tobias Walker's shiny new white barn, with classical detail, more up-to-date than his house, clearly demonstrated his whole-hearted acceptance of this classical image. He appreciated it because it was the dominant symbol of civic and agricultural improvement in rural New England and would continue to be until the twentieth century.

CONVENIENCE AND BEAUTY

Intertwined within most of the passages quoted from New England's agriculturalists has been this fundamental assumption: function and beauty are integrally united in the service of sound farming and building practices. This combination of functional and aesthetic criteria is evident in a typical exhortation to Maine farmers about the improvement of their farmsteads: "The judicious arrangement of buildings is a matter of no little importance and adds much to its beauty and convenience."[69] By mid-century, progressive agriculturalists had combined these concepts into a powerful message in promotion of farming and life-style improvements. In fact the term *convenience and beauty* became synonymous with excellence in farming and building.

The concept that function and beauty should be inextricably united was an Enlightenment idea applied by progressive agriculturalists to the problems of building and farming in America.[70] The European origin of this message is evident in a typical English building treatise of the early 1800s. In a suggestion for rural building improvement, the English author Gandy laments, "But the advancement of Public Taste requires more than this—that we should combine convenience of arrangement with elegance in external appearance; a point of much consequence to the general aspect of the country."[71] New England agriculturalists, like their European Enlightenment predecessors, believed that knowledge and scientific method would lead directly to a physical environment of beauty and good taste (although frequently classical inspiration or imagery provided the unstated aesthetic standard).[72] All early nineteenth-century agricultural journalists firmly believed that knowledge and the products of scientific experimentation had strong visual components and that science and knowledge would lead to beauty, and vice versa. This idea became a bedrock assumption that was captured in the expression *convenience and beauty* and became an extraordinarily central message to the early nineteenth-century rural reform movement.

But the relationship of the term *convenience and beauty* to the development of connected farmsteads is not simple or direct. Farmers like Tobias Walker who joined their houses and barns may never have used such terms to describe their construction projects. Many farmers probably never heard the expression. Yet most farmers who connected their house to their barn came to subscribe to the ideas behind those terms, which entailed increased attention to the visual components of the building arrangement and architectural order. The buildings documented in the previous chapters clearly show that during the nineteenth century New England farmers significantly increased the overall organizational and visual unity of their farms. Collectively they came to accept the idea that successful farming, which involved the application of scientific techniques and sound economic policies, was integrally related to the visual organization of the farm. Of course not every farmer believed this, and many retained their traditional arrangements and did not take part in modest aesthetic reforms. But during the course of the nineteenth century, a majority of farmers did reorganize their farms, and through their concerted actions they transformed much of the early nineteenth-century landscape of rural New England.

Another reason why New England farmers like Tobias Walker accepted the reform message of convenience and beauty was that it reinforced so many of their preexisting values and agricultural practices. The idea that function and beauty (or order) were inextricably united is one of the most fundamental tenets of a folk or vernacular value system.[73] The ideal of beauty in the folk system is intrinsic to the work of everyday life and is never detached from that life. The beauty of the farm flower is, therefore, integrated into the productive kitchen garden. The ornamental tree may be beautiful, but it also bears edible fruit and provides a border for productive fields. Therefore, when the "book farming" idea of convenience and beauty was offered to nineteenth-century New England farmers, it was not new, only a newly packaged folk idea. It did, however, provide an explicit, formal expression for their previous traditions, which New England farmers like Tobias Walker were to exploit when they reorganized their farms and connected their houses with their barns.

GENTEEL SENSIBILITIES AND VERNACULAR TRADITIONS

There are many aspects of the Romantic-Aesthetic movements of the nineteenth century that had little appeal for New England farmers like Tobias Walker. For example, the architectural styles associated with the Romantic movement, such as Gothic and Italianate, were largely ignored by most farmers. Two years after Tobias Walker adorned his barn in a sparse classical-vernacular style, he watched George Bourne turn his house and barn into a Romantic-Gothic fantasy known today as the Wedding Cake House of Kennebunk, Maine.[74] But this style must have appeared strange and alien to the Puritan folk sensibilities of Tobias Walker and his neighbors. Certainly no one in his neighborhood followed Mr. Bourne's example and only a very few farmers in New England built in this style.

Although the architectural styles of the Romantic movement were alien, distinct portions of its pastoral-picturesque message were to have a wide-ranging appeal for many farmers, principally because it gave clarity and voice to many of their existing farming and building practices. For example, the town-initiated movement for the planting of roadside trees spread quickly throughout New England during the first half of the nineteenth century and is properly associated with the influence of this Romantic-Aesthetic movement.[75] But this influence was not entirely one way. While it is true that rustic, tree-lined country roads may have excited the romantic sensibilities of townspeople, they had long made good sense to farmers, who had maintained traditions of roadside trees and had frequently relegated orchards to field boundaries. Sound nineteenth-century farming practices, which had placed a premium upon neatness and careful visual order, were now also found to be beautiful to city folk. In short, many traditional farm practices were relatively close to the new aesthetic appreciation of the Romantic-Aesthetic movement. (Remember too that both European and American Romantic movements developed their rural imagery, in part, from looking at, longing for, but never actually taking part in, real farms.)[76]

Whether to assign the source of the farmer's tree-lined roadside to picturesque or folk sources is an extremely difficult and controversial chicken-or-egg problem. Many of the reform practices that were gradually adopted by farmers in the nineteenth century contained the Romantic-Aesthetic characteristics advocated by genteel reformers, but many characteristics were also fundamental components of a more traditional folk system. Perhaps the most important effect of the Romantic-Aesthetic movements upon New England farmers was to give sharpness, clarity, and a visual image to their traditional customs of farm improvement. The message of aesthetic reform probably served to codify traditional (unarticulated) aesthetic principles held by many farmers into a powerful image of farm improvement. In this more fashionable form, it became a symbol of agrarian progressiveness in nineteenth-century New England.

Agricultural writers were strong proponents of visual order in support of scientific farming practices and frequently associated the visual order with the moral order of the farm.[77] They generally embraced the aesthetic-picturesque message but were also careful not to alienate farmers with a too urbane disregard for the necessities of farm function. As an agricultural writer clarified in 1842: "We wish to be distinctly understood, that we are in no degree desirous of seeing the useful and comfortable sacrificed to the ornamental; but the perfection of a homestead, we take it, is by proper location, shape, and arrangement of the buildings, to produce the most pleasing effect consistent with convenience and economy."[78] Tobias Walker gave a hint of his awareness of these genteel sensitivities on his only trip to Boston in 1835 where he "took a walk across the Commons which was very pleasant on account of the situation, the pond, the trees, the walks, etc."[79] Here Tobias Walker lists the important components of the picturesque aesthetic of the Boston Common. Fifteen years later he would reapply some of these concepts in a severely modified form to organize the buildings, trees, and fences about his newly remodeled house and barn.

A few gentlemen farmers actively championed this Romantic-Aesthetic message by completely reorganizing their farmsteads and closely attending to the visual composition of their farms. Most farmers, however, conducted more modest and less extensive improvements whose origins were entangled in both folk and genteel sources. But it is important to emphasize that although the sources for this visual reform of New England's rural landscape are complex and diverse, the results are clear and precise. Most farmers initiated a variety of functional-aesthetic reforms to their farmsteads during the nineteenth century, including roadside trees, front yard fences and shrubbery, and a general improvement in the overall appearance of the farm—as did Tobias Walker.

THE EVANGELICAL REFORM TRADITION

"Have decided to refrain from the use of ardent spirits."[80] On February 4, 1833 Tobias Walker vowed to give up liquor and, from every available indication, he stuck to his pledge for the rest of his life. We cannot know how much "spiritous liquor" Tobias consumed before he made his pledge, but we do know that alcohol consumption reached staggering proportions during the early years of the Republic. From all available information, the prohibition reform movements that swept New England between 1820 and 1860 involved a wrenching reversal of custom for a significant portion of the population.[81] But in many ways this was quite normal for rural New Englanders, who seemed to have a history of wrenching reform and have even been characterized as a reforming people.

Care must be taken not to see every era in New England as an age of great turmoil, change, and reform, but the pace of revivalist and reform movements in the first half of the nineteenth century was truly extraordinary. In a roughly overlapping chronology,

New Englanders experienced intensive periods of revivalist or reform activity including temperance, religious revivalism, and abolitionism, to which must be added the broader movements for educational and later social reform.[82] Although these movements occurred throughout America, in New England they were marked with a particular zealousness and evangelicalism.

It is one of the principal assertions of this study that the popular making of connected farms was also characterized by a kind of building evangelicalism with the purpose of reforming the New England farm. The degree to which this should be called a building reform movement, rather than just a normal phase of farmstead improvement, is evident in the following quotation from a Committee on General Farm Improvements, which toured Cumberland County, Maine, in 1859. Its goal was to award premiums for overall farm improvement, and the members commented on the efforts of each farmer they visited: "Now he [Jarey Green of Naples, Maine] proposes to clear rough land of trees and stones; to build stone walls; to improve his pastures and buildings. His soil is a gravelly loam, with stones, varying in size from a pebble to a boulder, scattered about in great profusion. His farm requires, and he has laid out for himself, labor enough to discourage a man of ordinary will and energy, but he satisfied us that, if he lives, he will perform it."[83] Green owned a very poor farm, but, like most of his New England neighbors, he was determined to improve it even if he worked himself to death.

This was not an isolated account but typifies nearly a hundred published by the Maine Board of Agriculture over a five-year period. Furthermore, it also typifies the normal level of farm improvement during the middle of the nineteenth century. From the record of building construction, it is clear that a farm reform movement of evangelical intensity spread throughout New England, but principally in the north, during the middle of the nineteenth century. This movement contributed to a redoubling of the normal efforts to improve the farm, and its boldest symbol was the connected farm organization.

From the outside, farmstead reform appears to be based upon a purely positivistic effort to improve the New England farm, but there were deeper motivations that sprang from a challenge to the very existence of the New England farming enterprise. Yankee farmers had a powerful reason to seek reform. The survival of the New England agrarian and social order was threatened by their inability to compete effectively with other agricultural areas, and their condition worsened as the nineteenth century advanced. In these circumstances, it was either reform or cease farming. So many farmers chose reform, with a vengeance.

Beginning in the early 1800s and increasing after 1840, farmers were constantly advised to reform their farms. They were told to make their physical surroundings orderly and attractive so as to turn the tide of farm failure in rural New England. They were asked to improve the physical quality of life for their children, so that they would not leave the hardships of the New England farm for the better agricultural prospects of the western states or the higher wages in southern New England factories. An early account in 1839 emphasizes this message by warning farmers that it was not enough just to have a comfortable farmhouse that was "neither painted inside or out—there is no door yard in front, nor shrubbery or shade trees about it, nor garden worthy of the name—no other fruit than common apples, few books in the library, and no interesting periodical taken. The children of such farmers have eyes that can see, feelings that can be gratified or wounded; they can contrast their cheerless looking houses and out-buildings with those of the professional man, traders, industrious and prudent mechanics and they can see about their situation an air of neatness, comfort and elegance they do not possess; home has but few attractions." [84] It was a poignant, all too obvious message for most of New England's rural population. This message of lament reached a high point in the 1850s and gradually diminished toward the end of the century when, perhaps, the self-chastising message could no longer be sustained by an obviously disadvantaged New England agricultural population. In the most painfully publicized way, New England's rural population was bombarded from press and pulpit with the specter of its own demise.

This plea for farm improvement and life-style reform could have fallen on deaf ears. But the message was heard by an evangelically conditioned audience of Yankee self-improvers in an increasingly difficult social and economic situation. A writer summarized the urgency of the need for environmental reform with this question: "How can the farmers of Maine, large and small, learned and unlearned, rich and poor, be led to make their homes more attractive, and thus check in some degree the out-flowing tide of bone, muscle and brains (our young men and women)?" [85] One of the options available to most farmers was a modest attempt at physical renewal of the farmstead, which they initiated by whitening, straightening, ordering, and beautifying. The message of visual domestic reform was, of course, a consistent component of Protestant social reform ideology and was heard in every corner of urban and rural nineteenth-century America. [86] But this message took on particular urgency in New England, where the tide of emigration and western agricultural competition had so fundamentally threatened the fabric of its rural society. Tobias Walker was in the forefront of this reform effort because he realigned his farm before many of his neighbors in southern Maine. His new buildings were certainly a model to other farmers in the Alewive neighborhood, who would gradually follow his example during the latter part of the nineteenth century.

In New England today the connected farmstead organization is perceived as an outmoded, old-fashioned arrangement of farm building. The reversals and declines of New England agriculture were so complete that even before the end of the century the connected farm organization became a mocking symbol of the failure of this reform effort. But this should not conceal the powerful original motivation behind the connected farm building plan: to improve and reform the New England farm, no matter how hopeless that task now seems in retrospect. The reason why Tobias Walker moved his woodshed from one side of his house to the other was to reform and improve his farm, and the connected farm arrangement was the most logical, practical, and fashionable plan available to him.

The Reasons for Making Connected Farm Buildings

Nineteenth-century New England farmers selected the connected farm building organization because it was a practical, efficient, and modestly fashionable arrangement of buildings to house their farming operation. Most farmers were motivated to consider reorganizing their previous detached house and barn system by declines in the agricultural economy caused by western agricultural competition and the effects of industrialization. With the survival of their rural society seriously threatened, they collectively reformed their farms to meet this challenge. The connected farm building arrangement was adopted because it met the requirements of a more commercially oriented, mixed-farming, home-industry operation, which had become the only viable means of farming in New England.

Although most did not convert their farms until the middle of the nineteenth century, the connected building concept had been known to New England farmers since the colonial period. Two diverse building traditions provided models for its popular development: Georgian and Federal period estate houses with extended outbuilding wings, and English vernacular housing and agricultural traditions following practices of incremental growth and clustered outbuilding construction. Although both traditions were widely practiced in 1820, the connected farm building organization was not popularly employed.

In the first quarter of the nineteenth century, New England yeomen farmers continued to build separate houses and barns, as they had done throughout the colonial period. But, significantly, they had developed a group of building customs that pointed toward the fully developed connected farm arrangement, which became popular during the next fifty years. These early nineteenth-century developments included: the construction of long, multifunctional ells; the standardization of workrooms in these ells linking the kitchen, workroom, woodshed, and vehicle shed; the spatial unification of the entire farm landscape, particularly the geometric alignment of house and barn with the road; the adoption of a new barn type with a door in the gable end; and the building of houses and barns in closer proximity than in the previous century. Each of these practices was to be continued and reinforced within the connected farm arrangement.

By the 1820s the organization and function of a typical New England farm approximated the fully connected 1880 arrangement, except that several new ideas and motives were required to displace the custom of separating house and barn. An influential new concept was developed by prosperous merchants and gentlemen farmers in the small towns of New England, who connected their houses to carriage houses or barns, following the older Georgian and Federal style estate house tradition. But this genteel building form might have remained the selection of a small minority of wealthy farmers had it not also appealed to common farmers who sought to reform their farms during the same period. The attraction was two-sided; it was stylish and fashionable, but more important, it worked well and was close enough to their existing arrangement to permit widespread emulation. Despite its outwardly radical departure from traditional practices, the new connected farm system actually dovetailed smoothly with many popular, preexisting, vernacular building customs. The application of the new connected idea often required only that a farmer realign or modestly readjust preexisting buildings, and perhaps clapboard and paint a facade. The New England custom of building movement was particularly useful in this regard since a house-to-barn connection could often be accomplished by simply moving a building or a shed between an existing house and barn. The connected farm organization could never have become such a popular organization for New England farmers had it required massive rebuilding expenses. But the ease of its accomplishment for most farmers does not mean that its impact was minor or that its application was of little consequence. The difference between the pre- and post-connected farm was dramatic and substantial, and its application symbolized a fundamental break (at least outwardly) with an old agricultural and social order and the adoption of a more modern, commercial orientation.

The new connected building formula allowed most New England farmers to adapt their existing buildings to the new style while maintaining the fundamental characteristics of their small-scale, mixed-farming, home-industry methods, which were, and always had been, the only viable economic and social strategy available to them. The connected farm organization may even be seen as the flowering development of a long tradition of New England's mixed-farming, home-industry agriculture. What was so unusual about the reform movement that generated connected farms was that it actually reinforced the older mixed-farming system behind a greatly remodeled facade. In retrospect it appears that New England farmers carried the gospel of reform as far as they could: they reformed the way the farm looked, but they could not reform the way it worked (even though they repeatedly attempted to do so).

The most unusual aspect of the connected farm organization, however, was the insistence, on the part of its builders, that the architectural refinement usually reserved for the house be applied to the entire connected complex, including the barn. This was an extreme act with little precedent for common farmers. It marks a significant effort to reorganize, unify, and finally to reform the farm and the entire farm landscape. The architectural result was a unified architectural ensemble from house to barn in which the barn became physically and symbolically linked to the visual and architectural order of the house. While many farming regions in America reorganized and dressed up their agricultural building in the nineteenth century, no other region so consciously unified and balanced what had previously been held physically and conceptually separate and unequal—the house and the barn. The reasons for this unusual extension of architectural order and unity to house and barn (in terms of the vast majority of American farmers) must finally be attributed to a strong collective sanction of farm self-improvement, even overachievement, and reform. This characteristic has consistently typified the New England enterprise, especially during this time of challenge to its very existence. In the face of this severe threat, Yankee farmers reformulated their traditionally ordered buildings into a powerful image of a shining classical dwelling. They did so because that was the image of reform in nineteenth-century New England, and the new connected farm was clearly intended to symbolize farm reform. Today even a casual observer is struck by the dynamic force of these rhythmic, unified compositions. It took an undauntable collective will to improve the farm and to conduct such an optimistic building experiment in the face of a stiff struggle just to continue farming. Yet that is what they accomplished; and, for a while, they succeeded.

The decision to improve and reform the farm must finally be seen within an increasingly harsh context of historical and economic conditions that narrowed the options available to most New England farmers. Yet, within this tightening circle of opportunities, New England farmers had choices. They could have moved to more productive western lands or left the farm for southern New England factories (as many chose to do). They could have continued to farm and build modestly by merely continuing their previous practices, or by following the building examples of more prosperous agricultural regions of the country. But they did not choose these options. Instead, they chose to build forcefully, even courageously, by following their own regional customs and new reform ideas to produce a powerful architectural arrangement that was a testament to their determination to succeed at farming. The ultimate fate of these New England farmers was to be no different from that of small farmers in other areas of the country, but the dogged persistence of their labor and the grandeur of their dreams are still evident in the design of their farmsteads.

Notes

1 Appearance and Actuality

1. During lectures I have conducted at various Maine historical societies, over fifty elderly listeners indicated their familiarity with the verse. Most said it was a childhood rhyme. Charlotte Lawrence of Yarmouth, Maine, remembers the verse repeated to children's games. An old farmer from Greenwood, Maine, recalled a satirical version comparing playmate's farms. Richard Lunt, author of *The Maine Folklife Index*, was told the verse in the children's mate selection game, "She loves me, she loves me not."

2. No indigenous name for these structures has been recorded in literature or suggested by local inhabitants. Other studies have labeled them: "the New England connecting barn" (Zelinsky 1958, 540); "extended farmhouse groups of northern New England" (Keune and Replogle 1961, 38); "connected farm plan" (Glassie 1968, 186); and "continuous architecture" (Sloane 1974, 46).

3. Percentage figures throughout the book are derived from 120 measured and photographed farms in Maine and New Hampshire. Visits to over 400 farms and extensive travel by car throughout New England have corroborated these findings.

4. An article describing the efficiency of the connected farm building plan also states, "The interior is arranged for the comfort and convenience of the farm family. . . ." Maine, Board of Agriculture, *Second Annual Report of the Secretary, 1857*, 36. See also "Changing Attitudes toward Farm Building," Chapter 7, herein.

5. Clayton 1880, facing 220.

6. Although titled a county history, it was actually a record of some of the county's wealthiest families. The fifty-to-seventy-five dollar fee for a family history was beyond the resources of all but a few farmers. When asked to have their farms recorded, most, like Edwin Walker of Kennebunk, Maine, "declined to do so." Tobias Walker Diary, December 24, 1879.

7. Visits to many of the pictured farm-steads reveal that irregularities in buildings and landscape were frequently eliminated by the artist. For example, the ground surface and buildings on the Byron Kimball farm in figure 9 were represented as more uniform than they actually were in 1880.

8. Of the following sources, only Zelinsky's offers any analysis of connected farm buildings, and his findings differ from those of this study. Zelinsky 1958, 540–53; Arthur and Witney 1972, 142–46; Keune and Replogle 1961, 38–39; Sloane 1974; Walcott 1936, 233; Glassie 1968, 184–87; Hart 1975, 127.

9. *Cultivator*, June 1843, 96.

10. As, for example, Zelinsky 1958, 540–53; Keune and Replogle 1961, 38–39; and Walcott 1936, 233.

11. For example, an extensive exhibit of paintings entitled "The Landscape of Change: Views of Rural New England, 1790–1865" (Old Sturbridge Village, Sturbridge, Massachusetts, 1976) showed many examples of detached houses and barns including: *Golbe Village*, ca. 1822; *Franklin Ruggles' House*, Hardwick, Massachusetts, 1840; and *Farm Scene*, 1840–1850. The 1980 exhibit, "New England Prospect" (Currier Gallery of Art, Manchester, New Hampshire) included maps and prints depicting detached arrangements including: the David Ogden farm, Fairfield, Connecticut, 1769; the B. Perkins farm, Ipswich, Massachusetts, 1717; and the William Thompson farm, Chelsea, Massachusetts, 1753. Both exhibits also included early examples of pre-1820 connected structures, but most were town houses or larger country estates. Common farms before 1820 were shown in a separated house and barn plan. Other scenes or accounts of the detached tradition can be found in wills: John Robinson, Paris, Maine (copy recorded in the courthouse, South Paris, Maine); samplers (Krueger 1978, 36, fig. 73); and diaries (see Tobias Walker farm account in Chapter 6).

12. Garvan 1951, 112.

13. Kimball 1950, 53–61.

14. Kimball 1950, 58, 75–81; Pal-ladio 1738, 46–59, plates 29–51.

15. Robinson 1976, 17–20, 24–31.

16. Kimball 1950, 59–60. Farms and rural retreats with attached wings were frequently shown in the early 1800s, as in Gandy 1805, plates 28, 30; and later Loudon 1836, 354–75, 540–66.

17. Most studies of English vernacular farm architecture reveal these incremental traditions, as in Harvey 1970, 92; Brunskill 1970, 134–37; Peters 1969, 51–53.

18. Eaton 1874, 8.

19. Harvey 1970, 54–55.

20. Addy 1905, 207–10.

21. Barley 1961, 4–5, 15; Garvan 1951, 111.

22. The late eighteenth- and nine-teenth-century development of the common English farmstead is extremely complex, but a common arrangement was a U-shaped courtyard design with detached house. Peters 1969, 50–51.

23. The outer boundary of connected farms in figure 18 is based upon a map by Zelinsky (1958, 543). Density zones were compiled from fieldwork by the author.

24. Fitchen 1968.

25. For example, the English farmers of central Virginia. Glassie, *Folk Housing*, 1975, 143–45.

26. The particularly New England contribution to the development of the western states is more difficult to distinguish than, for example, German influence, but it was profound. See, for example, Holbrook 1950; Roos 1937, 41–49; Hamlin 1944, 258–60.

27. For example, Glassie 1968, 8–12, 35; Kniffen 1960, 22. In fact, the ethnic retention of characteristic house forms allows historians to track the diffusion of particular groups, as in Raitz 1975. No regional architectural study or farm inventory has revealed the presence of the connected farm organization in any of the northern tier of states heavily settled by emigrant New England farmers, as, for example, Glassie 1974.

28. Jacobs 1970, 93–105; Schmidt 1975, plates 2–12, 23; and the author's travel by car through western New York State.

29. The hardships of New England farming were continually emphasized by western speculators (Holbrook 1950, 13–26) and recognized by supporters of New England's agricultural interest (Greenleaf 1816, 69, 139, 142).

30. Wilson 1967, 56–66.

31. Dole 1964, 202–6.

32. d'Entremont 1972, 24–25.

33. Arthur and Witney 1972, 115–42.

34. The early exodus from Connecticut has been particularly well recorded, as, for example, by Olmsted 1859, 7–16; Rosenberry 1934, 1–7; Purcell 1918, 140–49.

35. Nineteenth-century New England agriculturalists strongly felt that industrialization had a negative effect on agriculture, for example, Henry Colman 1838, 13–14. Agricultural historians have agreed with this assessment. Pabst 1940–41, 111–13; Clive Day 1935, 6–7, 28–30; Olson 1935, 17–25.

36. Lockridge 1974, 13, 76–79; Winston 1930, 9–13, 16–17.

37. The homogeneity of rural New England stands in sharp contrast to the ethnic diversity of other agricultural regions in the North and West, as, for example, southeastern Pennsylvania. Lemon 1972, 43–51.

38. Gould P. Colman links a farmer's willingness to accept new ideas with the presence of innovators in a farm community (Colman 1968, 174–75, 187). It is hypothesized here that one of the factors that sustained rural New England homogeneity was that both innovators and followers all came from the same English cultural background and that even innovation took on a particular New England character.

39. For one of the finest statements outlining the problems of popular architectural study see Glassie, *Folk Housing*, 1975, 1–18.

2 The Buildings

1. The Smith house raising is recorded in the William Walker Diary, May 9, 1877 and cited in family records belonging to Anna Smith LeBlanc, 1980.

2. In 1800 Timothy Dwight, president of Yale College, used the term to describe a uniform house type found on Cape Cod (Dwight 1821, III, 97). Although today the term is imprecisely applied to a wide variety of one-story colonial houses, it appropriately describes a low-posted, center-chimney, two-rooms-deep house found on Cape Cod and throughout New England (Connally 1960, 47–56). In West Bridgton, Maine, 25 percent of the pre-1900 farm dwellings are Cape Cod houses, and this percentage is generally consistent throughout much of rural New England.

3. In the surveyed farm neighborhoods of southwestern Maine, 75 percent of all post-1850 dwellings were variations of the side-hall Greek Revival house type.

4. Various New England house type classification systems are found in Cummings 1979, 22–39; Connally 1960, 49–53; Glassie 1968, 124–31; Candee 1969, 105; and Garvan 1951, 116–24.

5. The English source of the one-room-deep house is described in Cummings 1979, 3–17; and Garvan 1951, 120, 149.

6. Various interpretations of the England/New England development of the saltbox house have been offered by Glassie 1982, 767; Garvan 1951, 116–21; and Cummings 1979, 31.

7. The development of two-rooms-deep houses is described in Candee 1976, 41; Cummings 1979, 41; and Glassie 1982, 767.

8. Candee 1976, 41. See also Chapter 2, n. 2 above.

9. The usage of the farm parlor is described in Cummings 1950, 78; Ulrich 1980, 35–36; and Cummings 1979, 28.

10. Beard 1976, revised 1981, 4–9; Tolles 1979, xx–xxii.

11. *The History of Waterford*, 1879, 72.

12. Cummings 1979, 22–27.

13. The practice of locating a kitchen in an attached ell appears to have become popular for all levels of society at the beginning of the nineteenth century. In North Yarmouth, Maine, it was not popularly established until after 1800, as in the Staples-Hill house, ca. 1801.

14. A commercial building with its major gable and doorway toward the road was a common early 1800 structure in the small towns of New England. Some examples are located around the town common of Sturbridge, Massachusetts.

15. Sources and documentation for the Hamilton house analysis are filed at the North Yarmouth Historical Society archives, and include measured architectural drawings, detailed field notes, photographs, population and agriculture census returns, deed and title search from 1790, and tax returns from 1810.

16. English vernacular structures employing a major side wall are shown in Innocent 1916, 73–90.

17. The seventeenth century development is described in Cummings 1979, 98–100. Although England has no equivalent major-rafter, minor-purlin system as developed in New England, various minor-purlin systems have long been employed (see, for example, Peters 1969, 221–23). Therefore English precedent provides a broad source for the development of the major-rafter, minor-purlin system.

18. The rapid development of the New England house cellar is described in Cummings 1979, 29–30.

19. William Walker Diary, December 3, 1849.

20. Stachiw 1980, 39.

21. Many characteristics of the modern balloon frame (Handlin 1979, 44; and Fitch 1973, 121) were introduced by early nineteenth-century New England framers before 1830. These innovations included the standardization and modularization of plan measurements, structural members, and elaborate joints of the ancient mortise-and-tenon system.

22. The term *little house* was used in a nineteenth-century farm diary to describe the kitchen ell. Tobias Walker Diary, August 18, 1831.

23. The popularity of the half-house is cited in Garvan 1951, 127–28; and Candee 1976, 21, 39, 41.

24. A farm sale advertisement of 1849 described the dwelling as "a large one-story double house" (*Maine Farmer*, January 11, 1849, 3). The term *double house* has also been used by architectural historians to describe a symmetrically divided center-door house (for example, Candee 1969, 105; and Connally 1960, 50).

25. Nineteenth-century town histories frequently cite the small half-house as the first permanent (framed) structure, as in Clayton 1880, 221 and facing 229; Corliss 1877–1885, reprint 1977, 1136; and Lapham 1886, 55. Where the earliest house type is known, 25 percent of the surveyed farms had a half-house as the first permanent structure.

26. For example, in Cummings 1966, 34, and in the ell of the David Trickey house, North Yarmouth, Maine.

27. The most common half-house plans in the survey areas of southwestern Maine measured 16 feet by 19 feet and 18 feet by 20 feet. Typical examples contained six slightly flared gunstock posts and a major-rafter, minor-purlin roof framing system.

28. The Acts and Resolves of the Province of Massachusetts Bay, 1761–64, XVII, 175. This standardized house

plan specification was a typical requirement of many eighteenth-century Massachusetts land grants, as observed by Clark 1970, 193–94.

29. Maine, Board of Agriculture, *Twelfth Annual Report of the Secretary, 1867*, 30.

30. Henry Glassie develops this general idea in his study of central Virginia folk housing (Glassie, *Folk Housing*, 1975, 134–36). John Kouwenhoven has observed that the modular building system is a particularly American technological development (Kouwenhoven 1948, 79–93).

31. Tobias Walker Diary, April 27, 1840.

32. The term *back house* was a common designation for English domestic outbuildings in the sixteenth and seventeenth centuries. Skeat and Britten 1879, 58.

33. In the Alewive neighborhood of Kennebunk, Maine, the earliest dated New England barn type was built in 1833. By 1850 all new barns were built in this new gable-door arrangement. Tobias Walker Diary, 1828–93.

34. Glassie 1974, 182.

35. Garvan 1951, 111, 112; and Glassie 1974, 182.

36. The American combination of the hay and cow barn is described in Hart 1975, 124–28.

37. Deane 1790, 17–18.

38. Older agricultural areas of southern New England, such as Topsfield, Massachusetts, have approximately equal numbers of English and New England barns. It is rare, however, to find an area in northern New England with densities of older English barns over 20 percent. In the survey areas of southwestern Maine, only 5 percent of the existing barns were side-door English barns.

39. Innocent 1916, 77.

40. Data obtained from John Mott, agricultural interpreter, Old Sturbridge Village Research Department, 1979. After 1875 the major-purlin, common-rafter system began to be adopted in areas of eastern New England; for example, the Nevers-Bennett farm, Sweden, Maine. It is unusual to find a common-rafter barn built in this region before 1875. Such a rare example is the Nutting barn of Otisfield, Maine, built ca. 1825.

41. Barn cellars were recommended by Henry Colman 1838, 80; and *New England Farmer*, October 9, 1824, 81.

42. *Maine Farmer*, January 4, 1840, 412.

43. Various gable-door barns are shown in Arthur and Witney 1972, 59–84; and Glassie 1974, 182.

44. In only five of eighty New England barns were the two side bays equal in width, thus producing a centered barn door. All five were built after 1890.

45. A comparison of barn bay widths throughout the nineteenth century shows that the sizing of the haymow and cow tie-up bays became more uniform toward 1900. For example, the 10 feet, 12 feet, 16 feet front bay ratio of the Carlson barn, Harrison, Maine, ca. 1830 was typical of the early 1800s barn, and the 13 feet, 12 feet, 13 feet front bay ratio of the Johnson barn, Denmark, Maine, ca. 1890 was typical of the late 1800s barn.

46. The roofs of five balloon-framed gambrel barns observed for this study were placed on traditional mortise-and-tenon, heavy-timbered walls.

47. An 1824 article titled "On the Construction of Barns and Stables, Etc." describes windows over the barn door as if they were a new, innovative feature. "There were twelve squares of glass arranged over the door to admit the light when the large doors were shut." *New England Farmer*, October 9, 1824, 18.

48. An article in 1838 criticized the common practice of clapboarding and painting only the front sides of houses and barns. *Maine Farmer*, September 25, 1838, 257.

49. *Cultivator*, June, 1847, 185.

50. Maine, Board of Agriculture, *Third Annual Report of the Secretary, 1858*, 1859, 53–56.

51. Brunskill 1970, 138–53; and Chapin 1981, 25.

52. The popularity of oxen is described by Russell, 1976, 357; and Bidwell and Falconer 1925, 404. Articles comparing the merits of oxen versus horses were common after 1840, for example *Maine Farmer*, March 7, 1840, 68; and Maine, Board of Agriculture, *Second Annual Report of the Secretary, 1857*, 1859, 53–56.

53. Clarence Day 1954, 103–6, 187; Howard Russell 1976, 351–53; and Bidwell and Falconer 1925, 110, 406–11.

54. Clarence Day 1954, 141; and Rutman 1967, 54.

55. Maine, Board of Agriculture, *Second Annual Report of the Secretary, 1857*, 1858, 170–71.

56. Howard Russell 1976, 509–10.

57. Although separate corncribs are recorded in the early 1800s (Howard Russell 1976, 367), most existing corncribs with distinctive slanted walls like the one shown in figure 51 were constructed after the Civil War.

58. These regulations came into force in the 1930s. Clarence Day 1963, 69.

59. Bidwell and Falconer 1925, 243. An early apple barn, ca. 1860, is located on the Dawes-Denison farm, Harrison, Maine.

60. Early silo development in New England is described in Russell 1976, 441; Maine, Board of Agriculture, *Twenty-Fourth Annual Report of the Secretary, 1880*, 13–25; and Noble 1981, 11–12.

61. The English practice of building field barns is described in Brunskill 1970, 151.

62. "Ten-footers" are described in Hunter 1980, 134, but the term does not appear to have been used before 1900.

63. Icehouse construction is outlined in *Maine Farmer*, August 29, 1840, 265 and January 11, 1849, 1.

3 The Buildings and the Land

1. *Maine Farmer*, September 2, 1829.

2. Maine, Board of Agriculture, *Twenty-Second Annual Report of the Secretary, 1877*, 97.

3. Cobbett 1819, 13.

4. Glassie 1972, 271–79; J. B. Jackson 1951, 3–7; and Glassie, *Folk Housing*, 1975, 158–71. Of these sources, Henry Glassie's *Folk Housing in Middle Virginia* contains the most forceful interpretation of the antinaturalistic/functionalist American folk aesthetic.

5. Stilgoe 1982, 164–65; and Favretti and Favretti 1978, 11–25.

6. Stilgoe 1982, 168.

7. For example, the overmantel painting from the Hathaway house, South Paris, Maine, used on posters and brochures for the exhibit "Maine at Statehood, the Forgotten Years—1783 to 1820," 1983.

8. William Walker Diary, November 27, 1856.

9. Emmet 1981, 8.

10. Stilgoe 1982, 168. In 1875 a maple tree was planted in front of the Nutting farm, Otisfield, Maine, to mark the birth of Silas Dexter Nutting.

11. William Walker Diary, May 12, 1858.

12. Stilgoe 1982, 25.

13. The relationship between the physical and moral order of the farmstead was one of the most consistent themes of the mid nineteenth-century farm literature, for example, *Maine*

Farmer, December 1839, 385.

14. Cobbett 1819, 319.

15. Deane 1790, 18.

16. Ibid., 69–70. This advice was repeated in the *Maine Farmer*, April 24, 1841, 126.

17. Various supplementary crops included broomcorn, tobacco, onions, seeds, hay, silk, nuts, and market vegetables. Howard Russell 1976, 373–83.

18. For example, Deane 1790, 70.

19. The four-field system reflects the Von Thünen model of agricultural productivity. Chisholm 1964, 21–22, 33.

20. Deane 1790, 70.

21. William Walker Diary, May 7, 1858.

22. The idea of a "systematic rotation of crops" was foreign to a group of Maine's leading farmers at a meeting in 1858. Most farmers rotated their crops only when fields became exhausted. Maine, Board of Agriculture, *Second Annual Report of the Secretary, 1857*, 1858, 76–77.

23. Howard Russell 1976, 37.

24. Atherton 1820, 21.

25. As described in *The Farm and Household Cyclopaedia*, 1885, 27.

26. Wagner 1971, 118.

27. Wilson 1967, 125; and Satterthwaite 1976, 27. Throughout the survey region of southwestern Maine, the overwhelming choice for farm sites was along the upper ridges of gently sloping hills. Ingalls Hill Road in Bridgton, Maine, is a typical example of this settlement pattern.

4 **Permanence and Change**

1. The data for the Nutting farmstead analysis was based upon six site visits and interviews with Mr. and Mrs. Albert D. Nutting between 1979 and 1982. Sources and documentation include measured architectural drawings, photographs, agricultural and population census records, deed and title search from 1780, and family papers in the Nuttings' possession.

2. New England log dwellings are described in Coffin 1855, 87; Candee 1976, 27–37; and Noyes 1852, 29.

3. No other barns in the surrounding area are known to have employed this structural system. See Chapter 2, n. 40.

4. As a general rule early nineteenth-century New England barn roofs were low-angled and were gradually steepened throughout the century.

5. *New England Farmer*, October 9, 1924, 82.

6. The decline in New England wheat production is described by Bidwell and Falconer 1925, 324; and Howard Russell 1976, 334–35.

7. Domestic reform literature in the second half of the nineteenth century emphasized the necessity for a distinction between food preparation areas and dining areas (Handlin 1979, 56, 375–77, 406). American and European folk traditions had long maintained a unity of the food preparation and eating areas (Glassie 1982, 382).

8. The sources and documentation for the Bacon farm analysis are filed at the North Yarmouth Historical Society archives and include measured architectural drawings of the entire complex, detailed field notes, photographs, population and agricultural census returns, deed and title search from 1780, tax returns from 1813 to 1900, and local interviews.

9. Maine, Board of Agriculture, *Eighteenth Annual Report of the Secretary*, 1873, 80.

10. *New England Farmer*, August 10, 1822, 12.

11. The anglophile idea of naming a farm after a feature of the natural landscape was practiced only after 1880, and then by a minority of farmers and gentlemen farmers.

12. The sources for the Nevers-Bennett farm analysis were derived from six site visits between 1978 and 1982 and three interviews with Charles M. Bennett, grandson of Charles W. Bennett, and include measured architectural drawings of the entire complex, detailed field notes, photographs, agricultural and population census returns, deed and title search from 1800, and local interviews.

13. Pike, n.d.

14. The sources and documentation for the Woodsum farm analysis were derived from five site visits between 1978 and 1982 and include measured architectural drawings of the entire complex, detailed field notes, photographs, farm and population census returns, deed and title search from 1800, and local interviews.

15. The present New England barn is constructed of sawn 8 inch by 8 inch structural members with a segmented plate construction (see fig. 45) typical of barns in the second half of the nineteenth century. Of the fifty-five New England barns documented for this study, only two large ones could be dated before 1840, and it is highly unlikely that

a common farmer like Benjamin Woodsum would have constructed his before 1850.

16. Russell 1976, 427.

5 **Pattern in Building and Farming**

1. Cummings 1958, revised 1974, 6; Connally 1960, 49. For example, the big house on the Samuel Nevers farmstead, Sweden, Maine, ca. 1790, faces south at a 45-degree angle to the road.

2. *Maine Farmer*, January 6, 1830.

3. The transition from a medieval-agrarian to modern-industrial social and technological orientation has been treated by various New England historians, for example, Richard Bushman 1967, 73–76, 107–19; Gross 1976, 75–79, 190–91; and Clive Day 1935, 28–30. Robert Gross has labeled this cultural reorientation an agricultural revolution (1982, 42), and his overall assessment of this profound reorientation experienced by nineteenth-century Massachusetts farmers is supported by the findings of this book.

4. Deane 1790, 102.

5. Vitruvius 1899, revised 1960, 183.

6. The various methods by which building practices are maintained and transformed within folk tradition are analyzed by Glassie, *Folk Housing*, 1975, 19–21, 34, 66–68.

7. A southward orientation for dwellings, therefore, links the pre-1830 houses of rural New England with the post-1970 solar-oriented houses.

8. For example, only a few of the early buildings shown on twenty town commons (Stilgoe 1982, 7–36) are oriented in a nonfrontal, nonrectilinear relationship with the geometry of the common and its roads.

9. As shown in Peters 1969, 48–59; and Brunskill 1970, 136–37.

10. The ability to manipulate independent portions of the architectural ensemble (the position of the barn) while maintaining the overall dependent arrangement (the connected building organization) is one of the primary methods by which folk designers achieve individuality within a traditional pattern of building. See also Glassie, *Folk Housing*, 1975, 38–40.

11. Maine, Board of Agriculture, *Second Annual Report of the Secretary, 1857*, 1858, 36.

12. The practice of separating house and barn has been consistent throughout the history of American agricultural development. Hart 1975, 127–36.

13. *Cultivator*, June 1843.

14. The practice of creating differentiated zones between uniform areas of a building is one of the most consistent architectural design strategies for achieving spatial variety, interest, and multiple interpretations. This strategy is analyzed by Cullen 1977, 97–142; and Kleinsasser 1982, 1–22.

15. Ulrich 1980, 27; Tryon 1917, 225–35.

16. Maine, Board of Agriculture, *Twelfth Annual Report of the Secretary*, 1867, 30.

17. The introduction of stoves in New England is described in Keep 1931, 70–87; and Edwin Jackson 1935–36, 55–56.

18. Between 1829 and 1835 a burst of stove patent activity marked the beginning of the popular ascendancy of the stove. Keep 1931, 87.

19. Cummings 1979, 37–38. See also Chapter 2, n. 13.

20. Forty percent of the 120 documented farms contained two kitchens within the connected building complex. In 12 farms there is evidence of simultaneous usage.

21. Cummings 1979, 31–33.

22. The introduction of modified balloon-framing techniques, coupled with the flexibility of multiple stove chimney placement, theoretically allowed New England builders a greater freedom of planning possibilities over the strictly organized center-chimney, heavy-timbered house. Yet it is interesting to note that New Englanders did not take advantage of these planning possibilities but quickly standardized the basic room organization of the side-hall, Greek Revival style house into a two-parlor arrangement. This basic plan was consistently produced throughout the second half of the nineteenth century. In this case, the availability of a wide variety of plan choices did not produce a wide variety of houses.

23. Rumford 1874–1875, reprint 1969, vol. 3, 91–122, 269–81.

24. Benjamin 1806, reprint 1972, plates 34, 36.

25. Advertisements for metal pumps appear in the second quarter of the nineteenth century, for example in the *Yankee Farmer*, March 20, 1841.

26. A wooden piping system was observed by the Reverend Paul Coffin at Sunday River, Maine, in 1796. Coffin 1855, 333.

27. Advertisements for hydraulic rams appear at mid-century, for example in the *Maine Farmer*, September 6, 1849, 1; and May 16, 1850, 1.

28. Fifty-five percent of the pre-1930 dwellings in the town center of Bridgton, Maine, are arranged in many variations of the basic three-part, connected town house design.

29. While an important factor for classifying high-style or architect-designed structures, the record of stylistic change has been shown to be insufficient for classifying folk architecture. Glassie, *Folk Housing*, 1975, 8–12, 71–75.

30. The strategy of studying the rules that guide architectural competence, as well as the product of that competence, has been championed by Henry Glassie. Glassie, *Folk Housing*, 1975, 19–40.

31. Ibid., 166.

32. *Maine Farmer*, September 25, 1838, 257.

33. The distinction between the monumentality of the public front and the nonmonumentality of the private back has been a consistent, if unstated, characteristic of urban and monumental buildings worldwide. Since the late 1960s architects have chosen to exploit the ambiguity and tension within this front/back relationship in the design of their buildings. Venturi 1966, 88.

34. For example, Beard 1976, revised 1981, 4–21.

35. The application of a limited vocabulary of classical styles to an understructure of vernacular architecture is cited in Garvan 1951, 123; Hitchcock 1969, 121; and Hamlin 1944, 163.

36. Hamlin 1944, 163–64.

37. Glassie, *Folk Housing*, 1975, 67–68.

38. Stilgoe 1982, 169.

39. Henry Glassie has observed that farmers in nineteenth-century central Virginia manipulated a sparse stylistic vocabulary according to a system of vernacular design strategies, including: frontality, bilateral symmetry, decoration subordinate to form, and various dialectical relationships such as inside/outside, public/private, and natural/man-made. Glassie, *Folk Housing*, 1975, 158–68.

40. As observed by Garvan 1951, 123; and Hamlin 1944, 163–64. Even when ornamentation from a nonclassical vocabulary was applied to common farmhouses, it was often detailed in a classical-vernacular style; for example, the Gothic dormer on the Woodsum house was trimmed with a modified Greek Revival cornice and painted white (see fig. 84). An analysis of contemporary popular housing confirms this fundamental bias toward unity, as in Hubka 1980, 70–71, and this is certainly the

historical vernacular bias, as in Glassie, *Folk Housing*, 1975, 120–22. Architects and designers have often acted in disregard of this popularly accepted idea, for example, Pile 1979, 139–40, and have consequently had little impact on the contemporary housing market.

42. Circular and multisided barns constructed throughout America in the second half of the nineteenth century are the product of a small minority of prosperous farmers who defied traditional building practices. See Arthur and Witney 1972, 146–171.

43. The isolation of northern and rural New England from ethnic migrations is demonstrated in maps in Zelinsky 1973, 28–33. Yankee cultural homogeneity did not, however, mean isolation with respect to new ideas about building and construction. Literature describing construction practices in other regions was widely circulated; for example, the description of a Pennsylvania barn in the *New England Farmer*, June 14, 1823, 361.

44. Weeden 1891, 804.

45. Horne 1963, 81–83; and Ellis and Millard, 1980, 26–27.

46. Most New England farmers interviewed for this study had moved buildings on their farms, and they frequently recalled that their fathers and grandfathers had also done so. Many, like Albert Mosher of Gorham, Maine, had moved buildings so many times that it was difficult for them to remember the precise sequence of placement. So ingrained was this custom in New England and throughout America that its frequency went largely unrecorded until European observers, like Frances Trollope, reacted with surprise at the ease and regularity of this phenomenon. Trollope 1832, reprinted 1927, 73.

47. Weeden 1891, 804.

48. Jefferson 1787, reprinted 1972, 133, 164–65; Tocqueville 1862, reprinted 1945, I, 63; 1945, II, 42–45, 148–50, 223–24.

49. This model for depicting permanence and change in the building system was inspired by Henry Glassie's description of the pattern of thought and motivation in the minds of folk designers. Glassie, *Folk Housing*, 1975, 160–63.

50. The variety of competing building systems is outlined in Candee 1976, 27, 37.

51. Kouwenhoven 1961, 62–75. It is this modified, heavy-timbered, mortise-and-tenon construction system that is described in Chapter 2, The Staples House.

52. This trend toward simplification

has been emphasized by Glassie 1974, 228; and Glassie, *Folk Housing*, 1975, 134, 135, 162. It is particularly evident in New England in a comparison of English barns of the early 1800s with the New England barns of the late 1800s; see Chapter 2, Barn.

53. *Work-rhythms* is the term that E. P. Thompson has used to describe the daily and seasonally timed activities of agrarian people (Thompson 1967, 57–58). The relationship between work and all phases of folk culture, including its art, has been a consistent theme in the work of Henry Glassie. Glassie 1982, 462, 469.

54. Tobias Walker Diary, April 10, 1849.

55. William Walker Diary, July 21, 1850.

56. Compiled from the years 1848 to 1852, Tobias Walker and William Walker Diaries.

57. The Tobias Walker Diary, 1828–93 and William Walker Diary, 1846–83 record a total of 130 house and barn raisings.

58. Although not typical, two women who maintained independent households are described in Ulrich 1980, 55–60; and Noyes 1852, 146.

59. In the twenty family histories compiled for this study, the nuclear family arrangement was selected by all parties when it was possible to do so. The factors of wealth and death, however, greatly restricted the ability to achieve this goal.

60. Mitchell 1978, 92–97.

61. Dwight 1821–22, III, 205; and Bidwell and Falconer 1925, 116.

62. The relationship between separate but mutually reinforcing gender work roles has been described by Thompson 1963, 291–96, 416.

63. *Maine Farmer*, June 17, 1829.

64. Tobias Walker Diary, April 13, 1855.

65. The importance of the New England town as a major political and social unit has been emphasized by Zuckerman 1978, 19–45; and Danhof 1969, 132–33.

66. The sixty-five-year Tobias Walker Diary reveals that he and his sons consistently cooperated with a group of fifteen to twenty families within the Alewive neighborhood of Kennebunk, Maine.

67. Powell 1963, 14–18; and Blum 1971, 164–66.

68. The 1840 and 1871 maps of school districts in Bridgton, Maine, closely reflect the changes in neighborhood organization between the two periods. Shorey 1974, 225–34.

69. The organization of an English road district is described in Powell 1965, 31.

70. By far the most common type of work exchange between neighbors was a direct labor exchange, or "changing work."

71. The English tradition of mutuality involving elaborate traditions of communal assistance and mutual cooperation has been analyzed by Thompson 1963, 234–40, 423–30, 732–39.

72. Each of these neighborhood craftspeople was hired by Tobias Walker between 1830 and 1860.

73. Spurr 1944, 603.

74. In the nineteenth century, the New England burying ground was transformed from a place symbolizing death to a place symbolizing beauty and pastoral life, as outlined by Stilgoe 1982, 228–30. The change from the colonial church burying ground to the neighborhood burying ground and finally to the late nineteenth-century town burying ground has not received sufficient investigation. The history of many rural New England towns will substantiate this hypothesis, for example, Bridgton, Maine. Shorey 1974, 460–65.

75. Beam 1957, 20.

76. The term *mutuality* has been emphasized by E. P. Thompson in his analysis of the cooperative traditions of the English working classes (1963, 17–22).

77. The Yankee balance between individualism and social responsibility has been analyzed by such diverse writers as Beam 1957, 162–63; Lockridge 1974, 191–97; and Zuckerman 1978, 48–50.

6 Tobias Walker Moves His Shed

1. Sources for the Tobias Walker farm analysis were derived from the Tobias Walker Diary, Maine Historical Society Library, the William Walker Diary, Mr. and Mrs. Robert Walker, and five site visits and interviews with Mr. and Mrs. Warren Morse, present owners of the Tobias Walker farm. Additional sources and documentation include measured architectural drawings of the entire building complex, detailed field notes, photographs, agricultural and population census returns, deed and title search to 1770, Kennebunk Town Records, 1820–60, and local interviews. Similar sources were used to reconstruct the building and social histories of thirty farmsteads that comprised the Alewive neighborhood where the Walker farm is located.

2. Remich 1911, 126.

3. The rapid turnover in pioneer land settlement has been noted by Candee 1969, 67; Wagner 1971, 9; and Clarence Day 1954, 75.

4. Remich 1911, 126.

5. Noyes 1852, 25.

6. Almost half of the 800 individual buildings investigated for this study were made from some building materials (usually structural members) from earlier structures.

7. Eliphalet Walker is described as a tanner by Remich 1911, 126. Tobias Walker continued the tanning business and employed a yearly average of three apprentices and day laborers until he went out of business in 1844.

8. Tobias Walker Diary, November 29, 1829; June 11, 1831; September 5 and 8, 1831.

9. Ibid., September 29, 1828.

10. Ibid., May 26 and 27, 1831.

11. As also described in Cummings 1966, 94.

12. Tobias Walker described this three-part division by naming each of the three parts. Tobias Walker Diary, May 26, 1831.

13. Clarence Day 1954, 145.

14. Tobias Walker Diary, June 7, 1836.

15. Maine, Board of Agriculture, *Second Annual Report of the Secretary, 1857*, 1858, 91–93.

16. Tobias Walker Diary, December 31, 1834.

17. Ibid., May 15 and 30, 1838.

18. Previously the hogs had been housed under the barn.

19. There is no direct evidence of Tobias Walker's newspaper subscriptions, but circumstantial evidence suggests that he did refer to farm journals, for example: his son, Edwin, formed a New York Tribune (a leading farm information paper) club (Tobias Walker Diary, December 31, 1860); he sold 190 lbs. of old paper to a peddler in 1863 (ibid., May 18, 1863); and his thirty-seven-year contribution to the diary attests to his commitment to literacy and a concern for education, which would have made his subscribing to one of many New England farm journals very likely.

20. Ibid., August 22, 1840.

21. As recommended in Deane 1790, 18; and the *New England Farmer*, October 9, 1824.

22. During the thirty-seven years To-

bias Walker kept his diary, he recorded more than one trip per week into the villages of Kennebunk and Kennebunkport, and his typical route took him past a wide variety of some of the finest dwellings in southern Maine.

23. Benjamin 1830, reprint 1972, plate 28.

24. Seth Emmons had his house frame raised in 1840 (Tobias Walker Diary, May 30, 1840) and the stairway was probably constructed at that time.

25. Ibid., September 27, 1842.

26. The popular misconception that average farmers designed, built, and detailed their houses and barns has found support in various publications including Alexander 1964, 46–54; and Rudofsky 1964, preface. Yet nearly every detailed study of American vernacular architecture has revealed the presence of skilled craftsmen-builders behind the design and building of most vernacular structures; for example, Cummings 1979, 40–51.

27. Cummings 1966, 94. Tobias Walker hired different master builders for his house and barn construction projects and so did his son, William, when he built a new house and a new barn.

28. Tobias Walker Diary, April 27, 1840.

29. Ibid., November 30, 1840.

30. Ibid., September 8, 1843.

31. Ibid., March 27, 1850.

32. Ibid., April 11, 1850.

33. The traditions by which folk peoples develop and pass on planning decisions have been described as "unselfconscious," (Alexander 1964, 29–55), but the full complexity by which this process achieves individual choice within tradition has only recently been explored. Glassie 1977, 1–44; and Glassie, *Folk Housing*, 1975, 19–40.

34. For example, Maine, Board of Agriculture, *Second Annual Report of the Secretary, 1857*, 1858, 26–38.

35. Amasa Walker 1852, 56–59.

36. The terms *long floor* to describe a New England type barn and *short floor* for an English barn have been used by older farmers, such as Albert Nutting of Otisfield, Maine.

37. Tobias Walker Diary, November 29, 1850.

38. Ibid., May 31, 1852.

39. Ibid., June 2, 1852.

40. Maine, Board of Agriculture, *Third Annual Report of the Secretary, 1858*, 1859, 53.

41. Tobias Walker Diary, June 3, 1852.

42. Ibid., June 7, 1852.

43. Ibid., July 13, 1852.

44. Ibid., September 26, 1853.

45. Ibid., June 10, 1851.

46. Ibid., April 29, 1852.

47. Ibid., May 28, 1842.

48. The development of New England tanning and shoemaking industries is described in Watkins 1961, 108; and Leblanc 1969, 60–71.

49. Tobias Walker Diary, April 25, 1851.

50. Ibid., March 22, 1877.

51. Ibid., October 2, 1851.

52. *Yankee Farmer*, March 20, 1841, 95.

53. Deeds: Book 237, p. 69, York County Court House, Alfred, Maine.

54. Tobias Walker Diary, June 10, 1863.

55. *Maine Farmer*, January 11, 1849, 1.

56. Tobias Walker Diary, June 27, 1893.

7 Why Tobias Walker Moved His Shed

1. *New England Farmer*, October 9, 1824, 81.

2. Deane 1790, 21–23.

3. *New England Farmer*, October 9, 1824, 82.

4. Ibid., June 14, 1823, 361.

5. Hart 1975, 128; and Deane 1790, 21.

6. Maine, State Agricultural Society, *Report of the Secretary, 1855*, 1859, 28.

7. A typical endorsement for barn cellars appeared in *Maine Farmer*, January 4, 1840, 412.

8. Maine, Board of Agriculture, *Second Annual Report of the Secretary, 1857*, 1858, 164.

9. Agricultural writers recommended a south-facing house as late as 1830, for example, *Maine Farmer*, January 6, 1830.

10. *New England Farmer*, August 10, 1822, 12.

11. Ibid., June 7, 1823, 353–54.

12. *Maine Farmer*, November 16, 1839, 346.

13. Various types of connected farm buildings occur throughout the long history of English farming. Brunskill 1970, 136–37; and Harvey 1970, 76–82.

14. Maine, Board of Agriculture, *Third Annual Report of the Secretary, 1858*, 1859, 52.

15. Maine, Board of Agriculture, *Second Annual Report of the Secretary, 1857*, 1858, 36–38.

16. Black 1950, 36–38.

17. Smith et al. 1982, 182–86; Barron 1982, 205–8.

18. Jorgensen 1977, 78–80.

19. Frederic 1979, 3–4.

20. Charles Clark 1970, 174; Wagner 1971, 9; and Richard Candee 1969, 67.

21. Howard Russell 1976, 112–24.

22. Many factors contributed to the inability of New England farmers to adopt modern technological methods, as described in Wilson 1967, 124–32.

23. Richard M. Candee 1976, 21–27.

24. Struik 1948, 237–38; and Leblanc 1969, 30–35.

25. Greenleaf 1829, 143–53.

26. Agricultural writers lamented the half-lumbering and half-agricultural practices of many New England farmers because they were aware of the long-term disadvantages of this system (*Maine Farmer*, July 3, 1838, 163). But for the majority who farmed, it was the only viable method.

27. Clarence Day 1954 and 1963.

28. By focusing on a decreasing number of successful farms, it is possible to show that New England farmers made substantial gains in their overall production and standard of living throughout the nineteenth century. Munyon 1978.

29. From a high point in 1880, the number of farms in New England has dropped steadily during each census year. Black 1950, 250–269.

30. Clarence Day 1954, 155–60; Raup 1966, 4–6; and Wilson 1967, 56–66.

31. Howard Russell 1976, 352–54; Clarence Day 1954, 103–6, 187.

32. Howard Russell 1976, 325–341.

33. Ibid., 437–44; Wilson 1967, 184–85; and Munyon 1978, 83–84.

34. Howard Russell 1976, 366–73.

35. New England farmers were repeatedly advised to grow a single cash crop, but with few exceptions they were unable to do so. *Maine Farmer*, July 3, 1838, 163.

36. During the nineteenth century the term *mixed farming* (or *mixed husbandry*) was used to describe both the most positive characteristics (United States, Commissioner of Agriculture, *Report for the Year 1870*, 1871, 260) and the most negative characteristics (Maine, Board of Agriculture, *Sixth Annual Report of the Secretary, 1861*, 87–88) of the diversified farming system.

37. United States, Commissioner of Agriculture, *Report for the Year 1870*, 1871, 260.

38. Bidwell and Falconer 1925, 437–39.

39. Clarence Day 1976, 302–7.

40. Maine, Board of Agriculture, *Eighteenth Annual Report of the Secretary, 1873*, 3.

41. *Maine Farmer*, February 12, 1836, 12.

42. Wagner 1971, 44. Almost one-third of William Walker's farm income between 1849 and 1853 was generated from lumbering activity, which was usually conducted in the winter. William Walker Diary, 1849–53.

43. *Maine Farmer*, August 10, 1839, 236.

44. Carter 1977, 24.

45. Cummings 1950, 81–84; Wilson 1967, 30; and Tryon 1917, 145.

46. Tryon 1917, 243–46.

47. Of the twenty farm family incomes investigated for this study, none achieved substantial economic growth without a major nonfarming source of income, of which lumbering and home industries were the most important.

48. Between 1790 and 1820 southern New England farmers experienced the first major impact of industrialization in America. Clive Day 1935, 6–20.

49. Henry Glassie's definition of building context includes two components: a particularistic context of physical setting, and an abstract context of ideas that surround and give meaning to the physical setting. Glassie, *Folk Housing*, 1975, 114–15.

50. The individual and collective motivation behind decision making in a folk or popular culture has been investigated by Henry Glassie (1977).

51. Tobias Walker Diary, September 4, 1869.

52. Maine, Board of Agriculture, *Third Annual Report of the Secretary, 1858*, 42.

53. Miller 1953, 396–416; and Bercovitch 1977, 15–34, 136–38.

54. May 1976, 153–55, 181–84.

55. Geertz 1973, 110–13.

56. McLoughlin 1978, 112–15.

57. Hart 1975, 115–36.

58. Marx 1964, 203–9; and Boorstin 1978, 37–48.

59. Holbrook, 1950, 313–35.

60. Kasson 1976, 3–5.

61. Kouwenhoven 1948, 15.

62. Howard Jones 1964, 214; Hamlin 1944, 3–6.

63. Howard Jones 1964, 252–55.

64. Honour 1968, 126; and Marx 1964, 126–29.

65. *Yankee Farmer*, August 14, 1841, 257; and Marti 1979, 201.

66. Cha's. The'o. Russell 1850, 9.

67. The William Lord house is one of the many that line Summer Street in Kennebunk, Maine, and that display various interpretations of the Federal and Greek Revival styles.

68. Hart 1975, 115–36.

69. *Maine Farmer*, November 16, 1839, 346.

70. Nineteenth-century agriculturalists combined functional and aesthetic characteristics into a uniform, quasi-religious appeal for farm improvements. The message of beauty and convenience is one of the most frequently used themes of mid nineteenth-century agricultural literature; for example, the *Maine Farmer*, November 16, 1839, 346.

71. Gandy, *Designs for Cottages*, 1805, iii.

72. References to classical literature and myths appear regularly in nineteenth-century New England agricultural literature. For example, in an article criticizing the building of large, wasteful farmhouses, a writer cites Socrates' preference for intimate rooms and tasteful scale in a general appeal for neatness and orderliness on the farmstead. *Maine Farmer*, September 23, 1829.

73. Glassie, *Folk Housing*, 1975, 469.

74. Murphy 1978.

75. Stilgoe 1982, 27–30.

76. Williams 1975, 120–26; and Marx 1964, 93–96.

77. For example, Maine, Board of Agriculture, *Fourth Annual Report of the Secretary, 1859*, 229.

78. *Eastern Farmer*, April 14, 1842, 63.

79. Tobias Walker Diary, August 31–September 5, 1835.

80. Ibid., February 4, 1833.

81. The effects of liquor consumption and the temperance movements in Maine are described in John Abbott 1892, 540–44. Temperance debates were common in New England town meetings during the second quarter of the nineteenth century. Kennebunk Town Records, I, 1820–40, pp. 161, 281.

82. McLoughlin 1978, 98–122.

83. Maine, Board of Agriculture, *Fourth Annual Report of the Secretary, 1859*, 56–57.

84. *Maine Farmer*, November 16, 1839, 348.

85. Maine, Board of Agriculture, *Fifteenth Annual Report of the Secretary, 1870*, 81.

86. Handlin 1979, 1–60.

Bibliography

Abbott, John S. C. *The History of Maine*. Portland: Brown Thurston, 1892.

Abbott, Richard H. "The Agricultural Press Views the Yeomen: 1819–1859." *Agricultural History* vol. XLII, no. 1 (Jan. 1968).

Acts and Resolves of the Province of the Massachusetts Bay, 1761–1764, vol. XVII. Boston: Wright and Potter, 1910.

Addy, Sidney Oldall. *The Evolution of the English House*. London: Swan Sonnenschein, 1905.

Alexander, Christopher. *Notes on the Synthesis of Form*. Cambridge, Mass.: Harvard University Press, 1964.

Andrews, Persis Sibley. Persis Sibley Andrews Journal. Maine Historical Society Library, Portland, Maine.

Armstrong, John Borden. *Factory Under the Elms*. Cambridge, Mass.: M.I.T. Press, 1969.

Arthur, Eric, and Witney, Dudley. *The Barn, A Vanishing Landmark in North America*. Greenwich, Conn.: New York Graphic Society, 1972.

Atherton, Charles H. *Address to the Hillsborough Agricultural Society*. Amherst, N.H.: Elijah Mansur, 1820.

Baier, Ursula, ed. *North Yarmouth, 1680–1980*. North Yarmouth, Maine: North Yarmouth Historical Society, 1980.

Barley, M. W. *The English Farmhouse and Cottage*. London: Routledge and Kegan Paul, 1961.

Barron, William R. "Eighteenth-Century New England Climate Variation and its Suggested Impact on Society." *Maine Historical Society Quarterly* vol. 21, no. 4 (Spring, 1982).

Bassett, T. D. Seymour. "The Cold Summer of 1816 in Vermont." In *The New England Galaxy*, edited by Roger Parks. Chester, Conn.: Globe Pequot Press, 1980.

Beam, Lura. *A Maine Hamlet*. New York: Wilfred Funk, 1957.

Beard, Frank A. *200 Years of Maine Housing*. 3d ed. rev. Augusta: Maine Historical Preservation Publications, 1981.

Benes, Peter. *The Masks of Orthodoxy*. Amherst: University of Massachusetts Press, 1977.

———, and Zimmerman, Phillip D. *New England Meeting House and Church: 1630–1850*. (No location) Boston University and Currier Gallery of Art, 1979.

Benjamin, Asher. *The American Builder's Companion*. 1806. Reprint. New York: Da Capo Press, 1972.

———. *The Practical House Carpenter*. 1830. Reprint. New York: Da Capo Press, 1972.

———. *Practice of Architecture*. 1833. Reprint. New York: Da Capo Press, 1972.

Bercovitch, Sacvan. *The American Jeremiad*. Madison: University of Wisconsin Press, 1978.

———. *The Puritan Origins of the American Self*. New Haven, Conn.: Yale University Press, 1977.

Berry, Wendell. *The Unsettling of America, Culture and Agriculture*. New York: Avon Books, 1977.

Bidwell, Percy Wells, and Falconer, John I. *History of Agriculture in the Northern United States, 1620–1860*. Washington, D.C.: Carnegie Institute of Washington, 1925.

Black, John Donald. *The Rural Economy of New England*. Cambridge, Mass.: Harvard University Press, 1950.

Blum, Jerome. "The European Village as Community: Origins and Function." *Agricultural History* vol. XLV, no. 3 (July 1971).

Boorstin, Daniel J. *The Americans*. New York: Random House, 1974.

———. *The Republic of Technology*. New York: Harper and Row, 1978.

Bouchard, Louis. *Traité des constructions rurales*. Paris: Librairie d'Agriculture et de Horticulture, 1866.

Bourne, Edward E. *The History of Wells and Kennebunk*. Portland, Maine: Thurston, 1875.

Bradbury, Charles. *History of Kennebunkport*. Kennebunk, Maine: James K. Remich, 1837.

Bradley, Robert L. *Maine's First Buildings*. Augusta: Maine Historical Preservation Commission Publications, 1978.

Bridges, William E. "Family Patterns and Social Values in America, 1825–1875." *American Quarterly* vol. XVII, no. 1 (Spring 1965).

Brooks, Van Wyck. *The Flowering of New England, 1815–1865*. New York: E. P. Dutton, 1936.

———. *New England: Indian Summer 1865–1915*. New York: E. P. Dutton, 1940.

Brunskill, R. W. *Illustrated Handbook of Vernacular Architecture*. London: Faber and Faber, 1970.

———. "Recording the Buildings of the Farmstead." *Transactions of the Ancient Monuments Society* vol. 21 (1976).

———. "A Systematic Procedure for Recording English Vernacular Architecture." *Transactions of the Ancient Monuments Society* vol. 13 (1965–66, abridged edition, 1975).

———. *Vernacular Architecture of the Lake Counties*. London: Faber and Faber, 1974.

Buist, Robert. *The Family Kitchen Garden.* New York: J. C. Rikes, 1849.

Bushman, Claudia L. *A Good Poor Man's Wife.* Hanover, N.H.: University Press of New England, 1981.

Bushman, Richard L. *From Puritan to Yankee.* Cambridge, Mass.: Harvard University Press, 1967.

Candage, R. G. F. *Historical Sketches of Bluehill, Maine.* Ellsworth, Maine: Hancock County Publishing, 1905.

Candee, Richard. "The Architecture of Maine's Settlement: Vernacular Architecture to About 1720." In *Maine Forms of American Architecture*, edited by Deborah Thompson. Camden, Maine: Downeast Magazine, 1976.

————. "A Documentary History of Plymouth Colony Architecture, 1620–1700." *Old-Time New England* vol. LIX, no. 3 (Jan.–Mar. 1969).

Cantor, Jay E. "The Landscape of Change: Rural Views of New England, 1790–1865." Slides of exhibit. Archives, Old Sturbridge Village, Sturbridge, Mass.

————. "The Landscape of Change: Views of Rural New England, 1790–1865." *Antiques* vol. 109 (Apr. 1976).

Carter, Timothy. Testimony before the Committee of Agriculture, House of Representatives, Washington, D.C. 1977. *Report on the Loss of Farmland.* Maine Environmental Network and Maine Council for the Humanities and Public Policy.

Chadbourne, Ava Harriet. *Maine Place Names.* Portland, Maine: Bond Wheelwright, 1955.

Chamberlain, Samuel. *Six New England Villages.* New York: Hastings House, 1948.

Chandler, Alfred D., Jr. *The Visible Hand.* Cambridge, Mass.: Harvard University Press, Belknap Press, 1977.

Chapin, R. Curtis. "The Early History and Federalization of the Codman House." Edited by Abbott Lowell Cummings. *Old-Time New England* vol. LXXI, no. 258 (1981).

Chisholm, Michael. *Rural Settlement and Land Use.* London: Hutchinson University Library, 1964.

Clark, Andrew Hill. "Suggestions for the Geographical Study of Agricultural Change in the United States, 1790–1840." *Agricultural History* vol. 46, no. 1 (Jan. 1972).

Clark, Charles E. *The Eastern Frontier.* New York: Alfred A. Knopf, 1970. Reprint. Hanover, N.H.: University Press of New England, 1983.

————. "History, Literature, and Belknap's Social Happiness." *Historical New Hampshire* vol. XXXV, no. 1 (Spring 1980).

————. *Maine, A Bicentennial History.* New York: W. W. Norton, 1977.

Clayton, W. Woodford. *A History of Cumberland County, Maine.* Philadelphia: Everts and Peck, 1880.

Cobbett, William. *A Year's Residence in the United States of America.* London: Sherwood, Neely, and Jones, 1819.

Coffin, Paul. *The Memoir and Journals of Rev. Paul Coffin, D.D.* Portland, Maine: B. Thurston, 1855.

Colman, Gould P. "Innovation and Diffusion in Agriculture." *Agricultural History* vol. XLII, no. 3 (July 1968).

Colman, Henry. *First Report on the Agriculture of Massachusetts, County of Essex, 1837.* Boston: Dutton and Wentworth, 1838.

————. *Second Report of the Agriculture of Massachusetts, County of Berkshire, 1838.* Boston: Dutton and Wentworth, 1839.

————. *Fourth Report of the Agriculture of Massachusetts, Counties of Franklin and Middlesex.* Boston: Dutton and Wentworth, 1841.

Connally, Ernest Allen. "The Cape Cod House: An Introductory Study." *Journal of the Society of Architectural Historians,* May 1960.

Coolidge, John. *Mill and Mansion.* New York: Columbia University Press, 1942.

Corliss, Augustus W. *Old Times of North Yarmouth.* 1877–1885. Reprint. Somersworth: New Hampshire Publishing, 1977.

Cullen, Gordon. *The Concise Townscape.* New York: Van Nostrand Reinhold, 1977.

Cummings, Abbott Lowell. *Architecture in Early New England.* Sturbridge, Mass.: Old Sturbridge Inc. 1958, revised 1974.

————. *The Framed Houses of Massachusetts Bay, 1625–1725.* Cambridge, Mass.: Harvard University Press, 1979.

————. "The House the Parson Built." *Old-Time New England* vol. LVI, no. 4 (Apr.–June 1966).

————. "Notes on Furnishing A Small New England Farmhouse." *Old-Time New England* vol. XLVIII, no. 3 (Jan.–Mar. 1950).

Cushing, John D. "Town Commons of New England, 1640–1840." *Old-Time New England* vol. LI, no. 3 (Jan.–Mar. 1961).

Dabney, John. *An Address to Farmers.* Newburyport, Mass.: Blunt and March, 1796.

Dalzell, Robert F., Jr. "The Rise of the Waltham-Lowell System and Some Thoughts on the Political Economy of Modernization in Ante-Bellum Massachusetts." *Perspectives in American History* vol. IX (1975).

Danhof, Clarence H. *Change in Agriculture: The Northern United States, 1820–1870.* Cambridge, Mass.: Harvard University Press, 1969.

Day, Clarence Albert. *A History of Maine Agriculture, 1604–1860.* Orono, Maine: University Press, 1954.

————. *Farming in Maine, 1860–1940.* Orono: University of Maine Press, 1963.

————. "The Humble Potato." In *A History of Maine,* edited by Ronald F. Banks. Dubuque, Iowa: Kendall/Hunt Publishing, 1976.

Day, Clive. "The Rise of Manufacturing in Connecticut 1820–1850." Tercentenary Commission of the State of Connecticut, pamphlet no. XLIV. New Haven, Conn.: Yale University Press, 1935.

Dean, G. A. *Essays on the Construction of Farm Buildings and Labourers' Cottages.* London: Simpkin, Marshall, 1849.

———. *Selected Designs of Country Residences*. London: Knight and Mardon, 1867.

Dean, William H. "Decay of Rural New England." *Saturday Review* LXX, London (Oct. 18, 1890).

Deane, Samuel. *The New England Farmer or Georgical Dictionary*. Worcester, Mass.: Isaiah Thomas, 1790.

Demos, John. *A Little Commonwealth*. London: Oxford University Press, 1970.

Dibner, Martin, ed. *Portland*. Portland, Maine: Greater Portland Landmarks, 1972.

Dole, Philip. "The Calef Farm: Region and Style in Oregon." *Journal of the Society of Architectural Historians* vol. XXIII, no. 4 (Dec. 1964).

———. "Farmhouse and Barn in Early Lane County." *Lane County Historian* vol. X, no. 2 (Aug. 1965).

———. "Farmhouses and Barns of the Willamette Valley." In *Space, Style and Structure: Building in Northwest America*. Portland: Oregon Historical Society, 1974.

Downing, A. J. *The Architecture of Country Houses*. 1850. Reprint. New York: Da Capo Press, 1968.

———. *Rural Essays*. New York: George A. Leavitt, 1853.

———. *A Treatise on the Theory and Practice of Landscape Gardening*. New York: Orange Judd Agricultural Book Publisher, 1865.

Dublin, Thomas. *Women at Work*. New York: Columbia University Press, 1979.

Durnin, Richard G. "A Town's District Schools: Then and Now." *Maine Life*, Dec. 1973.

Dwight, Timothy. *Travels in New England and New York*. 4 vols. New Haven: Timothy Dwight, 1821–22.

Eaton, Lilley. *Genealogical History of the Town of Reading*. Boston: A. Mudge and Son, 1874.

Ellis, Leola C., and Millard, Kera C. *Early Cornish (1666–1916)*. West Baldwin, Maine: Nelson's Print Shop, 1980.

Emerson, Ralph Waldo. "Self Reliance." In *Essays*. New York: Grosset and Dunlap (no date).

Emmet, Alan. "The Codman Estate—'The Grange': A Landscape Chronicle." *Old-Time New England* vol. LXXI (1981).

d'Entremont, Clarence. "The Acadians in New England." In *The French in New England, Acadia and Quebec*, edited by Edward Schriver. Orono, Maine: University of Maine, 1972.

The Farm and Household Cyclopaedia. New York: F. M. Lupton, 1885.

Favretti, Rudy J., and Favretti, Joy Putman. *Landscapes and Gardens for Historic Buildings*. Nashville, Tenn.: American Association for State and Local History, 1978.

Ferguson, Eugene S. "The American-ness of American Technology." *Technology and Culture* vol. 20, no. 1 (Jan. 1979).

Fessenden, Thomas G. *The Complete Farmer and Rural Economist*. Boston: Lilly, Wait; and George C. Barrett, 1834.

———. *The Complete Farmer and Rural Economist*. Boston: Otis, Broaders, 1840.

Festinger, Leon. *A Theory of Cognitive Dissonance*. Stanford, Calif.: Stanford University Press, 1957.

———, Riecken, Henry W., and Schachter, Stanley. *When Prophecy Fails*. Minneapolis: University of Minnesota Press, 1956.

Fitch, James Marston. *American Building*. New York: Schocken Books, 1973.

Fitchen, John. *The New World Dutch Barn*. Syracuse, N.Y.: Syracuse University Press, 1968.

Frederic, Paul B. "Post Civil War Intra-Town Population Movements in Central Maine." Paper read at the New England-St. Lawrence Valley Geographical Society, Newport, R.I., November 1979.

———. "Wealth and Poverty in Rural Maine: A Distribution and Management Problem." Paper read at the International Geographical Union Symposium on Rural Development, Fresno, Calif., April, 1981.

Fuess, Claude M., ed. *The Story of Essex County*, vol. I. Salem, Mass.: Essex Institute, 1935.

Gandy, Joseph. *Designs for Cottages, Cottage Farms and Other Rural Buildings*. London: John Harding, 1805.

———. *The Rural Architect; Consisting of Various Designs for Country Buildings Accompanied with Ground Plans, Estimates and Descriptions*. London: John Harding, 1805.

Gans, Herbert J. *Popular Culture and High Culture*. New York: Basic Books, 1974.

Garvan, Anthony N. B. *Architecture and Town Planning in Colonial Connecticut*. New Haven, Conn.: Yale University Press, 1951.

Gates, Paul W. *The Farmer's Age*. New York: Holt, Rinehart and Winston, 1960.

———. "Two Hundred Years of Farming in Gilsum." *Historical New Hampshire* vol. XXXIII, no. 1 (Spring 1978).

Gaustad, Edwin Scott. *The Great Awakening in New England*. New York: Harper Brothers, 1957.

Geertz, Clifford. *The Interpretation of Culture*. New York: Basic Books, 1973.

Ginzburg, Carlo. *The Cheese and the Worms*. Baltimore: Johns Hopkins University Press, 1980.

Glassie, Henry. "Barns Across Southern England: A Note on Transatlantic Comparison and Architectural Meaning." *Pioneer America* vol. VII, no. 1 (Jan. 1975).

———. "Folk Art." In *Folklore and Folklife: An Introduction*, edited by Richard M. Dorson. Chicago: University of Chicago Press, 1972.

———. *Folk Housing in Middle Virginia*. Knoxville, Tenn.: University of Tennessee Press, 1975.

———. "Meaningful Things and Appropriate Myths: The Artifact's Place in American Studies." In *Prospects*, vol. III, edited by Jack Salzman. New York: Burt Franklin, 1977.

———. *Passing the Time in Ballymenone*. Philadelphia: University of Pennsylvania Press, 1982.

———. *Pattern in the Material Folk Culture of the Eastern United States*. Philadelphia: University of Pennsylvania Press, 1968.

———. "The Variation of Concepts Within Tradition: Barn

Building in Otsego County, New York." *Geoscience and Man*, vol. 5 (June 10, 1974).

Gloag, John. *Mr. Loudon's England*. Newcastle upon Tyne: Oriel Press, 1970.

Greenleaf, Moses. *A Statistical View of the District of Maine*. Boston: Cummings and Hilliard, 1816.

———. *A Survey of the State of Maine*. Portland, Maine: Shirley and Hyde, 1829.

Gregor, Howard F. *Geography of Agriculture*. Englewood Cliffs, N.J.: Prentice-Hall, 1970.

Greven, Philip. *The Protestant Temperament*. New York: Meridian Books, 1979.

Greven, Philip J., Jr. *Four Generations: Population, Land, and the Family in Colonial Andover, Massachusetts*. Ithaca, N.Y.: Cornell University Press, 1977.

Griswold, A. Whitney. *Farming and Democracy*. New York: Harcourt, Brace, 1948.

Gross, Robert A. *The Minutemen and Their World*. New York: Hill and Wang, 1976.

———. "Culture and Cultivation: Agriculture and Society in Thoreau's Concord." *Journal of American History* vol. 69, no. 1 (June 1982).

Hall, Allan M. "The Shaker Response to Industrialism." Master's Thesis, University of Maine, Orono, 1979.

Halsted, Byron D. *Barn Plans and Outbuildings*. New York: Orange Judd, 1911.

Hamlin, Talbot. *Greek Revival Architecture in America*. London: Oxford University Press, 1944.

Handlin, David P. *The American Home*. Boston: Little, Brown, 1979.

Harris, Seymour E. *The Economics of New England*. Cambridge, Mass.: Harvard University Press, 1952.

Hart, John Fraser. *The Look of the Land*. Englewood Cliffs, N.J.: Prentice-Hall, 1975.

Hartt, Rollin Lynde. "New England, The National Wallflower." *Century* vol. XCII (1916).

Harvey, Nigel. *A History of Farm Buildings in England and Wales*. Newton Abbott, England: David and Charles, 1970.

Hawthorne, Nathaniel. *The House of the Seven Gables*. New York, New American Library, 1961.

The History of Waterford, Oxford County, Maine. Portland, Maine: Hoyt, Fogg, and Donham, 1879.

Hitchcock, Henry-Russell. *Architecture: Nineteenth and Twentieth Centuries*. Harmondsworth, England: Penguin Books, 1969.

Hoffman, Richard C. "Medieval Origins of the Common Fields." In *European Peasants and Their Markets*, edited by William N. Parker and Eric L. Jones. Princeton, N.J.: Princeton University Press, 1975.

Hofstadter, Richard. *The Age of Reform*. New York: Random House, 1955.

Holbrook, Stewart H. *The Yankee Exodus*. New York: Macmillan, 1950.

Holmes, E. *Transactions of the Agricultural Societies in the State of Maine 1850, 1851, 1852*. Augusta, Maine: William T. Johnson, 1853.

Honour, Hugh. *Neo-Classicism*. Harmondsworth, England: Penguin Books, 1968.

Horne, Ruth B. D. *Conway Through the Years and Whither*. Conway, N.H.: Conway Historical Society, 1963.

Hoskins, W. G. *The Midland Peasant*. London: Macmillan, 1957.

Howells, John Mead. *The Architectural Heritage of the Piscataqua*. New York: Architectural Book Publishing, 1965.

Hunter, Ethel A. "The Ten-Footers of New England." In *The New England Galaxy*, edited by Roger Parks. Chester, Conn.: Globe Pequot Press, 1980.

Hubka, Thomas C. "Just Folks Designing." *Journal of Architecture Education*. vol. XXXII, no. 3 (Feb. 1979).

———. "Maine's Connected Farm Buildings." *Maine Historical Quarterly*, Part I, vol. 18, no. 3 (Winter 1978), Part II, vol. 18, no. 4 (Spring 1979).

———. "The Vernacular as Source: A Vernacular Point of View." In *Proceedings of the ACSA 68th Meeting*, edited by John Meunier. New York: Association of Collegiate Schools of Architecture, 1981.

Innocent, C. F. *The Development of English Building Construction*. Cambridge: Cambridge University Press, 1916.

Isaacson, Philip. "Records of Passage: New England Illuminated Manuscripts in the Fraktur Tradition." *Clarion*, Winter 1980–81.

Jackson, Edwin. "New England Stoves." *Old-Time New England* vol. XXVI (1935–36).

Jackson, J. B. "Ghosts at the Door." *Landscape* vol. 1, no. 2, Autumn, 1951.

———. *The Necessity for Ruins*. Amherst, Mass.: University of Massachusetts Press, 1980.

Jacobs, Stephen W. *Wayne County: The Aesthetic Heritage of a Rural Area*. New York: Publishing Center for Cultural Resources, 1970.

Jefferson, Thomas. *Notes on the State of Virginia*. Edited by William Peden. 1787. Reprint. New York: W. W. Norton, 1972.

Jewett, Sarah Orne. *The Country of the Pointed Firs*. Garden City, N.Y.: Doubleday, 1956.

Jones, Horace. Horace Jones Diaries, 1856–1864. New Hampshire Historical Society Library, Concord, N.H.

Jones, Howard Mumford. *O Strange New World*. New York: Viking Press, 1964.

Jorgensen, Neil. *A Guide to New England's Landscape*. Chester, Conn.: Globe Pequot Press, 1977.

Kalett, Jim. "New England's Connected Architecture." *Country Journal* vol. III, no. 9 (Sept. 1967).

Kasson, John F. *Civilizing the Machine*. New York: Grossman Publishers, 1976.

Kaufmann, Emil. *Architecture in the Age of Reason*. Cambridge, Mass.: Harvard University Press, 1955.

Keep, William J. "Early American Cooking Stoves." *Old-Time New England* vol. XXII, no. 2 (Oct. 1931).

Kelly, John. *Sketch of Hampstead (New Hampshire)*. New Hampshire Historical Society Collections, V, 1835.

Kennebunk, Maine. Kennebunk Town Records. Vol. 1 (1820–49). Kennebunk Town Office.

Kent, W. W. "The Franklin Stove." *Antiques*, July 1922.

Keune, Russell V., and Replogle, James. "Two Maine Farm-houses." *Journal of the Society of Architectural Historians* vol. XX, no. 1 (Mar. 1961).

Kimball, Fiske. *Domestic Architecture of the American Colonies and of the Early Republic*. New York: Dover Publications, 1950.

Kirk, Jeffrey. "The Family as Utopian Retreat from the City: The Nineteenth Century Contribution." In *The Family, Communes, and Utopian Societies*, edited by Sallie TeSelle. New York: Harper and Row, 1972.

Klamkin, Charles. *Barns*. New York: Hawthorn Books, 1973.

Kleinsasser, William. *Synthesis*. Eugene: University of Oregon, 1982.

Kniffen, Fred. "To Know the Land and Its People." *Landscape* vol. 9, no. 3 (Spring, 1960).

Kouwenhoven, John A. *The Beer Can by the Highway*. Garden City, N.Y.: Doubleday, 1961.

———. *Made in America*. Garden City, N.Y.: Doubleday, 1948.

Krueger, Glee. *New England Samplers to 1840*. Sturbridge, Mass.: Old Sturbridge Village, 1978.

Lancaster, Clay. *Architectural History of Nantucket*. New York: McGraw-Hill, 1972.

Lapham, William Berry. *Centennial History of Norway, Oxford County, Maine 1786–1886*. Portland, Maine: Brown, Thurston, 1886.

Larkin, Oliver W. *Art and Life in America*. New York: Holt, Rinehart, and Winston, 1960.

Laslett, Peter. *The World We Have Lost*. New York: Scribner, 1965.

Leblanc, Robert G. *Location of Manufacturing in New England in the 19th Century*. Geographic Publications at Dartmouth no. 7, 1969.

Lemon, James T. *The Best Poor Man's Country*. Baltimore: Johns Hopkins University Press, 1972.

Lewis, Peirce F. "Axioms for Reading the Landscape." In *The Interpretation of Ordinary Landscapes*, edited by D. W. Meinig. New York: Oxford University Press, 1979.

Lewis, R. W. B. *The American Adam*. Chicago: University of Chicago Press, 1968.

Lienhard, John H. "The Rate of Technological Improvement Before and After the 1830's." *Technology and Culture* vol. 20, no. 3 (July 1979).

Lipke, William C. "Changing Images of the Vermont Landscape." In *Vermont Landscape Images 1776–1976*, edited by William C. Lipke and Philip N. Grime. Burlington, Vt.: Robert Hull Fleming Museum, University of Vermont, 1976.

———, and Grime, Philip N., eds. *Vermont Landscape Images 1776–1976*. Burlington, Vt.: Robert Hull Fleming Museum, University of Vermont, 1976.

Lockridge, Kenneth A. *Literacy in Colonial New England*. New York: W. W. Norton, 1974.

———. *A New England Town, the First Hundred Years*. New York: W. W. Norton, 1970.

Loehr, Rodney C. "Self-Sufficiency on the Farm." *Agricultural History* vol. 26 (Apr. 1952).

Lord, John P. *The Maine Townsman*. Boston: White, Lewis and Potter, 1844.

Louden Barn Plans. Fairfield, Iowa: Louden Machinery Company, 1914.

Loudon, J. C. *An Encyclopaedia of Agriculture*. London: Longman, Orme, Brown, Green, and Longman, 1839.

———. *An Encyclopaedia of Cottage, Farm, and Villa Architecture and Furniture*. London: Longman, Rees, Orme, Brown, Green, and Longman, 1836.

———. *Hints on the Formation of Gardens and Pleasure Grounds*. London: Gale, Curtis and Fenner, 1813.

Lovett, Robert W. "A House and Its Inhabitants." *Essex Institute Historical Collections* vol. CIV, no. 1 (Jan. 1968).

Lowenthal, David. *George Perkins Marsh, Versatile Vermonter*. New York: Columbia University Press, 1958.

Lunt, Richard. *The Maine Folklife Index*. Orono, Maine: University of Maine, 1981.

McHenry, Stewart G. "Eighteenth-Century Field Patterns as Vernacular Art." *Old-Time New England* vol. LXIX, no. 1–2 (Summer–Fall 1978).

McLoughlin, William G. *Revivals, Awakenings, and Reform*. Chicago: University of Chicago Press, 1978.

Maine. Board of Agriculture. *First Annual Report of the Secretary, 1856*. Augusta, Maine: Fuller and Fuller, 1857.

———. *Second Annual Report of the Secretary, 1857*. Augusta, Maine: Stevens and Sayward, 1858.

———. *Third Annual Report of the Secretary, 1858*. Augusta, Maine: Stevens and Sayward, 1859.

———. *Fourth Annual Report of the Secretary, 1859*. Augusta, Maine: Stevens and Sayward, 1859.

———. *Fifth Annual Report of the Secretary, 1860*. Augusta, Maine: Stevens and Sayward, 1860.

———. *Sixth Annual Report of the Secretary, 1861*. Augusta, Maine: Stevens and Sayward, 1861.

———. *Twelfth Annual Report of the Secretary, 1867*. Augusta, Maine: Stevens and Sayward, 1867.

———. *Fifteenth Annual Report of the Secretary, for the Year 1870*. Augusta, Maine: Sprague, Owen and Nash, 1871.

———. *Seventeenth Annual Report of the Secretary, for the Year 1872*. Augusta, Maine: Sprague, Owen and Nash, 1873.

———. *Eighteenth Annual Report of the Secretary, for the Year 1873*. Augusta, Maine: Sprague, Owen and Nash, 1873.

———. *Nineteenth Annual Report of the Secretary, for the Year 1874*. Augusta, Maine: Sprague, Owen and Nash, 1874.

———. *Twenty-Second Annual Report of the Secretary, for the Year 1877*. Augusta, Maine: Sprague, Owen and Nash, 1877.

———. *Twenty-Fourth Annual Report of the Secretary, for the Year 1880*. Augusta, Maine: Sprague and Son, 1880.

Maine State Agricultural Society. *Report of the Secretary, 1855*. Augusta, Maine: Fuller and Fuller, 1859.

Marti, Donald B. *To Improve the Soil and the Mind*. Ann

Arbor, Mich.: University Microfilms International, 1979.

Marx, Leo. *The Machine in the Garden*. New York: Oxford University Press, 1964.

May, Henry F. *The Enlightenment in America*. Oxford: Oxford University Press, 1976.

Mayr, Otto. "Yankee Practice and Engineering Theory: Charles T. Porter and the Dynamics of the High-Speed Steam Engine." *Technology and Culture* vol. 16, no. 4 (Oct. 1975).

Miller, Perry. *The New England Mind*. Cambridge, Mass.: Harvard University Press, 1953.

Mitchell, Robert J. "Tradition and Change in Rural New England: A Case Study of Brooksville, Maine, 1850–1870." *Maine Historical Society Quarterly* vol. 18, no. 2 (Fall 1978).

Moore, Pauline W. *Blueberries and Pusley Weed*. Kennebunk, Maine: Star Press, 1970.

Mordant, John. *The Complete Steward*, vol. I. London: W. Sandby, 1756.

Mortimer, John. *The Whole Art of Husbandry*. London: Printed by J.H. for H. Mortlock, 1708.

Mumford, Lewis. *Sticks and Stones*. New York: Dover Publications, 1955.

Munyon, Paul Glenn. *A Reassessment of New England Agriculture in the Last Thirty Years of the Nineteenth Century*. New York: Arno Press, 1978.

Murphy, Thomas W., Jr. *The Wedding Cake House*. Kennebunk, Maine: Thomas Murphy, 1978.

Myers, Denys Peter. *Maine Catalog, Historic American Building Survey*. Augusta: Maine State Museum, 1974.

New Hampshire Board of Agriculture. *The New Hampshire Agricultural Repository*. Concord, N.H.: Hill and Moore, 1822.

New Hampshire Department of Agriculture. *New Hampshire Farms Available for Farming or Summer Homes*. Concord, N.H.: State of New Hampshire, 1916.

Noble, Allen G. "The Diffusion of Silos." *Landscape* vol. 25, no. 1 (1981).

Noble, David F. *America by Design*. Oxford: Oxford University Press, 1979.

Norton, Bettina A. *Edwin Whitefield, Nineteenth Century North American Scenery*. Barre, Mass.: Barre Publishing, 1977.

Noyes, David. *The History of Norway*. Norway, Maine: David Noyes, 1852.

Nylander, Robert Harrington. "Jason Russell and His House in Menotomy." *Old-Time New England* vol. LV, no. 2 (Oct.–Dec. 1964).

———. "The Jepson Family of New Sweden, Maine." *Old-Time New England* vol. LI, no. 4 (Apr.–June 1961).

Olmsted, Frederick Law. *Walks and Talks of an American Farmer in England*. Columbus, Ohio: Jos. H. Riley, 1859.

Olson, Albert LaVerne. "Agricultural Economy and Population in Eighteenth-Century Connecticut." Tercentenary Commission of the State of Connecticut, pamphlet no. XL. New Haven, Conn.: Yale University Press, 1935.

Pabst, Margaret Richard. "Agricultural Trends in the Connecticut Valley Region of Massachusetts, 1800–1900." *Smith College Studies in History* vol. 26, no. 1–4 (Oct. 1940–July 1941).

Palladio, Andrea. *The Four Books of Andrea Palladio's Architecture*. London: Isaac Ware, 1738.

Palmer, Seth. Seth Palmer Diary 1846–1860 vols. 4, and 5. Maine State Museum Archives, Augusta, Maine.

Parker, Thomas. *History of Farmington, Maine From its Settlement to the Year 1846*. Farmington, Maine: J. S. Swift, 1875.

Pearson, Danella. "Shirley-Eustis House Landscape History." *Old-Time New England* vol. LXX (1980).

Peters, J. E. C. *The Development of Farm Buildings*. Manchester, England: Manchester University press, 1969.

Pike, Clifford L. "Genealogy of the Early Inhabitants of Sweden, 1795–1890." Unpublished paper, Lovell Library, Lovell, Maine.

Pile, John F. *Design*. New York: W. W. Norton, 1979.

Polanyi, Karl. *The Great Transformation*. Boston: Beacon Press, 1957.

Portland, White-Mountain and Montreal Rail-Road Guide. Portland, Maine: Foster, Gerrish, 1853.

Portman, Derek. "Vernacular Building in the Oxford Region." In *Rural Change and Urban Growth 1500–1800*. Edited by C. W. Chalkin and M. A. Havinden. London: Longman, 1974.

Powell, Sumner Chilton. *Puritan Village*. Garden City, N.Y.: Doubleday, 1965.

Pullen, John J. "The Extended Dwelling." *County Journal*, Dec. 1979.

Purcell, Richard J. *Connecticut in Transition*. Washington, D.C.: Oxford University Press, 1918.

Quinan, Jack. "Asher Benjamin and American Architecture." *Journal of the Society of Architectural Historians* vol. XXXVIII, no. 3 (Oct. 1979).

Raitz, Karl B. "The Barns of Barren County." *Landscape* vol. 22, no. 2 (Spring 1978).

———. "The Wisconsin Tobacco Shed." *Landscape* vol. 20, no. 1 (Oct. 1975).

Rapoport, Amos. *House, Form and Culture*. Englewood Cliffs, N.J.: Prentice-Hall, 1969.

Raup, Hugh M. "The View from John Sanderson's Farm." *Forest History* vol. 10, no. 1 (Apr. 1966).

Redfield, Robert. *Peasant Society and Culture*. Chicago: University of Chicago Press, 1956.

Remich, Daniel. *The History of Kennebunk From Its Earliest Settlements to 1890*. Kennebunk, Maine: Daniel Remich, 1911.

Robinson, John Martin. "Model Farm Buildings of the Age of Improvement." *Agricultural History* vol. 19 (1976).

Roos, Frank J. "Reflections of New England's Architecture in Ohio." *Old-Time New England* vol. XXVII, no. 2 (Oct. 1937).

Rosenberry, Lois Kimball Mathews. "Migration From Connecticut After 1800." Tercentenary Commission of the State of Connecticut, pamphlet no. LIV. New Haven, Conn.: Yale University Press, 1935.

———. "Migrations From Connecticut Prior to 1800." Tercentenary Commission of the State of Connecticut, pamphlet no. XXVII. New Haven, Conn.: Yale University Press, 1934.

Rowe, William Hutchinson. *Ancient North Yarmouth and Yarmouth, Maine*. 1937. Reprint. Somersworth, N.H.: New England History Press, 1980.

Rudofsky, Bernard. *Architecture Without Architects*. Garden City, N.Y.: Doubleday, 1964.

————. *The Prodigious Builders*. New York: Harcourt Brace Jovanovich, 1977.

Rumford, Count (Benjamin Thompson). *Collected Works of Count Rumford*, vol. III. Edited by Sanborn C. Brown. Cambridge, Mass.: Harvard University Press, Belknap Press, 1969.

Rundlett-May Notebooks, vol. I. Society for the Preservation of New England Antiquities, Library. Boston, Mass.

Russell, Charles. Charles Russell Journal 1802–1855. Maine Historical Society Library, Portland, Maine.

Russell, Cha's. The'o. *An Address Delivered Before the Agricultural Society of Westborough and Vicinity, September 25, 1850*. Boston: Charles Moody, 1850.

Russell, Howard S. *A Long, Deep Furrow: Three Centuries of Farming in New England*. Hanover, N.H.: University Press of New England, 1976.

Rutman, Darrett B. *Husbandmen of Plymouth*. Boston: Beacon Press, 1967.

Sadler, Julius Trousdale, Jr., and Sadler, Jacquelin D. J. *American Stables*. Boston: New York Graphic Society, 1981.

Satterthwaite, Sheafe. "Pucker Brush, Cellar Holes, Rubble: Observations on Abandonment in Vermont." In *Vermont Landscape Images 1776–1976*, edited by William C. Lipke and Philip N. Grime. Burlington, Vt.: Robert Hull Fleming Museum, University of Vermont, 1976.

Schafer, Joseph. *The Social History of American Agriculture*. New York: Macmillan, 1936.

Schmidt, Carl F., and Smith, Roger B. *The Early Architecture of Genesee Valley*. Geneseo, N.Y.: Genesee Council on the Arts, 1975.

Scofield, Edna. "The Origin of Settlement Patterns In Rural New England." *Geographic Review* vol. XXVII, no. 4 (October 1938).

Sennett, Richard, and Cobb, Jonathan. *The Hidden Injuries of Class*. New York: Alfred A. Knopf, 1973.

Sherbourne, Andrew. *Memoirs of Andrew Sherbourne: A Pensioner of the Navy of the Revolution*. Utica, N.Y.: Williams, Williams, 1828.

Sherman, Rexford B. "One Year on a New Hampshire Farm, 1888." *Historical New Hampshire* vol. XXXII, nos. 1 and 2 (Spring/Summer 1977).

Shettleworth, Earle G., Jr. *Norlands, The Architecture of the Washburn Estate*. Augusta: Maine Historic Preservation Commission Publications, 1980.

————, and Barry, William David. *Mr. Goodhue Remembers Portland, Scenes from the Mid-19th Century*. Augusta: Maine Historical Preservation Commission Publications, 1981.

Shorey, Eula M., ed. *Bridgton, Maine 1768–1968*. Bridgton, Maine: Bridgton Historical Society, 1974.

Sinclair, John. *The Code of Agriculture*. London: Sherwood, Neely, 1821.

Skeat, W. W., and Britten, James, eds. *Reprinted Glossaries and Old Farming Words*. London: Trubner, 1879.

Slepper, John S. *An Address Delivered Before the Agricultural Society of Westborough and Vicinity*. Boston: Gould, Kendall and Lincoln, 1841.

Sloane, Eric. *An Age of Barns*. New York: Ballantine Books, 1974.

Smith, David; Baron, William R.; Bridges, Anne E.; TeBrake, Janet; Borns, Jr., Harold W. "Climate Fluctuations and Agricultural Change in Southern and Central New England, 1765–1880." *Maine Historical Society Quarterly* vol. 21, no. 4 (Spring 1982).

Smith, Henry Nash. *Virgin Land*. New York: Random House, 1950.

Smith, J. T. and Yates, E. M. "On the Dating of English Houses from External Sources." *Field Studies* vol. 2, no. 5 (1968).

Smith, Merritt Roe. *Harpers Ferry Armory and the New Technology*. Ithaca, N.Y.: Cornell University Press, 1980.

Spiller, Nellie D. "The Parson Smith Homestead, South Windham, Maine." *Old-Time New England* vol. XLVII, no. 2 (Oct.–Dec. 1957).

Spurr, William Samuel. *A History of Otisfield, Maine*. Otisfield, Maine: William Samuel Spurr, 1944.

Stachiw, Myron O. "Cultural Change in Cambridge: The Cooper-Frost-Austin House and Its Occupants." *Old-Time New England* vol. LXX (1980).

Stilgoe, John R. *Common Landscape of America, 1580 to 1845*. New Haven, Conn.: Yale University Press, 1982.

————. "Folklore and Graveyard Design." *Landscape* vol. 22, no. 3 (Summer 1978).

————. "The Puritan Townscape." *Landscape* vol. 20, no. 3 (Spring 1976).

————. "Town Common and Village Green in New England: 1620 to 1981." In *On Common Ground*, edited by Ronald Lee Fleming and Lauri A. Halderman. Harvard, Mass.: Harvard Common Press, 1982.

Storms, Roger C. "A Century of Democracy in Parkman, Maine 1822–1922." Master's thesis, University of Maine, Orono, 1968.

Struik, Dirk J. *Yankee Science in the Making*. Boston: Little, Brown, 1948.

Tarule, Rob. "The Mortise and Tenon Timber Frame: Tradition and Technology." In *Tools and Technologies: America's Wooden Age*, edited by Paul B. Kebabian and William C. Lipke. Burlington, Vt.: Robert Hull Fleming Museum, University of Vermont, 1979.

Thomas, Robert B. *The (Old) Farmer's Almanack, 1833*. Boston: Carter, Hendree, 1833.

Thompson, E. P. *The Making of the English Working Class*. New York: Random House, 1963.

————. "Time, Work-Discipline, and Industrial Capitalism." *Past & Present*, number 38 (Dec. 1967).

Tocqueville, Alexis de. *Democracy in America*. 1862. Reprint. vols. I and II. New York: Vintage Books, 1945.

Tolles, Jr., Bryant F. *New Hampshire Architecture*. Hanover, N.H.: University Press of New England, 1979.

Towne, John H. *Topsfield Houses and Buildings*. The Historical Collections of the Topsfield Historical Society vol. VIII, edited by George Francis Dow. Topsfield, Mass.: Merrill Press, 1902.

Trollope, Frances. *Domestic Manners of the Americans*. 1832. Reprint. New York: Dodd, Mead, 1927.

Tryon, Rolla Milton. *Household Manufactures in the United States*. Chicago: University of Chicago Press, 1917.

Ulrich, Laurel Thatcher. "Good Wives: A Study in Role Definition in Northern Colonial New England, 1650–1750." Ph.D. diss., University of New Hampshire, 1980.

United States. Commissioner of Agriculture. *Report for the Year 1870*. Washington, D.C.: Government Printing Office, 1871.

Upton, Dell. "Architectural Change in Colonial Rhode Island: The Mott House as a Case Study." *Old-Time New England* vol. LXIX, nos. 3–4 (Jan.–June, 1979).

van Ravensway, Charles. *The Arts and Architecture of German Settlements in Missouri*. Columbia: University of Missouri Press, 1977.

Vitruvius, Pollio. *The Ten Books of Architecture*. 1899. Reprint. New York: Dover Publications, 1960.

Venturi, Robert. *Complexity and Contradiction in Architecture*. New York: Museum of Modern Art, 1966.

Wagner, James Burnham. "The First Century on the Eastern Frontier: Transitional Farming in Corinth, Maine." Master's thesis, University of Maine, Orono, 1971.

Walcott, Robert R. "Husbandry in Colonial New England." *New England Quarterly* vol. IX, no. 2 (June 1936).

Walker, Amasa. *Transactions of the Agricultural Societies in the State of Massachusetts for 1851*. Boston: Dutton and Wentworth, 1852.

Walker, Andrew. Andrew Walker Diaries, 1851–1897. Microfilm. The Brick Store Museum, Kennebunk, Maine.

Walker, Tobias. Tobias Walker Diaries vols. 1–8, 1828–93. Maine Historical Society Library, Portland, Maine.

Walker, William. William Walker Diary vols. 1–5, 1846–83. Mr. and Mrs. Robert Walker.

Watkins, Lura Woodside. "Shoemaking and the Small Town." *Old-Time New England* vol. LI, no. 4 (Apr.–June 1961).

Weeden, William B. *Economic and Social History of New England*. Boston: Houghton, Mifflin, 1891.

Wilson, Harold Fisher. *The Hill Country of Northern New England*. New York: AMS Press, 1967.

Williams, Raymond. *The Country and the City*. New York: Oxford University Press, 1975.

Winston, Sanford. *Illiteracy in the United States*. Chapel Hill: University of North Carolina Press, 1930.

Woodman, J. S. *An Address Delivered Before the Connecticut River Valley Agricultural Society at Haverhill, N.H., October 2nd, 1851*. Haverhill, N.H.: H. W. Reding, 1851.

Zelinsky, Wilbur. *The Cultural Geography of the United States*. Englewood Cliffs, N.J.: Prentice-Hall, 1973.

———. "The New England Connecting Barn." *Geographical Review* vol. 48 (1958).

Zuckerman, Michael. *Peaceable Kingdoms*. New York: W. W. Norton, 1978.

Glossary

Arch: A cellar chimney support, often a semicircular brick arch, used as a winter storage area for produce (see fig. 33).

Back house: Any building in the connected farm complex located between the kitchen and the barn. Also called the ell or shed. Back house may also refer to a privy or outhouse located in these buildings (see fig. 5).

Balloon frame: A framing system composed of lightweight, sawn members joined by nails. Between 1820 and 1870, this light "balloon" method replaced the standard heavy-timber system of medieval origin.

Baluster: A turned or rectangular upright supporting a stair rail or a fence rail.

Balustrade: A row of balusters topped by a rail forming a railing or fence.

Bank barn: A two-level barn, usually dug into a hillside, with entrances on both first-floor and cellar levels.

Bark house: A building for leather tanning used to store and process tree bark (usually oak). Animal skins were soaked in acidic solution derived from tree bark.

Bay: The space between major structural posts, as found in barns. The most common New England barn is three bays wide and three bays deep (see fig. 46).

Bent: The transverse framing section in a New England barn usually having four posts and erected as a single structural unit (see fig. 46).

Big house: The first or front building in the connected building complex containing the parlor and bedrooms (see fig. 5).

Boiler: A large iron pot or caldron set into a masonry firebox and used to boil water for kitchen-related tasks. Also called a set kettle (see fig. 96).

Borning room: A popular name for the small bedroom adjacent to the kitchen in a typical Cape Cod house. While births occurred there, the term does not appear to have been widely used before 1920.

Brace: A structural member set at a 45-degree angle between vertical posts and horizontal beams. Its purpose is to stiffen the frame and prevent racking and bending.

Byre: An English term for a cow barn.

Camp: Any temporary or unimproved shelter; often used for seasonal activities such as lumbering or hunting.

Camp meeting: An outdoor religious revival meeting usually held in the late summer.

Cape Cod house: A one-story, center-chimney house, two-rooms-deep, found throughout the New England region (see fig. 28).

Carriage house: A building to shelter horse-drawn vehicles and sometimes to stable horses.

Casing: Finish woodwork enclosing the opening of a door or window, usually molded or cut in a particular architectural style.

Chaise house: A carriage house named after the horse-drawn chaise.

Chamber: A room located on the second floor, usually a bedroom.

Cistern: A water storage reservoir usually located in the cellar or in the ground.

Classical-vernacular: The minimal architectural style of most nineteenth-century farms. It is composed of elements of the classical styles (from Georgian, Federal, and Greek Revival sources) and applied according to strict vernacular rules of organization and application.

Cooper shop: A building for making wooden barrel staves, assembling barrels, and making other wooden ware.

Corncrib: A building for storing corn, usually constructed with slatted boards for ventilation, slanted walls for weather protection, and set on stilts to deter rodents (see fig. 51).

Cornice: In common usage, a projecting molding below the edge of a roof.

Cow path: A fenced or stone-walled path to guide cows from the barn, past crop and mowing fields, and into pastures. Also called a "lane."

Cupola: A small ornamental structure placed at the crest of a house roof. A less ornate structure placed on a barn for ventilation was called a ventilator.

Dooryard: The outside area adjacent to the kitchen and the major barn door and used for farm work activities (see fig. 57).

Doric: The stylistic vocabulary derived from the oldest and simplest Greek architectural order.

Eave: The lower edge of a roof overhanging the wall.

Ell: Any building extending outward from the main or big house, usually an L-shaped arrangement. On a connected farmstead, the ell includes all the buildings linking the big house and the barn.

English barn: The dominant early New England barn type, brought from England and having the major door in the center of the side wall below the eave (see fig. 43).

Ensilage: The process of preserving animal food (usually corn) in an airtight container or silo.

Entablature: The upper section of a wall supported by columns, usually employing a Greek or Roman architectural style.

Federal: The architectural style of the early Republican period in America, 1790–1830, derived from classical forms.

Finisher: A carpenter or housewright employed for finish work on architectural details such as windows, doors, staircases, and paneling.

Fire frame: An iron fire-surround set into a fireplace to increase heating efficiency. A free-standing iron fireplace set out into a room is called a Franklin stove.

Fireplace surround: Wooden molding encasing a fireplace opening.

Framer: A carpenter responsible for structural framing and rough carpentry work.

Framing: The structural framework of a building.

Franklin stove: An iron firebox with an open mouth designed to be set into a room.

Front yard: The outside area in front of the big house in the connected building complex; often defined by a picket fence in the nineteenth century (see fig. 57).

Gambrel: A roof with a double slope; the lower one steeper than the upper.

Georgian: An architectural style derived from Greek and Roman precedents and employed during the colonial period, 1700–1790.

Girt: Any major horizontal structural member supporting ceilings and floors.

Gothic: The architectural vocabulary of medieval Europe. In America, Gothic is associated with the revival of this style between 1830 and 1890.

Greek Revival: The architectural style of ancient Greece revived in the second quarter of the nineteenth century.

Gunstock post: A major vertical structural member wider at the top to accept horizontal members. Also called a flared post.

Half-house: A common colonial house usually consisting of one room. Most were half versions of the hall-and-parlor house.

Hall-and-parlor house: A medieval house type with a center chimney and two major ground-floor rooms: a hall (or kitchen) and a parlor (see fig. 29).

Haymow: The bays along one side of a barn used for storing hay (see fig. 43).

Home industry: Various nonagricultural manufacturing occupations of the farm, for example: the production of cloth and clothes, soap, leather goods, and wooden items. The term may also include lumbering and any production activity of a farm.

Hop barn: A building for drying and storage of hops.

Hydraulic ram: A gravity-triggered pumping device that became popular after 1850.

Indian shutters: Sliding paneled window covers concealed within the walls of many colonial houses. Often assumed to be for protection against Indian attack, they were actually built for insulation and environmental control.

Intervale: Flat land in a river valley, often formed by a flood plain. In hilly New England, these were valuable farm lands.

Italianate: The architectural style derived from Italian Renaissance examples and popular in America between 1840 and 1880.

Joiner: A carpenter responsible for interior finish work and paneling. A cabinetmaker.

Joist: A small structural member supporting the floor. The term usually describes the balloon frame system of small, lightweight floor supports.

Lathing: Thin, narrow strips of wood nailed to structural walls and ceilings to provide a bonding surface for plaster finish.

Light: A single pane of window glass, as in a two-over-two light window.

Linter: The sheltered milking area for cows in a barn; the word is probably derived from the term *lean-to*.

Little house: The second building in the connected building complex containing the kitchen (see fig. 5).

Long floor: The wagon floor in a gable-end door New England barn. Its floor was longer than the short floor of the earlier side-door English barn.

Lyceum: A civic association for the promotion of public educational lectures and cultural activities.

Master builder: The head carpenter in charge of building a house or barn.

Mortise-and-tenon: An ancient method of all wood joinery by which a projecting member is inserted into a cut-out hole and held together by a wooden dowel called a treenail or pin.

Newel post: The lowest post supporting the stair rail; usually it is the largest and most elaborate post.

New England barn: A barn with its major door in the gable end, which became popular in the nineteenth century (see fig. 43).

Outbuilding: Any farm building not connected to the major house and barn.

Overmantel: Paneling or decorative woodwork positioned above the fireplace.

Ovolo molding: A rounded or quarter-round molding.

Palladian: Classical revival architecture based upon the works of Andrea Palladio.

Piazza: A porch or veranda inspired by Italian examples.

Pilaster: A structural post resembling a column (with a square section), engaged or attached to a wall.

Plate: A major horizontal framing member located at the junction of the vertical posts of the wall and the sloped rafters of the roof.

Post: A major upright structural member.

Purlin: A major roof-framing member running parallel with the ridge and supporting smaller common rafters or vertical sheathing (see fig. 32).

Rafter: Any roof-framing member running parallel with the slope of the roof (see fig. 32).

Raising: The process of erecting the structural members of houses and barns usually with the assistance of neighbors. Raising may also refer to the common practice of elevating a roof by steepening or adding additional wall height.

Ridge: The peak of a roof or the structural member at the peak.

Romantic-Aesthetic: Any manifestation of a literary, artistic and philosophical movement of the late eighteenth and early nineteenth centuries that emphasized imagination and emotional response. It was characterized by an appreciation of primitive naturalism and pastoral settings, especially in reaction to neoclassical, rational traditions. In America, the period between 1840 and 1880.

Rumford roaster: An elaborate cylindrical metal baking oven invented by Count Rumford.

Saddle board: A term for a fascia board at the junction of the roof and the gable wall. Also called a rake board.

Saltbox: A colonial house form with two stories in front and one story behind and a gable roof with the rear slope longer than the front slope.

Sap house: A building for boiling maple tree sap to produce maple syrup.

Screw jack: A rotating screw-operating device for lifting heavy loads such as houses.

Set kettle: *See* Boiler.

Sheathing: Covering boards encasing the framing members of a building. On houses these boards are covered by clap-boards or finish siding, while on barns the sheathing might be left exposed.

Shippon: The English term for a cow barn.

Shoes: Timbers used to support a building during a moving operation.

Short floor: The wagon floor of an English barn that was shorter than the long floor of the later New England barn.

Side-hall house: A house with its major door and stair hall located to one side of the gable end. In New England, this form was frequently built in the Greek Revival and Victorian styles between 1830 and 1900 (see fig. 27).

Sidelight: Narrow vertical windows placed on both sides of an exterior door. A common element in Federal and Greek Revival styles.

Sill: A major horizontal framing member resting on the exterior of the foundation and supporting the vertical posts and studs of the walls.

Silo: A tall, usually cylindrical structure used to store animal feed. Most silos are sealed to exclude air and promote the fermentation of green fodder without spoilage.

Skids: A timber in contact with the ground used to drag a building during the moving operation.

Stair ends: The exposed ends of stairs often finished with decorative molding. Also called stairs brackets.

Stud: A small vertical structural member inserted between the sill and plate forming the nailing surface for interior and exterior walls.

Summer kitchen: A kitchen workroom where the cookstove was temporarily moved during the hottest summer months for kitchen comfort (see fig. 93).

Ten-footer: A small, detached home-industry shop.

Threshing floor: The central floor of a barn used for flailing grain to separate the seeds from the chaff.

Tie-up: The milking area for cows in a barn.

Town house: Any residential building common to the small towns and cities of New England.

Well sweep: A fulcrum and lever device for easing the task of raising water from a well (see fig. 53).

Index

Agriculturalists, attitudes of, 13, 181–86
Agriculture: changes in, 179–80, 186–87, 203; conditions of, 187–93; mixed-farming, home-industry, small-scale, 9–10, 13, 120–22, 180, 187–93, 204; reform of, 18, 188, 200–202, 204
Anderson farm (Windham, Maine), 59–60
Animal shelters, 61–63
Architectural style. *See* Style, architectural
Aroostook County potato barn, 65

Back house, 6, 50–52, 122–28, 167–68
Bacon farm (North Yarmouth, Maine), 95–101
Barn, 6, 9, 52–61, 98, 99, 104–5, 109, 110, 111–12; cellar of, 58, 92, 174–75, 183; centralization of, 182–83; change from English to New England, 52, 59–60; English (side-door), 28, 52–55, 87–88, 104, 165; exterior of, 6–9, 30, 58, 92; New England (gable door), 28, 52, 55–61, 90–92, 174–76; in relation to house, 28, 120–22, 143, 183–85; structural system of, 54–55, 56–58, 92, 105, 142–43
Barnyard, 6, 80–81, 116
Benjamin, Asher, 16, 170; *American Builder's Companion*, 128, 136
Bethel, Maine, 75
Big house, 6, 32–44; cellar of, 41–42, 87, 90, 98; after 1850 (side-hall with stove chimney and kitchen in ell), 32–35, 38–39, 42–44, 93–95, 169–70; before 1820 (with center fireplace chimney and kitchen in house), 32–37, 39–42, 87–88, 96–98, 109–10, 163–65; exterior of, 100, 102; interior of, 37, 42, 44, 98, 102, 136–37, 170; in relation to barn, 28, 120–22, 143, 183–85; structural system of, 39–41, 44, 101–2, 142
Borning room, 37
Boundaries (walls and fences), 84–85

Bridgton, Maine, 59
Building movement, 139–40, 172–74, 176, 203

Camps (cabins), 68
Cape Cod house, 32, 35, 39–42, 87, 90–94, 109–10, 111. *See also* Big house
Carriage house, 50, 61–62, 94, 95, 104, 111, 129–33, 168, 185. *See also* Town house
Cobbett, William, 73, 80
Codman, John, 75
Concord, Massachusetts, 14
Connected farm buildings: attitudes toward, 10, 181–86; reasons for, 12–14, 18, 120–22, 172–74, 186–204
Connecticut, 14–16
Construction techniques, 138, 142–44, 167–68; of barn, 54–55, 56–58, 92, 142–43; of big house, 39–41, 44, 101–2, 142; and professional carpenters, 170–71, 175
Convenience and beauty, 198–99
Cow path, 83–84

Dawes-Denison farm (Harrison, Maine), 25–27
Deane, Samuel, 81–82, 83–84, 116, 181
Dooryard, 6, 9, 13, 73, 76, 77–80, 116
Double house, 47–48
Downing, A. J., 16

Ell. *See* Back house; Little house

Family, 147–50
Fences, 28–30, 84–85, 168, 200; picket, 70, 105, 176
Fields, 81–84
Fire, threat of, 13–14, 18
Freeport, Maine, 14
Front yard, 6, 70–77

Gandy, Joseph, 16, 198
Geographic distribution, of connected farm buildings, 10, 18–25; outside New England, 20–22

Gibbs, James, 16
Greek Revival style house, 32, 35, 38, 42, 109, 169–70

Half-house, 47–48, 109
Hall-and-parlor house, 35, 88–90, 165
Hamilton house (North Yarmouth, Maine), 39–42, 44, 126–28
Harrison, Maine, 25–27, 65. *See also* Woodsum farm
Home industry, 9–10, 120–22, 180, 188–89, 192–93; workshops for, 66–67, 98–99, 111, 165, 167, 176

Icehouse, 67, 94–95, 105, 178
Improvement, spirit of, 194–95, 204
Inventive tradition, 195–96

Kasson, John: *Civilizing the Machine*, 196
Kennebunk, Maine, 16–18, 25–27, 161–62, 197, 199. *See also* Walker farm
Kitchen, 9, 93–94, 98, 122–28; improvements to, 129, 176; interior of, 49–50, 176; summer, 6, 104, 172; two in one house, 94, 148–50, 177. *See also* Little house

Little house, 6, 44–50, 116, 122–28; ell, 38, 39, 42–43, 48–49, 90, 93–94, 98–99, 104–5, 110–11, 116, 165–67, 169–70; exterior of, 49–50; half- and double, 47–48, 109; interior of, 49–50, 136–37. *See also* Kitchen
Loudon, J. C., 16

Maine Farmer, 184
Marston-Lawrence farm (North Yarmouth, Maine), 122, 128
Mills, 68, 98
Milton, New Hampshire, 130
Minot, Maine, 72, 73, 76
Mutuality, 152–58, 175, 193

Neighborhoods, 150–58
Nevers-Bennett farm (Sweden, Maine), 3–5, 28–30, 62, 67, 70, 87, 101–5, 118

North Yarmouth, Maine, 122–28. *See also* Bacon farm; Hamilton house; Staples house
Nutting farm (Otisfield, Maine), 87–95, 127

One-room-deep house, 35, 37–38, 47–48
Orchards, 72, 81, 84
Organization, of connected farm buildings, 5–6, 9–10, 114–22, 129–33, 182–85; connecting, 120–22; linking, 119–20; siting, 96, 114–19, 164–65, 169, 175–76, 183
Otisfield, Maine. *See* Nutting farm
Outbuildings, 61–69; pattern in, 68–69
Outhouse, 6, 52

Pain, William, 16
Permanence and change, 138–42. *See also* Remodeling
Pigsty, 62, 168–69, 174, 178
Porch (piazza), 49, 95, 100, 105, 111, 112
Portland, Maine, 16
Portsmouth, New Hampshire, 16, 128
Privy, 6, 52
Produce storage structures, 63–65, 94–95

Reform, agricultural, 18, 188, 200–202, 204
Remodeling, 28–30, 49–50, 111–12, 138–42, 169–72, 176–77
Road orientation, 96, 114–19, 164–65, 169, 175–76, 183

Romantic-Aesthetic movement, 199–200

Saltbox house, 35
Sawyer-Black farm (Sweden, Maine), 5, 116, 129
Set kettle, 128, 172
Side-hall house, 35, 38–39, 42–44
Smith (Samuel) farm (Kennebunk, Maine), 32
Stable, 50, 61–62, 94, 104, 105, 111
Staples house (North Yarmouth, Maine), 42–44, 128
Stores, 67, 105
Stove, introduction of, 105, 111, 125–28, 172
Style, architectural, 133–38; classical, 16, 196–98; classical-vernacular, 134–38; Federal, 16, 102, 134–36; folk (vernacular), 16–18, 199–200; and frontality, 133–34, 175; functional-aesthetic, 198–200; Georgian, 16, 35, 136; Greek Revival, 32, 35, 38, 42, 105, 109, 133, 136, 170, 197; incremental-juxtapositional and uniform-formal, 133; precedents for, 14–18, 37, 203; Romantic-Aesthetic, 199–200; unity of (dissipation), 6–30, 9, 105, 134, 175, 185–86, 197–98, 204
Summer kitchen, 6, 104, 172
Sweden, Maine. *See* Nevers-Bennett farm; Sawyer-Black farm

Thompson, Benjamin (Count Rumford), 128
Topsfield, Massachusetts, 37

Town houses, connected, 13, 16, 130–33, 185, 203
Trees, 73, 100, 105, 168; orchard, 72, 81, 84; roadside, 76–77, 199–200
True farm (North Yarmouth, Maine), 122, 128
Two-rooms-deep house, 35, 36–37, 47–48, 87, 96–98, 101–4

Vehicle storage structures, 66, 92, 105

Walker farm (Kennebunk, Maine), 119, 137–38, 163–78
Walls, stone, 84–85
Ware, Isaac, 16
Water conveyance and storage, 99, 129, 176
Weather protection, 12–13, 187
Windham, Maine, 59–60, 130
Wood house, 6, 67, 99, 167. *See also* Little house
Woodsum Farm (Harrison, Maine), 48, 106–12
Work, 9; and cooperation, 153–56, 175; male and female, 144, 147–50; rhythms of, 144–47

Yankee Farmer, 181
Yards, 70–81; barnyard, 6, 80, 116; dooryard, 6, 9, 13, 73, 76, 77–80, 116; front yard, 6, 70–77

Figure Credits

Ashfield Historical Society, Ashfield, Mass., Copyright 1979, Howes Brothers, photographers, figs. 107, 120.

Bennett, Mr. and Mrs. Charles, photograph, fig. 2.

Benson, Scott, drawings, figs. 23, 30, 33, 35A, 46, 94B, 94C, 96, 108.

Bethel Historical Society, Bethel, Maine, photographs, figs. 3, 11, 48, 56, 59, 61, 104, 113B, 116.

Brown, Kurt, photographer, figs. 1, 6A, 40, 42, 51, 58B, 77, 85, 86, 90A, 99, 100.

Conant, Ben, photographs, figs. 39, 92, 113A.

Concord Antiquarian Museum, Concord, Mass., photograph, fig. 12.

Four Books of Andrea Palladio's Architecture, The, Andrea Palladio. London: Isaac Ware (Publisher) 1738 (plate 31), fig. 15.

Freeport Historical Society, Freeport, Maine, photograph, fig. 17.

Gould, William, drawings, figs. 22, 52.

History of Cumberland, Maine, W. Woodward Clayton. Philadelphia: Everts and Peck, 1880, photograph, fig. 9.

Holland, William and Stacey, Thomas, drawings, figs. 68, 69, 74, 75, 78, 79, 81, 82, 123–25, 128, 131, 133.

Hoover, Jeffrey, drawing, fig. 44.

Hubka, Thomas C., drawings, figs. 4B, 5, 7, 18, 20, 21, 26–29, 32, 37, 41, 43, 47, 49, 54, 55, 57, 65, 71, 72, 83, 87–89, 90B, 98, 103, 106, 110, 114, 126, 127, 129, 132; photographer, figs. 4A, 6B, 8, 19, 25, 38, 50, 67, 70, 80, 84, 101, 121; postcard, fig. 112.

Kennebunk Free Library, Kenneth Joy Collection, Kennebunk, Maine, photograph, figs. 16, 102.

King, B. A., photographer, fig. 10.

Kleinkopf, Robert, drawings, figs. 31, 34, 35B.

Landon, Ruth, photograph, fig. 118.

Lincoln County Cultural and Historical Association, Wiscasset, Maine, photographs, figs. 117, 119.

Martin, Hilary, photographs, figs. 122, 130.

Minot Historical Society, Susan Campbell Collection, Minot, Maine, photograph, fig. 58A.

North Yarmouth Historical Society, North Yarmouth, Maine, photographs, figs. 53, 60, 63C, 73, 76, 94A, 111, 115.

Rudd, William, drawing, fig. 45.

Society for the Preservation of New England Antiquities, Boston, Mass., photographs, figs. 13, 14, 63B, 66; Emma Colman, photographer, frontispiece; Fred Quimby, photographer, figs. 62, 64, 109.

Strong, George J., photograph, fig. 24.

Sussman, Nancy, drawing, fig. 93.

Vickery, James Berry, photographs, figs. 36, 95, 97.

Walker, Robert, photograph, fig. 63A.

Yarmouth Historical Society, Yarmouth, Maine, photograph, fig. 105.